PERSISTENCE *through* PERIL

PERSISTENCE *through* PERIL

Episodes of College Life and Academic Endurance in the Civil War South

— Edited by —

R. ERIC PLATT *and* **Holly A. Foster**

University Press of Mississippi / Jackson

The University Press of Mississippi is the scholarly publishing agency of the Mississippi Institutions of Higher Learning: Alcorn State University, Delta State University, Jackson State University, Mississippi State University, Mississippi University for Women, Mississippi Valley State University, University of Mississippi, and University of Southern Mississippi.

www.upress.state.ms.us

The University Press of Mississippi is a member of the Association of University Presses.

Manufactured in the United States of America

First printing 2021
∞

Library of Congress Cataloging-in-Publication Data available

LCCN 2021032570
ISBN 9781496835031 (hardback)
ISBN 9781496835048 (trade paperback)
ISBN 9781496835079 (epub single)
ISBN 9781496835024 (epub institutional)
ISBN 9781496835062 (pdf single)
ISBN 9781496835055 (pdf institutional)

British Library Cataloging-in-Publication Data available

For our families, friends, and pets

The struggle of today is not altogether for today—
it is for a vast future also.

—Abraham Lincoln

Contents

Acknowledgments

A few years back, we, the editors of this volume, engaged in a lengthy conversation about Southern college life during the American Civil War (1861–1865) and those existing texts related to the subject. Most relevant books and scholarly articles focused on the wartime closure of Southern colleges and universities and only briefly discussed what academic and social life was like for those students and faculty who remained engaged in higher education throughout the four tumultuous years of conflict. Deepening our inquiry, we came across interesting primary and secondary source accounts that depicted the lived wartime experiences of students and instructors at Southern institutions of higher learning. Granted, many college students and faculty left their academies to join the Confederate forces. However, others remained enrolled and continued their studies all while supporting the Southern secessionist cause. Further, we noted that some Southern colleges, unlike most of their regional peers, remained open for the duration of the war or shuttered for a brief stint and reopened quickly. Our interest was piqued. Beyond the fascinating accounts of students praising their Confederate army peers and professors managing rowdy pupils more interested in battles than arithmetic and academic oration, we became interested in the notion of academic endurance through this watershed moment in US history.

We queried: How had some Southern colleges and universities managed to remain open in the face of all-out war while so many nineteenth-century academies were shuttered? What was student, faculty, administrative, and community life like at these wartime institutions? What Civil War elements affected students' academic progress, challenged their administrative leaders, and challenged their organizational survival? Moreover, what archival evidence existed that could enhance readers' understanding of Southern Civil War academic endurance? Existing literature provides some insights into the lives of college students, faculty, and administrators at widely known institutions such as the College of William and Mary, the University of Alabama, the University of Mississippi, and the University of Tennessee prior to and after their wartime closure. But what of those students who remained at their institutions while their fellow college wards went off to fight? What of the faculty, the administration, and surrounding communities? What of the handful of academies that remained functional?

While countless college-age students engaged in battles and fought on the front lines, others remained in their classes and cheered on the Confederate war effort. As the war progressed, those students and professors who stayed behind experienced their own hardships—decreased food and clothing supplies, lack of contact with friends and families, and crumbling Southern morale as the war waned and the Confederacy fell to Union victories. Those institutions that remained open, like many of their closed counterparts, emerged from the war as changed bastions of Southern thought. Liberal arts instruction and upper-class mores no longer dominated the pedagogical scene—academic pragmatism, mercantilism, agriculture, mechanical curricula, and career attainment became common themes in Reconstruction-era Southern higher education. Indeed, those colleges and universities that persisted through the war experienced the full gamut of academic and social transformation. Instead of reopening as retooled academies ready to meet the needs of the New South, most of the institutions featured in this text held on to the Southern secessionist cause until the fall of the Confederacy; only after the war did they slowly adapt to changing regional standards of practical instruction and vocation-attainment ideologies.

Before the phenomena of college life and academic endurance in the Civil War South can be explored, we would like to thank a bevy of individuals who contributed to the production of this edited volume. First and foremost, the book editors would like to thank each chapter author for their hard work, archival investigations, and painstaking analysis. Without their dedication, this volume would never have come to pass. The editors and chapter authors would like to express a special debt of thanks to our friends, families, and pets for their support and fellowship. Having colleagues and loved ones to support one's work is invaluable. Therefore, this book is dedicated to them. We would like to extend our sincere appreciation to the Southern History of

Education Society (SHOES) and its esteemed members. Several chapters in this book were presented at past meetings and received various comments and suggestions for improvement. We thank our peer educational historians for their valued feedback, collaboration, and ongoing support. Likewise, we would like to thank Emily Bandy and Valerie Jones at the University Press of Mississippi as well as Vijay Shah (formerly at the University Press of Mississippi) for seeing worth in this project and promoting its success along the way. Emily, Vijay, the University Press of Mississippi staff, and associated peer reviewers were instrumental in shaping this text and seeing it through to completion. The book editors would also like to express our gratitude to Charisse Gulosino at the University of Memphis for crafting the highly informative map of relevant Southern colleges and universities that remained open during the Civil War. This map can be found in the pages that follow. We would also like to express gratitude to Diane Powell for organizing the index—an essential component to this and many other books. Index funding was graciously provided by the University of Memphis Fine Arts, Humanities, and Social Sciences Support Program: Professional Indexing Grant.

In addition to the abovementioned support, a host of archivists contributed to the research behind each chapter. Special thanks goes to the archival staff at the Albert and Shirley Small Special Collections Library, University of Virginia, Charlottesville, Virginia; Baptist and University Archives, Mercer University, Macon, Georgia; Clemson University Special Collections Library, Clemson, South Carolina; Daniel Archives and Library, The Citadel, Charleston, South Carolina; Duke University Archives, Durham, North Carolina; Houghton Memorial Library and Archives, Huntingdon College, Montgomery, Alabama; Leland Speed Library, Mississippi College, Clinton, Mississippi; Mississippi Baptist Historical Archives, Mississippi College, Clinton, Mississippi; New Orleans Province Collection, Jesuit Archives and Research Center, St. Louis, Missouri; Wesleyan College Archives and Special Collections, Macon, Georgia; Sandor Teszler Library and Archives, Wofford College, Spartanburg, South Carolina; South Caroliniana Library, University of South Carolina, Columbia, South Carolina; Spring Hill College Archives and Special Collections, Burke Library, Mobile, Alabama; University Archives and Special Collections, University of North Carolina Libraries, Chapel Hill, North Carolina; and Virginia Military Institute Archives, Lexington, Virginia.

Finally, we would like to offer our appreciation to those past and present authors who have done so much to chronicle the history of the American

Civil War, nineteenth-century higher education, the nature and development of nineteenth-century college student life, Reconstruction-era social and ideological trends, and the changing nature of Southern higher education development pre- and post-war. Your diligent work and quality publications provided the bedrock for this research.

PERSISTENCE *through* PERIL

INTRODUCTION

Persistence through Peril

R. Eric Platt and Holly A. Foster

In 1861, a professor at former Louisiana College in East Feliciana Parish wrote in the institution's annals, "Students have all gone to war. College suspended; and God help the right" (Faculty Minutes 1840–90, 253). Statements like this have marked the introductions of various narratives that chronicle the closure of Southern higher education at the onset of, or during, the American Civil War (1861–1865) (Tewksbury 1932; Geiger 2000; Pace 2004; Morgan 2008). Despite the myth that the antebellum South lacked educational institutions (especially when compared to such Northern states as Michigan or Pennsylvania), recent research has done much to extol the significant presence of colleges, schools, academies, and educational promotors in Southern states prior to the Civil War (Bernath 2010; Hyde 2016; Williams 2015; O'Brien 2012). Even so, literature that recounts the history of nineteenth-century Southern higher education includes Civil War-related issues as part of a larger, longitudinal narrative and, in cases concerning the war years, focuses on the closure, destruction, and reformation of various regional colleges and universities due to student enlistment, the burning of buildings by Union troops, campus conversions to military barracks or army hospitals, etc. Few, however, focus completely on the Civil War South—even less provide detailed case examples that extol the persistence of some Southern colleges during the war.

Though most Southern institutions of higher education *did* close during the war, there were a handful of academies that remained open, weathering the storm and providing academic instruction to remaining students. Of the existing literature concerning college life in the Civil War South, a dominant theme is the departure of young men from institutions of higher learning to join Southern military regiments and fight on far-flung battlefields. These texts often describe students as desperate for soldierly life and the "glory of combat." Some books, however, chronicle the reluctance of other students to enlist and the struggle to enroll pupils during the post-Civil War Reconstruction era (Williams 2015). Either way, student enrollment remained an issue throughout the war. Even before the national conflict commenced, students left Southern colleges en masse to enlist in the Confederate army. This led to the suspension of such institutions as the College of William and Mary in Virginia, the Arkansas-based University of the Ozarks, and South Carolina College (later known as the University of South Carolina) in 1861 (University of the Ozarks 2019; University of South Carolina 2018; Heuvel and Heuvel 2013). In 1862, East Tennessee University's (present-day University of Tennessee) president, Joseph J. Ridley, fearing that Knoxville would be overrun by Union forces, left for North Carolina, and the institution closed shortly thereafter (Montgomery, Folmsbee, and Green 1984). Mirroring other Southern academies, the University of Georgia closed in 1863 due to the lack of wartime students and faculty (Flynt 1968).

As the war intensified, other Southern colleges and universities tried to remain open, but in vain. The Louisiana Seminary of Learning and Military Academy (present-day Louisiana State University) remained open during the first half of the war despite the resignation of its first superintendent (president) William Tecumseh Sherman. As a pro-Union supporter, Sherman left Louisiana following the state's secession. Not long after his egress, a string of institutional leaders followed. Col. George W. Lay was elected superintendent but left the position not long after his home state of Virginia seceded. West Point graduate William R. Boggs was elected to replace Lay, but he was called to serve the Confederate army in Florida before he could assume charge of early Louisiana State University (LSU). The college's professor of mathematics and natural philosophy, Anthony Vallas, assumed the superintendency, but was soon after replaced by Methodist reverend and former military officer, W. E. M. Linfield. The pro-secessionist Linfield, however, gave up his administrative post after students stole dishes and cutlery from the academy's mess hall, threw them into the campus water well, and proceeded to destroy kitchen furniture. These rowdy students were protesting the college administration's unwillingness to let them enlist. Though the seminary's professor of English, William A. Seay, was appointed superintendent to replace Linfield, all students were dismissed when Union soldiers were reported as approaching the campus in 1863 (Fleming 1936; Winters 1991; Hoffman 2020). As will be noted in the chapters that follow, consistent turnover in administration plagued Southern Civil War-era higher education and often hindered institutional progress.

For reasons similar to those that encumbered fledgling LSU, colleges and universities across the South closed. In the State of Mississippi, only the still-extant, Baptist-affiliated Mississippi College remained open throughout the war (Coulter, Stephenson, and Tindall 1967; Heuvel and Heuvel 2013). Likewise, Wesleyan Female College in Georgia and Wofford College in South Carolina remained open. Despite such examples of wartime "enduring" colleges, the history of Southern higher education during the Civil War is often described as devastated and barren. As historian Dan R. Frost elucidates, Federal troops "burned schools they suspected of aiding the Confederate effort and seized or destroyed university records. Both sides [Confederate and Union] plundered campuses for apparatus, art, books, and furniture" (Frost 2000, 39). Likewise, Joseph A. Stetar extols, "The War and its social and economic consequences had a profound influence upon Southern higher education. The region's colleges were all but destroyed, and their clientele and financial support lost" (1985, 343). A review of literature concerning Southern Civil War-era higher education shows an emphasis on the annihilation of college campuses which was, in fact, not experienced by all. Institutions such as Wake Forest University in North Carolina and Tulane University of Louisiana closed during the war but did not experience substantial campus damage (Dyer 1966; Flynt 1968). On the other hand, academies such as the Georgia Military Institute, LaGrange Military College in Alabama, and the Clinton, Mississippi-based Corona Female College were raided or commandeered and burned by Federal soldiers, never to reopen as independent institutions (Mayo 1901; Wyeth 1907; Miller 2002).

While related books and articles provide interesting insights regarding college student military service, the role some professors played as Confederate officers, and the Reconstruction emergence of Southern higher education, this text attempts to showcase *how* some colleges and universities remained open during the war via in-depth case "episodes" of eleven Southern institutions of higher education that, for various reasons, remained in existence for the entirety or majority of the war. While some institutions relied on preparatory departments that enrolled students too young to enlist, other academies garnered the support of local communities for material and human resources. Some institutions profited from parental perceptions that enrolling their children as boarding students would keep their progeny safe from the ravages of war (McCandless 2011). A few Southern colleges and universities benefited from geographic locales not heavily influenced by raiding troops or destructive cannon fire. At the same time, professors at other academies played host to Union soldiers in order to stave off campus destruction. Northern officers camped on campuses while students resided in academic buildings—a temporary residential sacrifice that spared some universities from the vicissitudes of war.

Whether by intentional efforts, locale removed from direct conflict, or a reliance on students that would not have otherwise enlisted—i.e., young boys and female students—the eleven chapters herein depict not only how some Southern colleges remained open during the war but also provide a deeper insight into the daily lives of students, faculty, and institutional leaders as they maintained academic practices during the four years of bloodshed. Granted, there are telling published accounts of the University of Mississippi's academic and administrative activities before its war-related closure in 1861. Similarly, some books and articles recount late-antebellum-era interactions between students, faculty and administrators at burgeoning Louisiana State University as well as the original Tulane University of Louisiana medical department. Other texts describe efforts to keep the University of Georgia open prior to its closure in 1863, the Civil War shuttering of the University of Florida and the involvement of cadets from the Florida Military and Collegiate Institute (present-day Florida State University) in the Battle of Natural Bridge, and the Union burning of the University of Alabama in 1865 despite protests from local citizenry (Fleming 1936; Platt and McGee 2017; Dyer 1985; Duffy 1984; Dodd 1952; Sellers 1953).

Given the litany of published accounts regarding Civil War college enrollment decline, institutional closures, and widespread campus destruction at Southern academies like the University of Alabama and the College of William and Mary, it is easy to see how these retellings overshadow narratives pertaining to institutions that kept their doors open or suffered little to no physical damage while continuing to offer pedagogical services. Considering such, this volume features historical narratives that shed light on the continued existence of several Civil War-era Southern colleges and universities chosen by regional scholars. Each chapter provides pertinent information that underscores events that occurred at each institutional site prior to, during, and after the war—founding events, war-related influence, efforts to maintain academic operations, and Reconstruction-era adaptations. Chapters, organized via state secession from the Union, provide detailed accounts of the South Carolina Military Academy (more commonly referred to as The Citadel), Charleston, South Carolina; Wofford College, Spartanburg, South Carolina; Mississippi College, Clinton, Mississippi; Spring Hill College, Mobile, Alabama; Tuskegee Female College, Tuskegee, Alabama (present-day Huntingdon College in Montgomery, Alabama); Mercer University, Macon, Georgia; Wesleyan College, Macon, Georgia; the University of Virginia, Charlottesville, Virginia; the Virginia Military Institute, Lexington, Virginia; the University of North Carolina, Chapel Hill, North Carolina; and Trinity College (present-day Duke University), Durham, North Carolina. For Southern states with multiple academies described herein, those institutional narratives have been organized by college founding date.

In addition to providing an insider's perspective as regards the persistence of some Southern colleges and universities in the wake of large-scale, Civil War-era higher education closure, this volume adds to the growing body of Civil War literature focused more on the lived experience of those who witnessed the war, than the overarching sociopolitical "War Between the States" portrayal. At the same time, this text, rather than comparing wartime academic experiences between select colleges in the American South, North, and West, acknowledges several Southern Civil War institutional histories that have not been well documented in existing literature. Still, some institutions featured in this book, such as Wesleyan Female College and the University of Virginia have been explored concerning war-related events but not to such detail as is provided in this book. Despite the fact that the colleges and universities included in this text remained open during the Civil War, ruined plantation vistas and cotton fields set ablaze by Union troops serve as contextual backgrounds to college students, university professors, and their war-influenced experiences both on and off of their campuses. Indeed, this volume goes to great lengths to provide examples that describe how some academies remained open during a watershed moment of American history. If anything, this book builds upon the growing body of literature concerning Civil War-era higher education in the American South via microhistorical investigation. Chapter authors delved into existing archives, scrutinizing remaining documents that chronicle not only how each featured college or university remained open but also what was occurring

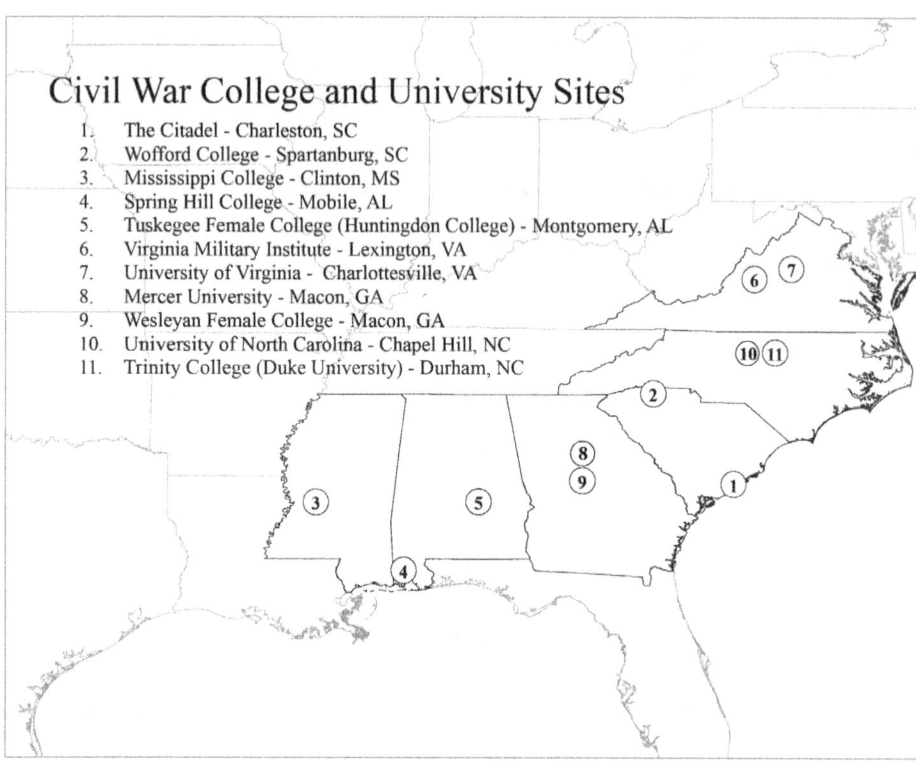

Civil War college and university sites. Map by Charisse Gulosino.

both inside and outside of each campus as the American South shifted from the antebellum, slave-holding plantation period to the long financial and political Reconstruction era that drastically changed the social landscape for all Southern residents.

Though this text focuses on Civil War experiences at extant colleges and universities in the former Confederate South, it should be noted that there were some Southern colleges that remained open during the war but have not survived to present day. For example, St. Charles College in Grand Coteau, Louisiana; the College of the Immaculate Conception in New Orleans, Louisiana; and Central Female Institute in Clinton, Mississippi, remained open for the duration of the war, though none of these academies exist in the modern era. The "higher education" division of the College of the Immaculate Conception was separated from the institution's preparatory department and closed in 1912. Though the institution's "lower division" was retained, it was relocated to the Carrollton suburb of New Orleans and was renamed Jesuit

High School. St. Charles College closed in 1922 following a directive from the Society of Jesus (Jesuits) to consolidate their Southern colleges. Central Female Institute, on the other hand, remained open until the early 1940s. Organized by the Central Baptist Association, this women's institution was renamed Hillman College in 1891 but merged with Mississippi College in 1942 (Balmer 2002; Drez 2012; Platt 2014). Given that over 150 colleges existed in the American South at the start of the 1860s, this work does not exhaust the entirety of Southern higher education history during the Civil War (Burke 1982; Brown 2020). Certainly not. Chapter authors were encouraged to construct institutional narratives based on historical interest and extant archival material. While the historical cases that follow provide interesting and informative accounts, the entirety of college life and academic experiences in the Civil War South is far greater than this text extols. If anything, this volume allows for deeper insights into academic persistence through turbulent years of battle and declining resources and might serve as a catalyst for further and deeper research on the operation of colleges and universities before, during, and directly after the war.

As has been mentioned, a significant portion of published literature describes the general closure of Southern higher education. While some institutions closed early in the war, others remained active until the latter half of the war before officially shutting their doors (Frost 2000; Sellers 1953). The significant loss of students, instructors, campus administrators, supplies, and the devastation of campus facilities caused a host of Southern institutions to shutter. Facilities were burned, buildings were ransacked, and academic buildings were converted into barracks, stables, or makeshift army hospitals. For example, Jefferson College in Convent, Louisiana, closed at the beginning of the war. Not long after, Federal troops invaded the surrounding area by means of the Mississippi River and, amongst various other sites, chose the Jefferson College campus to serve as an army barracks due to its proximity to the all-important waterway as well as its physical location halfway between New Orleans and Baton Rouge (Platt 2017). While stationed at the college-turned-barracks, Union officer F. G. Barnes lamented his own lack of higher education. Perusing the college's laboratory and the scattering of "first-year books," he considered taking a few texts for his personal edification. Seeing nothing wrong with purloining the abandoned volumes, Barnes wrote in a letter to his wife, "Everybody here is Secesh [secessionist] and I feel like spoiling them every chance I get." Despite his desire to take the introductory college books, Barnes could not find enough space in his saddlebag. Instead, he took with him a handful of unidentified French tomes (Barnes 1863).

Like the barracks conversion of Jefferson College, many institutions of higher education were also repurposed for a variety of wartime uses. Buildings at the University of Georgia in Athens were repurposed as an army hospital, quartermaster storage, and refuge for war-torn families. Two dormitories on the Howard College campus in Birmingham, Alabama, were repurposed as a Confederate hospital. Facilities at Wake Forest University were also used as makeshift army hospitals. Maryville College in Tennessee "served both armies as barracks, and then as horse stables" (Flynt 1968, 220–21; Montgomery, Folmsbee, and Greene 1984). While such repurposing often led to unintentional destruction due to the fact that such spaces were being used in ways they were not intended, other campuses were intentionally damaged by Union soldiers (Frost 2000). College libraries with rare books were destroyed, stairways were demolished, floorboards were torn up, and furniture was smashed (Nelson 1931). Though a handful of institutions were left relatively untouched by ravaging troops, all colleges and universities in the Civil War South were negatively influenced to a greater or lesser extent by the four years of military, political, and social hardship. Regardless of campus destruction, Southern higher education suffered due to the war effort long before they were subject to physical damage.

Apart from the large-scale Civil War closure of various college and universities, Southern institutions that remained open, such as Spring Hill College, Tuskegee Female College, and Mercer University (to name a few), continued to operate with low student numbers, scant resources, and faculty ranks stripped bare either by forced conscription or voluntary enlistment of white men aged eighteen to thirty-five (Sacher 2014). Those faculty who remained on their campuses subsisted on substantially reduced wages and, like their pupils, were cut off from families and friends. In the few texts dedicated to the subject, brief mention is given to the lived experiences of college students and their professors while residing at their institutions during the war itself. Some texts describe the significant social and intellectual changes experienced by faculty and pupils concerning their daily lives and classroom activities as the war progressed and resources diminished. On some campuses that managed to remain open, faculty wrote about the decreased food and clothing supplies in addition to progressively dwindling enrollment. While remaining professors concerned themselves with their institution's survival, various young men, bored with their academic activities, longed for the perceived honor of battle and were eager to join the fray. In his history of Spring Hill College, historian and Jesuit priest Michael Kenny described students as boys who "dreamed of the freedom of camp life, and military glory, and united to join the army even against the will of their parents" (1931, 213). Kenny also described those unable to enlist due to age or lack of parental consent as morose. Clearly these young men were depressed about remaining behind to study instead of joining their potential comrades in arms. There were even some students who attempted to run away and join the army to pursue the perceived excitement of war rather than the drudgeries of academic study (Platt 2014).

At other colleges, students helped with nursing duties as portions of their institutions were transformed into infirmaries. Unlike those academies that closed and were repurposed as hospitals, the University of Virginia in Charlottesville hosted an army hospital while offering classes to male students who opted not to enlist early in the war or those too young to join the Confederate armies later in the war. At academies with substantial military curricula, such as the Virginia Military Institute and the South Carolina Military Academy, cadet training, once meant to instill rigidity and a sense of gentlemanliness, became founts for Confederate officer training. Many such college cadets went into service not long after the war commenced or remained at their institutions to train incoming cadets (Andrew 2001; Green 2008). Indeed, militarism at several Southern institutions became a mainstay. While colleges like the Virginia Military Institute and The Citadel funneled student military men into Confederate ranks, other institutions, such as Mississippi College, also provided able-bodied young men to enlist, fight, and in some cases, die for the Confederacy.

Even though some institutions remained open during the war, nearly all such academies experienced enrollment decline—largely due to military enlistment. The shift in enrollment typically began with an initial drop at the start of the war during the 1860–1861 academic year, when the largest wave of students abandoned their studies to defend the South as soldiers. After this initial enrollment drop, many institutions experienced steady declines until the war's end. The University of North Carolina in Chapel Hill saw a sharp drop in enrollment in 1861, as students left daily to join their families or to enlist. Enrollment fell from 376 in the fall of 1860 to 91 in the fall of 1861. Despite declining enrollment, the University of North Carolina remained open during the war. Other colleges faced similar issues. Trinity College's founding president Braxton Craven described his institution in 1861 as one filled with political excitement and good student health despite dwindling enrollments. During the 1860–1861 academic year, 212 students were enrolled at Trinity College. This number dropped precipitously to 40 by the end of the 1863 academic year. Like the University of North Carolina, Trinity College continued to operate despite enrollment decline (Lindemann 2017). While most colleges dealt with significant enrollment drops as the war progressed, not all academies faced that particular problem. At Spring Hill College, the 1864–1865 academic year opened with an elevated enrollment as families were increasingly concerned that their sons might be drafted into military service if they were not enrolled in academic study. Despite their parents' best intentions, many students left the academy to fight (Platt 2014).

As enrollment dropped, so did tuition revenue. This was especially challenging as supplies became more expensive and more difficult to obtain. One student at the University of North Carolina wrote to his sister in 1862 that everything was expensive and scarce. He stated that the fee to board on campus was very high, and "there is but very little to eat" (Sessoms 1862). A Randolph-Macon College student in Boydton, Virginia, wrote to his father on May 1, 1861, that the "college will not suspend . . . for want of provisions—they are getting scarce" (Dunn 1861). In 1868, Randolph-Macon College was relocated to Ashland due to the Union destruction of important railways that connected Boydton to other Virginia cities and townships (Caknipe 2015). The "scarcity of provisions" occurred almost immediately on some campuses, and access to supplies was also affected by campus locations. Lack of provisions was exacerbated by the influx of Union forces in some areas. For example, Spring Hill College near Mobile, Alabama, was directly affected by the 1862 Federal occupation of New Orleans. Like several Gulf South cities, Mobile and surrounding areas relied on various exports from the Crescent City (Kenny 1931; Lang 2002). Due to the inflation of Confederate currency and the lack of comestibles, clothing, and other general supplies, students and faculty had to go without many of the comforts they had known prior to the war—fine quills for writing, well-tailored garments, substantial meals, etc. While some colleges were forced to close due to a lack of supplies, faculty and administrators at other institutions improvised and devised plans to ensure that students had enough resources for the lean years to come. University of Virginia faculty accepted food in lieu of tuition and administrators at Trinity College, in 1864, requested that students bring any books from home they could carry to offset the college's lack of literary supplies (Chaffin 1950).

Though this book does not portray every aspect of college life in the Civil War South, it does highlight important aspects relevant to student activities, faculty involvement, and academic life, while battles raged, often nearby. All chapters in this volume detail how each college or university remained open while so many other institutions closed. One institution, the Virginia Military Institute closed briefly during the first year of the war but was quickly reopened and remained in existence to train soldiers for Southern military ranks (Walker 1875). This is not to say, however, that the colleges and universities featured in this volume emerged from the Civil War well stocked with student, instructional, and financial resources. On the contrary, many academies that remained open throughout the war years fought to endure during Southern Reconstruction and the latter half of the nineteenth century. Not all were successful. Though Trinity College remained open during the war, it closed in the same month Gen. Robert E. Lee surrendered at Appomattox, Virginia. Trinity College closed in the spring of 1865 due to the intense operational strain resulting from lack of regional resources and the arrival of approximately twenty thousand war-torn Confederate soldiers who sought refuge on the college grounds. The private, North Carolina-based institution, later renamed Duke University, remained closed until the following year (Chaffin 1950).

Likewise, the South Carolina Military Academy in the heavily bombarded, war-torn city of Charleston remained opened throughout the war despite heavy shelling from Federal cannoneers. Though The Citadel persevered during the war, the fall of Charleston and Union occupation dealt a heavy blow to both the city as well as the military college. As a result, South Carolina's military institution closed and remained shuttered throughout the Reconstruction era (Andrew 2001; Conrad 2004). Suffering from the loss of institutional funds and a dearth of regional support, the University of North Carolina closed in 1871. However, it was reopened four years later (Snider 1992). Conversely, the University of Alabama closed in the final year of the war due to Federal troops destroying a large portion of the campus. Following the campus siege and the burning of various buildings, the Tuscaloosa-based institution closed on April 4, 1865, five days before Gen. Lee's surrender. The University of Alabama remained closed for seven years (Sellers 1953).

In the face of wartime hardships, college students, whether male or female, found ways to support the Confederacy and its military personnel. Certainly, students enflamed by Confederate patriotism did much to unify student bodies via their shared mindset and political purpose. While some students penned poetic verses that heaped glories on Confederate figures like Jefferson Davis, others practiced military drills in hopes of bolstering Southern battalions should they enlist. Students at Wesleyan Female College (renamed Wesleyan College in 1917) not only supported the war effort by forming their own military brigade complete with wooden rifles, some female pupils championed the secessionist South through speeches and debate (Bonnell 1864; Griffin 1996). The early days of war caused excitement among students at many colleges across the South. Female students at Tuskegee Female College in Alabama attended balls and soirées in support of the Confederacy (Ellison 1954). A student at Randolph-Macon College indicated that everyone was talking about the war. He wrote to his sister that "[t]he great topic of conversation now is the present state of our country. There is very much excitement here, and but little studying being done" (Dunn 1861). Even so, some university faculty plied their trade and maintained an air of academic rigidity. Instructors tried, though often in vain, to force their students to focus on studies rather than the excitement of far-off battles. Before the University of Georgia's closure in 1863, the institution's faculty reminded students that their studies must come first (Flynt 1968). To keep colleges open, exemption requests were made to state governors in hopes of retaining students who would otherwise be subject to conscription. In some cases, exemption requests were honored, but in other cases they were denied (Coulter 1968).

Requests for exemptions became more common as the war progressed. The faculty and members of the governing board at the University of Virginia wrote to the secretary of war, James A. Seddon, informing him that the conscription of all able-bodied men would "grievously jeopardize the school's existence without tangibly adding to the Confederacy's military strength" (Jordan 2017, para. 12). While students at the University of Virginia were not exempted from conscription, they were given a yearlong furlough. Other institutions were not so fortunate. University of North Carolina president David Lowry Swain requested a military conscription exemption in 1863, and while exemptions for the junior and senior students were granted that year, they were denied the following year. After the 1864 denial, conscription agents went to the university to remove students by force (Lindemann 2017).

Regardless of conscription denials, most of the academies featured in this text remained open despite the loss of students due to mandatory enlistment.

Not only were the lives of Southern college students affected by the war, so too were those of their professors. Indeed, faculty retention was often difficult due to enlistment and conscription. While some instructors avoided enlistment, others left the classroom to take up arms against the Northern foe (Flynt 1968). For those professors who stayed at their respective campuses, many were committed to ensuring their institutions remained open while also supporting the Confederacy, if not by serving as soldiers then via overt patriotic sentiment (Parks 1957). At all Southern colleges and universities described in this book, Confederate patriotism and support is evident. During the early Civil War years, Southern faculty, like their students, exhibited intense pro-Confederacy sentiment. However, as the war progressed, the cloistered campus experience resulted in low faculty morale, student boredom, and general irritation. As most students were not permitted to leave campus to visit friends and family, reports emerged depicting college life as far from exciting. For example, students at the University of Virginia described days of academic study amidst continued news of Confederate losses as tedious, depressing, and irksome. Students often wrote home and commented that their studies progressed despite changes to daily social life due to the war. These accounts sometimes display more monotony and general weariness than Confederate enthusiasm. One University of Virginia student, John Henderson, wrote to his mother on February 14, 1863, and commented on the dwindling sophomore class as well as the many students who were conscripted. He commented that he regretted to see his friends leave, but that they, the enlisted, went off in good spirits (Henderson 1863). Henderson wrote without the excitement often described in so many texts on early Civil War military life. Similarly, when Preston H. Sessoms, a student at the University of North Carolina, wrote to his sister on August 28, 1862, he mentioned the noticeable absence of his fellow students due to conscription and described the campus as very dull and lonesome (Sessoms 1862).

While all Southern college students experienced hardship in some form, the difficulties they experienced were not consistent across campuses. At Trinity College, rules were made more flexible as the excitement of war brought a "gradual relaxing of the social restrictions" that had previously been in place (Chaffin 1950, 230). Along with the relaxation of social restrictions, academic regulations at several colleges became disorganized.

Conversely, students at Trinity College in 1864 were described as healthy and attentive to their studies. Spring Hill College students, particularly in the final years of the war, however, were depicted as being in low spirits and humiliated by the presence of the Union troops who camped on the lawns of their college (Kenny 1931).

Southern militarism, regional pride, and Confederate nationalism, despite declining morale and ennui, pervade the narratives of all institutional cases herein. Issues germane to regional women's higher education, slavery and states' rights, Southern honor, and regional ideological preservation are highlighted throughout this book as well. In almost all chapters, the issue of slavery is addressed. Some chapters provide detailed illustrations of institutional connectedness to chattel servitude, administrative and faculty support for the institution of slavery, and student connections to plantation life. To be sure, slavery was socially connected to all individuals who enrolled in or were employed by Southern colleges and universities—just as it was a core tenant behind Southern secession, slavery was an undergirding factor that tied all pupils and their instructors to the greater social fabric of antebellum Southern life. Prior to the Civil War, several Southern colleges and universities profited from slave labor. For example, slaves were used to construct most of the buildings on the early campus of the University of Virginia (Goode 1966). Similarly, several college presidents, such as the Methodist preacher and first president of Trinity College, Braxton Craven, owned slaves (Craven 1860).

The role of women in Southern Civil War higher education is also explored. While institutions like Wesleyan Female College were focused on the mental fortification of young women who would, in time, lead households and rear Southern children, other colleges, including Trinity College and Mississippi College, admitted female students along with male students, if only for a short period of time. When the Civil War broke out, parents were relieved to send their daughters to reside at a safe academy, one seemingly, though not always, removed from the carnage of war. Though antebellum female colleges were far fewer than their male counterparts, the voices of female students residing at Southern women's institutions, as well as those women enrolled at early Wesleyan Female College, Trinity College, and Tuskegee Female College, are recounted in this book. Though not permitted to enlist, female support of the Confederate cause was no less passionate and, as will be illustrated, their vocal support for the South was evident.

Yet another theme that emerges in this book is that of religion. In various instances the Judeo-Christian denominational predilections of institutional leaders and students (Baptist, Catholic, Methodist) are overt. Students and instructors prayed for Confederate victories in Catholic Masses, Baptist conventions sponsored and supported Civil War-era higher education, and prominent Methodist preachers oversaw colleges while battles were fought in the surrounding countryside. The American South, prior to and after the Civil War, was an actively religious region of the United States. Though the nineteenth-century played host to several instances of denominational conflict between Catholics and Protestants, Southern colleges affiliated with said denominations were not only pedagogical sanctuaries in the war-torn South but also religious havens where those enrolled prayed for their enlisted brethren (Miller, Stout, and Wilson 1998; Miller 2007; Wilson 2011). As the war progressed, religion, at several of the institutions included in this volume, became a crucial morale booster, as hopes for Union defeat diminished. In almost all colleges that remained open through the war years, students struggled to maintain a positive outlook as the Confederacy weakened and eventually died. As a result, religion remained an important anchor for students and professors who, by the war's end, had lost faith in their Southern government but still prayed for a future in which their regional livelihoods would be maintained.

With the conclusion of the Civil War and the start of Southern Reconstruction, regional institutions of higher education emerged as entities in need of intellectual and instructional revision if they were to persist. While various Southern professors and former Confederate officers reopened shuttered institutions, the colleges and universities described in this book strove to maintain viability in a turbulent era of political, social, and physical rebuilding. Institutional leaders altered curricula to address vocational needs rather than liberal arts mores. A host of family fortunes were ruined by the war, and formerly wealthy Southern progeny had to refocus their academic efforts to engage in careers that would garner a steady paycheck: mercantilism, law, business, accounting, etc. (Frost 2000; Marsden 1994). At the same time that Southern academies were wrestling with curricular modernity against the backdrop of the region's crippled plantation-based economy, the newly freed African American population plied for education inclusive of college instruction (Follett 2016; Butchart 2013; Foner 2011). With financial support stemming from the Freedmen's Bureau, institutions such as Fisk University in Tennessee (1865), Howard University in Washington, DC (1867), and Tougaloo College in Mississippi (1869) were founded. While some states, such as South Carolina, experimented with early forms of college-level racial integration (in 1873, Henry E. Hayne became the first African American to enroll in medical classes at the University of South Carolina), Mississippi's Reconstruction-era legislators circumvented attempts at higher education desegregation by founding Alcorn State University (1871) to serve the state's freedmen (Foner 2014; Posey 2011). Despite some efforts at late-nineteenth-century racial integration and the establishment of several African American-serving institutions, higher education in the American South wrestled with racial segregation well into the latter half of the twentieth century. The Civil War may have been a significant economic, military, political, and social turning point for the United States, but it did not secure access to higher education for formerly enslaved people in spite of Abraham Lincoln's Emancipation Proclamation (1863), the abolition of slavery via the Thirteenth Amendment (1865), the recognition of freedmen as US citizens (1868), or the enactment of African American voting rights (1870). In fact, many of those Southern colleges that remained open during the war, or reopened thereafter, championed racial segregation even after the civil rights movement of the 1950s and 1960s (Anderson 1988; Kean 2013; Richardson 2001).

To date, no text focusing completely on college life during the Civil War has been published nor is there a volume that presents readers with examples of different institutions. As historian Wayne Flynt states, "there has been no attempt to construct an overview of Southern higher education in the war years" (1968, 211). Existing research on collegiate activities in the war-torn South focuses predominantly on the rebirth of higher education during Reconstruction (Burke 1982; Cohen 2012). However, these publications lack details about the daily life of students, faculty, and administrators who remained on campus. This volume broaches the topic of lived Civil War-era student and faculty experiences via chapters dedicated to individual institutions and provides insights into why these colleges and universities remained open while their peer institutions were shuttered. Responding to the call from fellow educational historians for a microhistorical, case-by-case examination of internal and external events related to academic persistence in the Civil War South, this book builds on existing educational history texts, Confederate-era narratives, and scholarship concerning higher education's war involvement. It also provides encouragement for scholars to further investigate Southern higher education in the mid-nineteenth century as related to religious activities, secession, Southern nationalism, slavery, student soldiers, women and higher education, wartime administrative struggles, changing curricular dynamics, institutional survival in the face of large-scale disaster, and the nature of higher education before, during, and after the American Civil War. Ultimately, this book gives readers the opportunity to see how some Southern colleges and universities remained open while so many of their peer institutions shut down during the deadliest internal conflict in American history.

REFERENCES

Anderson, James D. 1988. *The Education of Blacks in the South, 1860–1935*. Chapel Hill: University of North Carolina Press.

Andrew, Rod., Jr. 2001. *Long Gray Lines: The Southern Military School Tradition, 1839–1915*. Chapel Hill: University of North Carolina Press.

Balmer, Randall H. 2004. *The Encyclopedia of Evangelism*. 2nd ed. Waco, TX: Baylor University Press.

Barnes, F. G. 1863. Jefferson College. Letter to his Wife. March 23, 1863. Albany: New York State Library and Archives, Cultural Education Center.

Bernath, Michael T. 2010. *Confederate Minds: The Struggle for Intellectual Independence in the Civil War South*. Charlottesville: University of North Carolina Press.

Bonnell, John M. 1864. Impressments Draft Letter. John Mitchell Bonnell Papers, 1848–1864. Stuart A. Rose Manuscript Archives and Rare Book Library, Emory University.

Brown, Ray. 2020. "Index of Colleges and Universities that have Closed, Merged, or Changed their Names." College History Garden. Last modified November 6, 2020. https://collegehistorygarden.blogspot.com/2014/11/index-of-colleges-and-universities-that.html.

Burke, Collin. 1982. *American Collegiate Populations: A Test of the Traditional View*. New York: New York University Press.

Butchart, Ronald E. 2013. *Schooling the Freed People: Teaching, Learning, and the Struggle for Black Freedom, 1861–1876*. Chapel Hill: University of North Carolina Press.

Caknipe, John, Jr. 2015. *Randolph Macon College in the Early Years: Making Preachers, Teachers, and Confederate Officers, 1830–1868*. Jefferson, NC: McFarland & Company, Inc.

Chaffin, Nora Campbell. 1950. *Trinity College, 1839–1892: The Beginnings of Duke University*. Raleigh, NC: Duke University Press.

Cohen, Michael David. 2012. *Reconstructing the Campus: Higher Education and the American Civil War*. Charlottesville: University of Virginia Press.

Conrad, James Lee. 2012. *The Young Lions: Confederate Cadets at War*. Columbia: University of South Carolina Press.

Coulter, Ellis Merton. 1928. *College Life in the Old South*. Athens: University of Georgia Press.

Coulter, Ellis Merton, Wendell Holmes Stephenson, and George Brown Tindall. 1967. *A History of the South*. Baton Rouge: Louisiana State University Press.

Craven, Braxton. Braxton Craven Diaries, 1845–1874. Braxton Craven Records and Papers, Box 2, Folders 30–34. Duke University Archives, David M. Rubenstein Rare Book & Manuscript Library, Duke University.

Dodd, William George. 1952. *History of West Florida Seminary*. Tallahassee: Florida State University Press.

Drez, Ronald J. 2012. *Gallant Fighting Sons: The Jesuits, Louisiana, and Their School in New Orleans*. Old Saybrook, CT: Konecky & Konecky Ltd.

Duffy, John. 1984. *The Tulane University Medical Center: One Hundred and Fifty Years of Medical Education*. Baton Rouge: Louisiana State University.

Dunn, R. E. 1861. Letter to Father. April 19, 1861. J. Hubert Scruggs Postal History Collection, Birmingham Public Library Archives Department.

Dyer, John P. 1966. *Tulane: The Biography of a University, 1834–1965*. New York: Harper & Row.

Dyer, Thomas G. 1985. *The University of Georgia: A Bicentennial History 1785–1985*. Athens: University of Georgia Press.

Ellison, Rhonda. Coleman. 1954. *History of Huntingdon College 1854–1954*. Tuscaloosa: University of Alabama Press.

Faculty Minutes 1840–90. Centenary College of Louisiana Archives and Special Collections. College Archives. Magale Library, Shreveport.

Fleming, Walter L. 1936. *Louisiana State University, 1860–1896*. Baton Rouge: Louisiana State University Press.

Flynt, Wayne. 1968. "Southern Higher Education and the Civil War." *Civil War History* 14 (3): 211–25.

Follett, Richard. 2016. "Introduction." In *Plantation Kingdom: The American South and Its Global Commodities*, edited by Richard Follett, Sven Beckert, Peter Coclanis, and Barbara Hahn, 1–11. Baltimore: Johns Hopkins University Press.

Foner, Eric. 2011. "Abraham Lincoln, Colonization, and the Rights of Black Americans." In *Slavery's Ghost: The Problem of Freedom in the Age of Emancipation*, edited by Richard Follett, Eric Foner, and Walter Johnson, 31–49. Baltimore: Johns Hopkins University Press.

Foner, Eric. 2014. *Reconstruction Updated Edition: American's Unfinished Revolution, 1863–1877*. New York: Harper Perennial.

Frost, Dan R. 2000. *Thinking Confederates: Academia and the Idea of Progress in the New South*. Knoxville: University of Tennessee Press.

Geiger, Roger L. 2000. "Introduction: New Themes in the History of Nineteenth-Century College." In *The American College in the Nineteenth Century*, edited by Roger L. Geiger, 1–36. Nashville, Tennessee: Vanderbilt University Press.

Goode, James Moore. 1966. "The Confederate University: The Forgotten Institutions of the American Civil War." Master's thesis. Charlottesville: University of Virginia.

Green, Jennifer R. 2008. *Military Education and the Emerging Middle Class in the Old South*. New York: Cambridge University Press.

Griffin, Richard W. 1996. "Wesleyan College: Its Genesis, 1835–1840." *The Georgia Historical Quarterly* 50 (1): 54–73.

Henderson, John F. February 14, 1863. Letter to Mother. *Documenting the American South*. University of North Carolina: Chapel Hill. Last modified July 11, 2019. http://docsouth.unc.edu/unc/unc09-12/unc09-12.html.

Heuvel, Sean M. and Lisa L. Heuvel. 2013. *The College of William and Mary in the Civil War*. Jefferson, NC: McFarland & Company, Inc.

Hoffman, Paul E. 2020. *Louisiana State University and Agricultural and Mechanical College, 1860–1919*. Baton Rouge: Louisiana State University.

Hyde, Sarah L. 2016. *Schooling in the Antebellum South: The Rise of Public and Private Education in Louisiana, Mississippi, and Alabama*. Baton Rouge: Louisiana State University Press.

Jordan, Ervin L., Jr. 2016. "The University of Virginia during the Civil War." In *Encyclopedia Virginia*. Last modified May 10, 2020. https://www.encyclopediavirginia.org/University_of_Virginia_During_the_Civil_War_The.

Kean, Melissa. 2013. *Desegregating Private Higher Education in the South: Duke, Emory, Rice, Tulane, and Vanderbilt*. Baton Rouge: Louisiana State University Press.

Kenny, Michael. 1931. *The Torch on the Hill: Centenary Story of Spring Hill College, 1830–1930*. New York: The American Press.

Lang, James O. 2002. "Gloom Envelops New Orleans: April 24 to May 2, 1862." In *The Louisiana Bicentennial Series in Louisiana History, Volume 5*, edited by Arthur W. Bergeron Jr., 24–37. Lafayette: Center for Louisiana Studies, University of Louisiana at Lafayette.

Lindemann, Erika. 2017. "Civil War." *Documenting the American South*. University of North Carolina: Chapel Hill. Last modified November 12, 2020. https://docsouth.unc.edu/true/chapter/chp06-01/chp06-01.html.

Marsden, George M. 1994. *The Soul of the American University: From Protestant Establishment to Established Nonbelief*. New York: Oxford University Press.

Mayo, A. D. 1901. "The Organization and the Development of the American Common School in the Atlantic and Central States of the South, 1830 to 1860." In *Report of the Commissioner of Education for the Year 1899–1900, Volume 1*, 427–561. Washington, DC: Government Printing Office.

McCandless, Amy Thompson. 2011. "Women's Higher Education." In *The New Encyclopedia of Southern Culture, Volume 17: Education*, edited by Clarence L. Mohr, 142–46. Chapel Hill: University of North Carolina Press.

Miller, Mary Carol. 2002. *Lost Landmarks of Mississippi*. Jackson: University Press of Mississippi.

Miller, Randall M., Harry S. Stout, and Charles Reagan Wilson. 1998. "Introduction." In *Religion and the American Civil War*, edited by Randall M. Miller, Harry S. Stout, and Charles Reagan Wilson, 3–18. New York: Oxford University Press.

Miller, Robert J. 2007. *Both Prayed to the Same God: Religion and Faith in the American Civil War*. Lanham, MD: Lexington Books.

Montgomery, James Riley, Stanley J. Folmsbee, and Lee Seifert Greene. 1984. *To Foster Knowledge: A History of the University of Tennessee, 1794–1970*. Knoxville: University of Tennessee Press.

Morgan, Lee. 2008. *Centenary College of Louisiana, 1825–2000: The Biography of an American Academy*. Shreveport: Centenary College of Louisiana Press.

Nelson, William Hamilton. 1931. *A Burning Torch and a Flaming Fire: The Story of Centenary College of Louisiana*. Nashville, TN: Methodist Pub House.

O'Brien, Michael. 2012. *Intellectual Life and the American South, 1810–1860: An Abridged Edition of 'Conjectures of Order*. Chapel Hill: University of North Carolina Press.

Pace, Robert F. 2004. *Halls of Honor: College Men in the Old South*. Baton Rouge: Louisiana State University Press.

Parks. Joseph Howard. 1957. *Birmingham-Southern College, 1856–1956*. Nashville, TN: Parthenon Press.

Platt, R. Eric. 2014. *Sacrifice and Survival: Identity, Mission, and Jesuit Higher Education in the American South*. Tuscaloosa: University of Alabama Press.

Platt, R. Eric. 2017. *Educating the Sons of Sugar: Jefferson College and the Creole Planter Class of South Louisiana*. Tuscaloosa: University of Alabama Press.

Platt R. Eric and Melandie McGee. 2017. "The Educational Administration of William Tecumseh Sherman: A North Military Officer's Tenure at a Southern University Prior to the American Civil War." *Vitae Scholasticae* 34 (1): 48–75.

Posey, Josephine McCann. 2011. *Against Great Odds: The History of Alcorn State University*. Jackson: University Press of Mississippi.

Richardson, Heather Cox. 2001. *The Death of Reconstruction: Race, Labor, and Politics in Post-Civil War North, 1865–1901*. Cambridge: Harvard University Press.

Sacher, John M. 2014. "Searching for 'Some Plain and Simple Method': Jefferson Davis and Confederate Conscription." In *The Enigmatic South: Towards Civil War and Its Legacies*, edited by Samuel C. Hyde Jr., 133–49. Baton Rouge: Louisiana State University Press.

Sellers, James Benson. 1953. *History of the University of Alabama*. Tuscaloosa: University of Alabama Press.

Sessoms, Preston H. August 28, 1862. Letter to Penelope E. White. *Documenting the American South*. University of North Carolina: Chapel Hill. Last modified July 11, 2019. https://docsouth.unc.edu/true/mss06-10/mss06-10.html.

Snider, William D. 1992. *Light on the Hill: A History of the University of North Carolina at Chapel Hill*. Chapel Hill: University of North Carolina Press.

Stetar, Joseph M. 1985. "In Search of a Direction: Southern Higher Education After the Civil War." *History of Education Quarterly* 25 (3): 341–67.

Tewksbury, Donald George. 1932. *The Founding of American Colleges and Universities Before the Civil War*. New York: Bureau of Publication, Teachers College, Columbia.

University of the Ozarks. 2019. "The Cane Hill Years." History: Different is in Our DNA. Last modified November 30, 2020. https://ozarks.edu/about/history/.

University of South Carolina. 2018. "Civil War, Reconstruction." Our History. Last modified November 11, 2020. https://www.sc.edu/about/our_history/.

Walker, Charles D. 1875. *Biographical Sketches of the Graduates and Élèves of the Virginia Military Institute Who Fell During the War Between the States*. Philadelphia, PA: J. B. Lippincott & Co.

Williams, Timothy J. 2015. *Intellectual Manhood: University, Self, and Society in the Antebellum South*. Chapel Hill: University of North Carolina Press.

Wilson, Charles Reagan. 2011. "Religion and Education." In *The New Encyclopedia of Southern Culture, Volume 17: Education*, edited by Clarence L. Mohr, 106–13. Chapel Hill: University of North Carolina Press.

Winters, John D. 1991. *The Civil War in Louisiana*. Baton Rouge: Louisiana State University Press.

Wyeth, John Allan. 1907. *History of LaGrange Military Academy and the Cadet Corps, 1857–1862*. New York: The Brewer Press.

CHAPTER ONE

The South Carolina Military Academy during the Civil War

Training Ground for the Confederacy

Christian K. Anderson

Just after daybreak on the morning of January 9, 1861, four cadets from the South Carolina Military Academy (otherwise known as The Citadel) fired cannon shots on the *Star of the West* in Charleston Harbor. The vessel had been sent to resupply Union troops at Fort Sumter. Maj. Peter F. Stevens, superintendent of The Citadel, gave the order: "Commence firing!" and John Marshall Whilden, the cadet gun captain, passed on the order: "Number one, fire!" On receipt of the order, Cadet George Edward Haynesworth of Sumter pulled the lanyard, firing the first shot—a warning across the bow of the vessel. Cadet Samuel Bonneau Pickens fired the second shot, which struck and damaged the steamer, and then each of the four guns continued firing. The *Star of the West's* crew reversed course, abandoned their mission, and turned out to sea, returning to New York. Under their red palmetto flag, the cadets declared victory.

This was the first of many engagements in the Civil War by South Carolina Military Academy cadets from its two campuses, the Arsenal in Columbia and The Citadel in Charleston. While the attack on Fort Sumter on April 12, 1861, is generally regarded as the official "start" of the Civil War, it is the attack on the *Star of the West* that looms large in Citadel lore (Baker 1990; Marshall 1967; Wiles 1971). The cadets involved in the firing on the *Star of the West*, along with their commander, are memorialized in a mural that hangs in The Citadel's library. Several scholarships and awards are named

Star of the West mural depicting Citadel cadets firing on the ship on January 9, 1861, by David Humphrey Miller, c 1960. Image courtesy of the Citadel Archives and Museum, Charleston, South Carolina.

after the incident ("Star of the West Scholarship Awarded" 1960). Period Charlestonians and Citadel cadets alike regarded this small skirmish as the beginning of the war. The Charleston *Mercury* declared on January 10: "THE WAR BEGUN . . . CITADEL CADETS FIRED THE FIRST SHOTTED GUN . . . THE UNITED STATES FLAG HAULED DOWN" (quoted in Marshall 1967, 17). Citadel cadets used this incident as a rallying cry throughout the war and thereafter. The *New York Evening Post* reported that the crew of the *Star of the West* was impressed with the cadets' military skills: "Their line was perfect," and the one who had "charge of the guns knew his business" (quoted in Buckley 2004, 23).

Only weeks before, on December 20, 1860, the Ordinance of Secession passed unanimously (169–0) in Charleston, dissolving South Carolina's association with the United States to preserve the institution of slavery (Edgar 1998). The state's "Declaration of the Immediate Causes Which Induce and Justify the Secession of South Carolina from the Federal Union" issued on December 24, 1860, explained in no uncertain terms that its reasons for withdrawing from the Union was "the increasing hostility on the part of the non-slaveholding States to the Institution of Slavery." Citadel cadets gave a parade in honor of the secessionist convention delegates (Bond 1936).

Tensions mounted after the *Star of the West* attack, and by April, it was clear that war was inevitable. On April 9, 1861, The Citadel's Board of Visitors

Minutes read: "That in consequence of the imminent collision between the troops of the Confederate States, and the forces of the United States, in the immediate vicinity of the City of Charleston, the usual ceremonies of the [graduation] commencement be dispensed with" (Board of Visitors Minutes 1861–1865). While the institution may have cancelled the ceremony, The Citadel itself did not close (Baker 1990; Bond 1936; Thomas 1893). The military academy remained open and active throughout the war, despite the many cadets who enlisted. The institution not only remained open—enrollment swelled beyond capacity. In fact, in one year, as many as two-hundred recruits had to be turned away. Citadel cadets engaged in their own courses and provided basic training to conscripted soldiers and recruits in Charleston and Columbia. In the field, cadets guarded and transferred prisoners, among other tasks (Baker 1990; Bond 1936; Thomas 1893). While classes continued, the war effort occasionally took precedence over academics for some. Despite remaining open during the war, The Citadel was forced to close in February 1865, when union troops occupied Charleston and were garrisoned in The Citadel itself until 1879. The academy did not reopen until 1882.

THE MILITARY ACADEMY TRADITION IN THE SOUTH

In the years leading up to the Civil War, there were at least eighty-five military academies in the American South (Coulter 2017). While only a quarter of them survived the war, this antebellum number demonstrates the ubiquity of military training in contrast to the North, which had only thirty-two such institutions during the same period. Many Southern military institutes were founded in response to the Nullification Crisis of 1832, a dispute between Southern states and the Federal government over tariffs that could have jeopardized the institution of slavery (Kytle and Roberts 2018; Conrad 2004; Andrew 2001). The founding of these Southern military institutions can be traced to Alden Partridge, alumnus and former superintendent of the US Military Academy at West Point, who founded the first private military college in the United States—the Military College of Vermont (Andrew 2001). Vermont's military academy graduates evangelized Partridge's military college model, particularly in the South. As a result, dozens of military academies can trace their roots to him and his students, including The Citadel (Bond 1936).

The difference between Northern and Southern military academies, however, was not only a matter of numbers. Most Northern institutions were private, and not state sponsored like those of the South (Coulter 2017; Conrad 2004). In the case of West Point, it was decidedly a *national* academy with the express purpose of training future US Army officers, while the *state* academies in the South had broader aims of inculcating a culture of honor, where militarism was on par with republicanism (or patriotic citizenship). Militarism at these Southern academies was not simply about martial preparedness but rather part of a larger design: to create ideal young men with proper character and gentlemanly Southern virtues (Andrew 2001). As John Coulter explains: "The South's distrust of the Federal government, arising from clashes over states' rights issues and attacks on its 'peculiar institution' [slavery], combined with its martial tradition, provided greater impetus for the establishment of military colleges, academies, and preparatory schools than existed in the more secure and less military-oriented North" (2004, viii).

When the Confederate Conscription Act was activated in 1862, which required compulsory military service of all white men ages eighteen to thirty-five, there were no academic exceptions. Many Citadel cadets were younger than eighteen, sometimes enrolling as young as fourteen, but continuing as a student-cadet beyond the age of eighteen provided no protection from military service. Rather, many enrolled at military colleges for the express purpose of being able to better serve the Confederate military effort. This did not prevent the governors of Alabama, Georgia, South Carolina, and Virginia from attempting to stop or circumvent this law so that students could remain exempt until graduation (Coulter 2017; Sacher 2014). The cadets at the South Carolina Military Academy, the University Alabama, the Georgia Military Institute, and midshipmen studying at the Confederate Naval Academy in Richmond all saw combat or provided military services and support (Coulter 2017; Andrew 2001). Indeed, administrators at the Virginia Military Institute provided sixty-four cadets as escort to the governor of Virginia. The cadets also served as guards at the public execution of abolitionist John Brown in 1859 and served in several major battles during the war such as the Battle of New Market (Conrad 2004).

BIRTH OF THE CITADEL AND ARSENAL

Abolitionist Elihu Burritt wrote in 1851: "If there be a town in the United States, which might be regarded as the citadel and capital of American slavery, that town is Charleston, South Carolina." Historians Ethan J. Kytle and Blaine Roberts agree: "No American city rivaled Charleston in terms of the role that slavery played in its formation and success, nor in the political, economic, and ideological support it provided for the expansion of slavery in the United States. And no American city better illustrates the brutal realities of human bondage, realities that belie the whitewashed image of the peculiar institution crafted by its Old South and latter-day apologists" (2018, 12). Slavery was such an essential part of Charleston that, by the start of the Civil War, most city residents were black with a powerful white minority in control. Antebellum Charleston was one of the largest North American cities, and at one point had more slaves than Boston, New York, and Philadelphia combined. It was the most significant port city for the import of enslaved labor, and after the abolishment of the transatlantic slave trade it continued to be "a vital center of the internal American slave trade through the Civil War" (2018, 17).

It was this social context, heavily undergirded by chattel servitude, that gave birth to The Citadel. The Citadel was built in 1822 in response to the thwarted rebellion of former slave Denmark Vesey (Conrad 2004). Vesey had purchased his own freedom but was unable to do so for his family. He was one of the founders of the African Methodist Church later known as Mother Emanuel. Vesey crafted a plan wherein free blacks and slaves would "rise up" on July 14, 1822, Bastille Day, attack their white masters, and set sail for Haiti. The plot was foiled before it began, and Vesey was hanged along with thirty-four associates, while others were sold off (Kytle and Roberts 2018). In response, the Arsenal was constructed in the South Carolina capital of Columbia and a permanent municipal guard of 150 men was created to ward off any similar incidents. One of Vesey's biographers calls the imposing Citadel and former Arsenal campus as "the most impressive symbol of racial control" (quoted in Macaulay 2009, 10).

The Arsenal campus was created in 1833 to consolidate state munitions from three other arsenals in the capital city. At first, the Arsenal was just that, guarded storage for munitions. In 1841, Governor John P. Richardson suggested that state arsenals could function as military academies with cadets serving as guards. On December 20, 1842, a bill was passed establishing the Columbia-based Arsenal and a second Charleston-based arsenal as both the Arsenal Academy and The Citadel Academy. In 1845, the two academies were formally combined into one institution, with cadets spending their first year at the Arsenal campus and then transferring to The Citadel campus for three more years of instruction (Conrad 2004). This act of amalgamation was further solidified when South Carolina's legislature mandated on January 28, 1861, that, "the Arsenal Academy and Citadel Academy shall retain the same distinctive titles, but they shall together constitute and be entitled 'The South Carolina Military Academy'" (Thomas 1893, 108–9). The act stipulated that cadets would be organized into companies known as "The Battalion of State Cadets."

CIVIL WAR HIGHER EDUCATION IN THE PALMETTO STATE

While The Citadel and Arsenal stayed open and active during the Civil War, their academic neighbors had mixed fates. The Medical College of South Carolina in Charleston closed its doors for the duration of the war until November 1865. Most medical faculty, students, and graduates—nearly four hundred—entered Confederate service, providing their expertise to the Southern cause. Their transition from classroom and laboratory learning to hands-on practice was a harsh one, as they experienced all manner of wartime injuries, "from musket shot and cannonball wounds to pneumonia, measles, gangrene, yellow fever, typhoid and dysentery" (Matalene and Chaddock 2009, 41). Some students transferred to other Southern medical schools that had yet to suspend classes.

Many faculty and students from the College of Charleston also joined the Confederacy, but the institution did not close despite severely dwindling numbers (down to seven at one point) until 1864. The college closed just before Christmas of that year, "in consequence of events arising out of the progress of the War," according to the Faculty Minutes (quoted in Matalene and Chaddock 2006, 74) and did not reopen until February 1, 1866.

Excitement was high among South Carolina College students (presently the University of South Carolina) in Columbia, less than two miles from the Arsenal campus. Trustee John H. Means, ardent secessionist and former governor who had served on The Citadel's original Board of Visitors in 1842, supported South Carolina College students organizing their own cadet company and joining the war effort (Hollis 1951, 212–13; Bond 1936, 17). Of that college's 143 students, 106 enlisted. The faculty of South Carolina College reorganized the following term, but once more, many of the students left to serve the Confederacy (Hollis, 1951, 219–27). In 1862, South Carolina College's faculty held classes and attempted to recruit new students, but by the summer it was determined that the college would have to close for want of sufficient student numbers. It did not reopen for instruction until after the war. During the war years, the Confederate government rented campus buildings to serve as a hospital. Thus, when William Tecumseh Sherman burned much of Columbia, including the Arsenal campus, South Carolina College facilities were spared.

GOVERNANCE AND ADMINISTRATION

While the war raged on, The Citadel's faculty and administrators tackled both the routine and extraordinary issues that faced the military academy, especially enrollment and resource costs. During the war The Citadel campus was commanded by Maj. James B. White, superintendent and professor of civil and military engineering and astronomy, with five other professors (who also all held military rank), a surgeon, and a quartermaster/bursar under him. Capt. John P. Thomas commanded the Arsenal campus with three professors, a surgeon, and a bursar reporting to him (Official Register 1863). Most institutional records and artifacts were moved from The Citadel to the Arsenal in late 1864 for safekeeping but were destroyed when Sherman marched through Columbia in February 1865. The Board of Visitors Minutes survived and illustrate a thriving military academy.

The Citadel's governing board addressed all manner of issues, from faculty appointments and financial issues to student conduct and examinations. The minutes for November 30, 1861, show that the board wrestled with how to deal with the "high prices of almost all the commodities which are necessary for the support of these institutions [Arsenal and Citadel campuses], the board are apprehensive that, with their present means, they will not be able, as hitherto, to keep them from debt." The report continues that members of the board were unwilling to ask for additional financial assistance from the state, but that they were also "anxious to keep these schools within the reach of that larger class of our people who cannot afford to give their sons an expensive education" (Board of Visitors Minutes 1861).

On November 29, 1862, the governing board was left with no choice but to require cadets, "to furnish their own underclothing, including shirts, drawers and socks; also, their shoes, combs and brushes." They also raised tuition to $400 to be paid "one hundred dollars per quarter in advance." A year later, on November 28, 1863, the board passed a resolution with nearly identical wording (perhaps to reinforce the requirement for cadets to supply their own provisions), except that now tuition was doubled: Cadets were to "pay annually eight hundred dollars viz: two hundred dollars per quarter in advance." In 1864, pillowcases and sheets were added to the list of items cadets had to supply, and tuition was raised to $1,200 (Board of Visitors Minutes 1862–1863).

Cadets commented on such financial and personal supply issues in their letters home. Claudius L. Fike wrote on January 9, 1862: "The Superintendent told us all that in consequence of the state of the country, the $60 which are allowed to each cadet, would be insufficient to clothe us; and that we would have to get underclothing from home. You will therefore take notice and prepare." On April 20, Fike wrote an apology to his parents regarding their need to "borrow" funds to support his higher education: "I am also sorry that you were obliged to borrow the money for me; although I will need it all, yet I will take good care of it" (1862). In their December 1862 report to the South Carolina's General Assembly, The Citadel's governing board expressed that the issue of high cost was "one of the most serious obstacles" members of the board faced. In that report, the board detailed The Citadel's financial standing: $37,000 was acquired from the state, $26,850 from paying cadets, and $1,335.03 from the sale of supplies to officers. The largest expenditures were subsistence ($18,661.19), officers' salaries ($12,649.44), and cadet clothing ($12,452.17). Other costs included fuel, lights, books, stationery, medicine, washing, servants, and improvements and repairs to buildings. After all expenses, The Citadel had a cash reserve of $905.70 (Board of Visitors Minutes 1862).

In their report to the General Assembly on December 1, 1862, the governing board reported that examinations of Citadel and Arsenal cadets had been, "entirely satisfactory to the Board; and notwithstanding the excitement in all men's minds during the present year, occasioned by a state of war, good order has been generally maintained, and a high grade of proficiency has been reached in both institutions." The board also reported that thirty-seven cadets had deserted The Citadel in order to join the Confederate army: "One instance of insubordination, however, occurred in the month of June, at The Citadel academy, which resulted in the suspension of thirty-seven Cadets, who left the institution in a body, in violation of the regulations, and no other alternative was left the Board but to confirm their suspension, and consequently the offending cadets were dismissed from the Academy." Three years later, without explanation, the board passed a resolution on April 14, 1865, that any cadet, "solicited to deliver an address at the commencement exercises of the Academy, who shall make any material alteration or addition to his address, after it had been submitted to the Professor of Elocution for his revisal shall be reported to the Board of Visitors as for disobedience." If said disobedience was substantiated, the cadet would "incur a forfeiture of his diploma" (Board of Visitors Minutes 1862).

While other Southern colleges and universities were closing or operating on a reduced scale, The Citadel was faced with increasing demands for admittance. "From the increasing popularity of these institutions, [and] from the closing of other places of education, a much larger number of applications has been received this year than ever before. Besides a large number of the State [supported] Cadets, more than three hundred pay Cadets have applied for admission into the class of next year, of whom the Board regret to say they can only receive at the Arsenal Academy, twenty-seven State and one hundred and fifteen pay cadets" (Board of Visitors Minutes 1862). The board suggested that this type of increase in admission should continue and asked that the legislature fund the construction of new wings for the Arsenal campus and a new house for the superintendent, thus allowing his residence to be converted into housing for cadets. In the meantime, the governing board asked that the legislature, "place at the disposal of the Board a portion of the [South Carolina] College buildings, now unoccupied. They would endeavor to make arrangements to receive all who have applied [to the Arsenal campus]" (Board of Visitors Minutes 1861–1865). This request, however, was denied as the South Carolina College campus was already functioning as a Confederate hospital (Hollis 1951).

CURRICULUM

The curriculum at the Military Academy of South Carolina was typical of the military academies of the time: a mix of practical subjects with certain liberal arts courses, especially history and English. There was an emphasis on the study of the US Constitution, particularly John C. Calhoun's interpretation. The Arsenal's curriculum, unlike The Citadel's, was not as extensive; the Columbia-based campus focused on preparing first-year cadets in English, mathematics, and belles lettres. After completing this curricular gamut, cadets transferred to the Charleston-based Citadel campus, where the curriculum was more robust and applied as concerned militarism. Instruction at The Citadel comprised reading and memorizing the day's (or at least portions of the day's) lessons for a particular subject. Cadets would then "recite" these lessons to the course instructor in front of fellow pupils (Conrad 2004). Examinations consisted of both oral and written portions and were given twice each year.

Cadet Fike explained this in correspondence with his parents. On January 7, 1862, Fike wrote: "I have to recite English at 7 to 8 a.m. French, 9 to 10 and Mathematics 11 to 12. We drill squad drill 1/2 hr. at 12 n., dine at 1 p.m.; study till 1/2 hr. before sunset when we drill again. We have 1/2 hour after every meal for recreation." After listing the names of his professors, he continued, "I find English the hardest of all because the teacher calls upon any one of the class and starts him in the lessons anywhere and he has to say on till he tells him to stop. We get from 4 to 8 pages of English grammar at one time . . . French is the easiest."

Although not all instructors had a military background, they were assigned a military rank based on their professorial rank (Conrad 2004). Military academies generally attracted quality faculty and The Citadel was no exception. Sometimes the lack of military experience was conspicuous, such as when professor of physics and chemistry, Cr. William Hume, drilled students and "ordered" them: "Will you be kind enough, gentlemen, to shoulder arms?" (Conrad 2004, 16).

In his diary from 1862, Cadet John E. Boinest detailed a list of forty-four "Subjects on History" he was to learn that year, moving from the discovery of America to the arrival of early explorers at Plymouth and the Massachusetts Bay Colony (nos. 23 and 25), and finally, the "Carolinas under Royal Charter" (no. 44). While he did not provide details regarding his other courses, Boinest listed his weekly marks for English, French, and mathematics. He also provided a page dedicated to the number of demerits he received and the dates on which he received them. Atop this page, Boinest scrawled: "April 1st 1863, 195 demerits—Maximum number allowed 250. Less by 55 demerits." (The Citadel's Official Register of 1863 lists the maximum number of demerits at 200 on page 14 under the subheading "Explanation of Conduct Roll.")

In addition to the above listed student letters and diary entries, the life and writings of John Peyre Thomas (1833–1912) serve as a guide to the ideological views and social norms transmitted to students at The Citadel during the war. Thomas was involved with the military academy nearly all his life. Starting as a cadet at the Arsenal campus and later The Citadel campus (graduating at the top of the 1851 class), Thomas became a professor of belles lettres, French, and history, and the superintendent of the Arsenal. He eventually became a professor, superintendent (the first after its Reconstruction-era reopening), and trustee at The Citadel. Late in life, he resided in Charleston while his son served as The Citadel's professor of mathematics (Thomas 1964). Thomas participated in the attack on Fort Sumter, and when the cadets went to battle in 1864, he led Company B, which consisted of Arsenal cadets. One cadet remembered Thomas during the war as follows: "with his sword drawn, rushed in front of us and gave the command." (Thomas 1964, 9). Over the course of the war, Thomas rose in rank from lieutenant to captain and, eventually, to colonel (Thomas 1964).

Thomas was devoted to the ideas of John C. Calhoun—South Carolina statesman, political Democrat, and political theorist. He served as editor for *The Carolina Tribute to Calhoun* in 1857 (Calhoun died in 1850) and, in 1860, Thomas published, *Analysis of Calhoun's Disquisition on Government and Discourse on the Constitution and Government*, which was also published as "Calhoun's Theory of Government" in *Southern Magazine* in 1899. In a speech given at Clemson University on June 22, 1897, Thomas declared to both the cadets of Clemson and The Citadel, "It is conceded that Calhoun's standard in the science of government is so lofty as in some respects to be unattainable in our day and generation" (quoted in Thomas 1964, 40–41). In another speech, Thomas heaped praise on Calhoun's *Disquisition*, calling it "masterly" and a "profound exposition" on the liberties of the governed, declaring it "a work superior to the Politics of Aristotle" (Thomas 1890, 11). Cadet Tom Law, Citadel class of 1859, said that Thomas as speaker was "sublimely beautiful" (1942, 307).

Calhoun's published works are capacious, consisting of six volumes. Thomas focused primarily on making Calhoun's *Disquisition* accessible to his Citadel students. He explained that, in requiring this reading, he hoped the cadets would garner an appreciation of Calhoun's "noble legacy" as the South Carolina statesman provided "the highest standard of political ethics" (363). The central argument that Calhoun made, and that Thomas conveyed in his analysis and synthesis, was that government needed oversight to ensure that it did not abuse its power. "The question now is, how can government be prevented from abusing its powers without being made too weak to properly exercise its functions" (Thomas 1899, 368).

Thomas argued at length in favor of Calhoun's concurrent majority, that it had moral and political advantages for society. He explained this concurrent majority as follows: "It restricts government to its primary ends and keeps it in its proper sphere" (378), and "The *concurrent* or *constitutional* majority" as promoted by Calhoun is "the true majority" (372). This concurrent majority veto power over the majority is at the heart of Calhoun's Nullification Theory, which was the legal argument in favor of South Carolina's secession from the Union to protect the practice of slavery.

Calhoun rejected the idea that the United States needed a strong central government (the view of George Washington and Alexander Hamilton). Instead, he sided with Thomas Jefferson's "states' rights" argument. Calhoun feared that large "numerical majorities" could overtake minority interests. Subsequently, he adapted his idea of the "concurrent majority" to defend the right of political minorities to veto actions of the political majority, and cited Jefferson's proclamation to abolish and replace any form of government that becomes "destructive of life, liberty or the pursuit of happiness" (Thomas 1890, 17–18).

At the close of his analysis of Calhoun's *Discourse*, Thomas invoked the Lost Cause ideology, recognizing that with the Civil War, Calhoun's ideas had been beaten down but that they should come back: "So the thoughtful student may well say to the men who have broken down the bulwarks and safeguards of our old government and constitution: 'Give back, give back to the Union its slaughtered principle of State sovereignty, which ought to be the brightest jewel in the diadem of the country'" (395). Thomas regularly sang the praises of Confederate heroes: "In the Rise and Fall of the Southern Confederacy, you will find the loftiest exemplars. Study their lives. Imitate, if you can, Jackson's faith, the sublime reticence of Albert Sidney Johnston, the firmness of Jefferson Davis, and the unexcelled chivalry of Lee" (Thomas 1890, 26). In 1883, after the reopening of The Citadel, Thomas, in his capacity as the new superintendent, gave an oration celebrating the history of the institution. He remarked on the gift of the flag to the Battalion of Citadel Cadets from the Washington Light Infantry. This flag, he explained, was of great importance and should be "conspicuously displayed, as a symbol of the past, and as a hope for the future" (Thomas 1883, 3).

STUDENT AND CADET LIFE AT THE MILITARY ACADEMY OF SOUTH CAROLINA

The education of cadets was not limited to the classroom or the drill field during the Civil War. Admission to the military academy meant learning while posted to campus guard duty and, for some, service in the battlefield. Application for admission to the Military Academy of South Carolina was a relatively simple matter. An official document had to be submitted that certified that the adult filling out the form (no specifics on who had to write it were given) could attest to the applicant's age, height, health, and ability to read and write (Official Register 1863). If the potential student was applying for financial support from the State legislature, the letter needed to include the line that, "He [the applicant] is without pecuniary means in his own right, and his parents are unable to pay for his education," which had to be certified by the Commissioners of Free Schools attesting the applicant's financial situation. Applications were due at the end of November, and the new term started in January.

While West Point had been publicly accused of being elitist and aristocratic, Southern military academies were generally more egalitarian (Andrew 2001). For example, Citadel regulations for 1858 specified that "no difference shall be made in the treatment, or in the duties required, between the pay and State Cadets; nor shall any distinction between cadets be known in the Academy, other than arising from merit" (quoted in Andrew 2001, 17). Cadets were always to be in uniform and were prohibited from keeping civilian clothing. This dress code, it was believed, broke down social class barriers between cadets from the Low Country planter class and cadets heralding from poorer upstate farming families. Life was regimented and cut off from the world. Arsenal cadet Fike lamented in a letter to his parents (January 9, 1862) that "We don't get any news here no more, than if we were in a jail, except on Saturday when the Sup't. gives us all the cadets leave to go in the city. . . . When you write you must write the news [from home]." He explained that his penmanship was poor because he was so busy and "in a hurry. I am busy all the time."

Cadet diaries and letters make clear that religion and church attendance were key parts of the cadet experience. Cadet John Boinest recounted one Sunday sermon where the preacher was soliloquizing from St. Luke 4:22, "All spoke well of Him and were amazed at the gracious words that came from His lips. 'Isn't this Joseph's son [Jesus]?' they asked." Below that, in what must have been a note to a fellow cadet, Boinest inquires: "Do you know that young lady . . . I mean the one next to the door in the last pew?" to which a reply is scrawled that the woman's surname was Steel. Cutting off cadets from female companionship obviously did not dissolve their interest in the opposite sex, at least for this particular cadet. On the next page of his diary, Boinest copied the titular line from the period song, "Kiss me quick and go" (1862).

John B. Patrick, an 1855 Citadel graduate and later professor of mathematics at the Arsenal campus from 1859 to 1865, wrote frequently of religious life at the academy in his journal. "Read to the Cadets, at prayers, the 1st Chap. of Genesis, and a part of the last chapter and encouraged at the attendance and interest manifested in the good work. Attended church—heard a good sermon . . . Heb. iv.:9." (Patrick 1861). On Sunday, April 14, 1861, Patrick wrote: "Went to Sunday School. Four of our teachers are away—they are on the tented field . . . Feel sad as I look around and see the little ones whose Fathers have gone from home to engage in the contest and uncertainties of war. May God spare them and bring them back safe to their families! The ordinance of Baptism was administered to two candidates—one white and one colored. In the afternoon the Lord's supper was administered" (1861).

Fike reported on the religious influence of his Arsenal campus superintendent, John P. Thomas, in letters to his parents. Thomas promoted Christianity in his academic speeches as the ultimate source of morality and that private realm of religion and public sphere of government were "divinely joined . . . one in essence" (Thomas 1890, 6). The Christian religion should, Thomas argued, be an ideal "refining and ennobling influence . . . upon every form of legislation and every institution of the State" (Thomas 1890, 9). In 1961, a century after the start of the Civil War, The Citadel's mid-twentieth-century chaplain, Robert S. Hall, extoled that Southern pastors, with their "Spiritual Values in the Confederacy," were "among the first and most enthusiastic" to take up arms in support of the secessionist cause. To Hall, these clergy showed "the most amazing display of spiritual power ever witnessed among fighting men on the American continent" (Hall 1961, 14–15). Of the 240 cadets who had graduated from The Citadel by 1861, thirteen were clergymen (see also Blackwell 2003).

Religion aside, Citadel cadets were governed by an extensive list of regulations. Defying any meant receiving demerits. Accumulating too many demerits or engaging in a single, significant incident of bad behavior resulted in punishments, ranging from demotion in rank to confinement or even dismissal from the academy (Conrad 2004). The Citadel's 1862 Official Register outlines the weight of different offenses. It also details that senior cadets should know better than to break rules and, as a result, were more seriously penalized for similar "crime[s]" committed by new cadets. Furthermore, the regulations stipulate that, "No pay Cadet who may be discharged, dismissed or expelled, shall be entitled to be refunded any part of the money paid in advance" (Official Register of 1862, 26). Cadet Fike informed his parents that his roommates had been written up for all manner of offenses: sitting on a trunk, leaving books in a chair, leaning on the bed, and looking out of doors in study hours even though "There is no published rule for such [minor infractions] as these, but we have to learn by experience and observation" (January 10, 1862).

Cadets, tried and tested by rigorous military training and severe rule adherence, undertook various duties during the Civil War. Citadel cadets helped defend Charleston against a Union gunboat attack in November 1861. During the summer of 1864, cadets were called on to escort prisoners of war to the prison camp at Andersonville, Georgia, which was done using railroad cattle cars. The military students had to scrape manure from railcar floors before Union prisoners could be loaded. Cadets also guarded prisoners at Camp Sorghum, near Columbia, where they had to build huts due to a lack of permanent quarters. When Confederate president Jefferson Davis visited Columbia to give a speech, Citadel and Arsenal cadets took part in a special military muster. Cadets also drilled newly enlisted soldiers, men who were ignorant of military drill and unaccustomed to taking orders (Conrad 2004; Government Printing Office 1882). Mere weeks after the Confederate firing on Fort Sumter, Arsenal cadets demonstrated drill maneuvers for novice soldiers in the 4th South Carolina Volunteer Infantry. In June of 1861, cadets assisted Col. Wade Hampton's Legion in battle (Conrad 2004). By the start of the war, the South Carolina Military Academy had contributed "209 graduates in the Confederate forces, including four generals and forty-eight field officers" (Coulter 2017, 81). Of the 1,699 academy alumni, the majority served in the Confederate army throughout the war years.

Lt. John Patrick, professor of mathematics at the Arsenal campus, described the excitement associated with the comings and goings of Civil

War soldiers near the academy. On April 10, 1863, Patrick recorded in his journal that "one [military company and a detachment of soldiers] left Columbia for Charleston." The next day he wrote, "A large number of volunteers passed down the Charlotte R. R. en route [underline in original] for Charleston. I did not see them but heard their loud huzzas as they went through. May the blessings of Providence attend them. It is reported that Gen. B. [Beauregard] has demanded surrender of Fort Sumter." General Pierre Gustave Toutant Beauregard had indeed demanded Union surrender of the South Carolina fortification. Beauregard sang high praises of The Citadel men who fired upon the fort (Baker 1990). When the news arrived on April 13th that Fort Sumter had been taken, Patrick sang, "All honor and Glory to God for the news that has reached us this day!" He noted that the Arsenal cadets fired off seven guns in honor of the first Confederate victory.

The military engagements of Citadel cadets were summarized in a report titled "Calls to Duty." The report listed events as follows (Citadel Cadets n.d.):

Star of the West	1861, January 9
Wappoo Cut	1861, November
James Island	1862, June
Charleston & vicinity	1863, July–October
James Island	1864, June
Tulifinny	1864, December
James Island	1864, December–1865, February
Williamston	1865, May
Confederate States army.	

It is not clear what is meant by the final entry, and the list excludes one significant military engagement that holds a place in Citadel tradition: the attack on Fort Sumter, April 12, 1865. Though published histories of The Citadel indicate that no Citadel cadets were involved in the battle, several Citadel graduates turned Confederate officers played key roles at the bombardment (Civil War Engagements, n.d.).

Cadets, in addition to Citadel alumni, witnessed the horrors of war firsthand. On August 22, 1863, Cadet Julius Bartlette wrote, "The Yankees commenced shelling the city last night. The first shell was thrown between half past one and two o'clock this morning." Bartlette was stationed at a battalion guard tent and recounted the names of local churches and stores that were damaged by cannon fire. When the first shell was fired, Bartlette wrote, "It seemed to me that it was coming directly to the place where I was lying and made me feel a little queer as it was the first I had ever heard. They make an awful, shrieking noise; but I soon got used to it. Everybody was taken by surprise, as it was not known that the Yankees had a battery near enough to shell the city." Bartlette reported on rumors concerning Gen. Beauregard and a would-be request for truce to remove the city's women and children. He also reported that there was a "negro insurrection," but admitted "I don't know what to believe" (Bartlette 1863).

Cadets from both The Citadel and Arsenal campuses participated in the Battle of Tulifinny in December of 1864. Their support contributed to the Confederacy's victory against Federal troops marching to the sea (Baker 1990; Bond 1936). Cadets made up more than one-third of the Confederate battle force in the Tulifinny engagement. Citadel and Arsenal campus cadets were organized into Company A from The Citadel and Company B from the Arsenal. South Carolina Military Academy cadets were involved in both the first shots of the Civil War as well as the last. On May 9, 1865, John Peyre Thomas and his Company B were surprised by Union general George Stoneman's Raiders near Williamston. The cadets "promptly rallied under their flag and drove off the Raiders with their one casualty. It is recorded that this was the last shot of the war by an organized body east of the Mississippi" (Thomas 1964, 14).

A strong sense of Confederate loyalty can be found in many cadet letters and diary entries. In 1862 Cadet Boinest included lyrics from two popular Civil War songs in his diary. Both songs were written by Harry McCarthy, an Irish immigrant, songwriter, and entertainer. Taken from "Missouri and The Volunteer" Boinest copied the following in his diary:

> I leave my home and thee, dear,
> With sorrow at my heart,
> If it is my country's call, dear,
> To aid her I depart;
> And on the blood red battle plain,
> We'll conquer or we'll die,
> 'Tis for our honor and our name,
> We raise the battle cry.

The ideals of loyalty to the cause are reinforced in the cadet diary via verses taken from McCarthy's "Bonnie Blue Flag":

> We are a band of brothers
> And native to the soil
> Fighting for the property
> We've gained by honest toil
> And when our rights were threatened
> The cry rose near & far
> Hurrah! Hurrah! for the bonnie blue flag
> That bears a single star.

Boinest included the entirety of "Bonnie Blue Flag." The second verse included in the cadet's journal reads, "But when Northern treachery attempts our rights to mar, / We raise on high the bonnie blue flag that bears a single star" (1862).

THE WAR ENDS, THE SOUTH CAROLINA MILITARY ACADEMY CLOSES

By the end of 1864, the South Carolina Military Academy's Board of Visitors knew the institution's continued operation was precarious. In the governing board's report to the General Assembly on December 3, board members explained that, "The continued bombardment of the city of Charleston by the enemy has rendered the Citadel in that city a dangerous habitation and wholly unfit for the Academic duties of the Cadets" (Board of Visitors Minutes 1861–1865). As the end of the war neared and the safety of Charleston remained in doubt, much of The Citadel campus' equipment—including furniture from the mess hall and officers' quarters, scientific apparatuses, and more than eight thousand library books—was sent to the Arsenal campus in Columbia for safekeeping. However, the Arsenal campus was destroyed and all equipment and books were either burned or carried off by Federal troops under the command of Union general Sherman (Conrad 2004).

Cadet W. A. Johnson kept a detailed diary of the last months of the war. On February 17, 1865, he was on guard duty at The Citadel campus commissary when it came time to distribute rations to local residents. The distribution turned hazardous as "the crowd, men, women, & children, black and white, rushed on us and into the building in such disorder, that we were forced to fix bayonets and shove them out. They then went around the building and attempted to get over the fence. We loaded our guns and had to threaten them to keep out of the way. As it was, we could not distribute the food in any sort of system. We just shoved it out and let the mob do the distributing" (Johnson 1865). The next day Johnson wrote in his diary that he and his fellow cadets left their tents on The Citadel green at sunrise, due to the fact that, "Stores were being destroyed and batteries blown up all night last night. Over 300 men, women, and children, black and white, were killed and wounded by an explosion in the N.E.R.R. depot." Cadet Johnson described these horrors as follows: "This explosion happened just as we were leaving the city, and I saw lots of burned and almost naked sufferers running through the streets screaming from pain and fright. . . . As we marched out pandemonium took our place" (1865).

Soon thereafter, the city of Charleston fell to Union forces. On March 21, 1865, somewhere between four and ten thousand people, white and black, gathered on The Citadel Green to watch a parade of black Union soldiers. The *New-York Tribune* reported that the procession was, "a celebration of their deliverance from bondage and ostracism; a jubilee of freedom, a hosanna to their deliverers" (quoted in Kytle and Roberts 2018, 42). The soldiers were followed by "A Car of Liberty" carrying fifteen women who represented the Southern slave states. The Citadel Green, the site where cadets previously marched to celebrate the secession of South Carolina and prepare for war in defense of the institution of slavery, was now witness to a celebration of emancipation. Subsequently, the castle-like Citadel building was occupied by black soldiers of the Massachusetts 54th (Kytle and Roberts 2018).

Cadet Johnson described his final days as a Citadel student. On April 25, 1865, he wrote: "Many men plotting to go home and refuse to fight any more." A few days later, Johnson added: "Commenced to turn over our wagons and stock to Yankees." When April 30 came, he noted that he had been "Relieved by Yankees to-day," and on May 4, Johnson and his fellow cadets began to march home, leaving their academy behind (Johnson 1865). Even after the Southern surrender at Appomattox, members of the South Carolina Military Academy's governing board held onto the hope that the institution could remain open. At their April 27, 1865, meeting in Greenville, which included Governor Andrew Gordon Magrath, board members resolved that "in view of the present conditions in the state, it is expedient to increase the number of cadets in the two Military Academies to the largest amount capable of receiving instruction from the Professors of these Academies" (Board of Visitors Minutes 1865). However, the Arsenal campus lay in ruins, save the officer's quarters, and The Citadel campus was occupied by Federal troops. The Arsenal campus never reopened, and its remaining barracks were repurposed as the South Carolina governor's mansion in 1868.

On November 30, 1865, the Board of Visitors met to discuss the closure of the military academy. Board members suggested that buildings "now standing at the Arsenal and Citadel be rented out the ensuing year." The Board of Visitors Minutes include a final report dated December 1, 1865, that was submitted by John B. Patrick, board secretary. The report detailed the final activities of all Arsenal and Citadel cadets—in the classroom and on the battlefield—for that year. It also reported the grim financial condition of the military academy (Board of Visitors Minutes 1861–1865). The occupation of The Citadel campus continued well past the end of Reconstruction, until 1879. In the early 1880s, Confederate war veterans and Citadel alumni were successful in persuading South Carolina's legislature to reopen the military academy. Alumni stressed the "benefits of military education in character formation" and that such an education would infuse "discipline and notions of honor and integrity" (Andrew 2001, 39), which resonated with legislators' intent on maintaining a social order based on Old South mores of honor, tradition, and Southern gentlemanliness (Conrad 2004). The South Carolina Military Academy officially reopened in 1882 at The Citadel campus site. In 1910, the institution's name was changed to "The Citadel: The Military College of South Carolina." Twelve years later, the campus was relocated to the site of a racetrack. The former Citadel building in downtown Charleston currently serves as a hotel.

LEGACY OF THE CIVIL WAR AT THE CITADEL

In 1942, South Carolina's governor, Richard M. Jeffries, celebrated the Military Academy of South Carolina's "century of accomplishment," including the role the cadets played in the Civil War. "This great institution really resulted from the strong adherence of the people of this State to the undying rights of individual states. No greater heritage can any institution have than to know that its birth came from the strong impulses of honor, devotion to principles, and eternal allegiance to that which is called duty" (Jefferies 1942, 7). In a March 1943 *Saturday Evening Post* article on The Citadel's centennial, journalist Herbert Ravenel Sass explained that the institution's "militant Americanism" was a sign of the nation's "strength and patriotism." Sass elaborated on The Citadel's Confederate heritage and its patriotism, declaring that it would be difficult to find "a more inspiring demonstration of the basic strength and soundness of the Republic than this military college in Charleston, South Carolina, most loyal of Southern cities to the memory of and ideals of the Confederacy" (Macaulay 2009, 9).

This sentiment echoed in the halls of The Citadel both before and after the centennial celebration. In 1883, Citadel superintendent John P. Thomas detailed the virtues of military education, its ability to mold young men, imparting them with self-control, justice, courtesy, and courage—ideals that, to Thomas at least, were lost on most post-Civil War Southerners who had been stripped of their "former strength and purity" (Thomas 1890, 5, 24). While Charleston, South Carolina had served as the Cradle of the Confederacy, it later became a cradle of the Lost Cause (Kytle and Roberts 2018). The invocation of the Confederate Lost Cause was used as a rallying cry at both The Citadel and the surrounding community. As Rod Andrew explains, "The legend of the Lost Cause and the virtuous Confederate citizen-warrior provided energy, vitality, and legitimacy for Southern military education. All over the South, cadets in gray marched in Confederate Memorial Day celebrations, fired their muskets over Confederate cemeteries, and escorted old veterans to podiums, where the latter preached to them the values of duty, sacrifice, piety, and moral courage. The cadets themselves were indeed part of the pageantry and symbolism of the Lost Cause" (2001, 6). Southerners continued to connect the ideas of "martial virtues (courage, patriotism, selflessness, and loyalty) and moral rectitude" well into the twentieth century (Andrew 2001, 47). The use of Citadel-esque military training and tactics spread to other Southern colleges and universities. The Lost Cause mythology itself was not the only impetus for the spread of military curricula. This strict pedagogical structure was also believed to aid in the development of well-rounded young men emboldened by religion and Southern nationalism. Indeed, at Southern military academies the words, "Warrior, Christian, Patriot" were practically synonymous and well aligned with Confederate justifications for secession, war, and, in time, Lost Cause ideology (Andrew 2001, 63).

One hundred years after the inception of the Civil War, the Confederate cause was still celebrated at The Citadel. In the *Association of Citadel Men Alumni News* for December 1960, several articles announced upcoming Civil War cadet commemorations, including a reenactment of the firing on the *Star of the West* (Durham 1961; "Star of the West Centennial to be Observed" 1960). It was also announced that winners of the institution's *Star of the West Medal* would be announced and that a new mural would be unveiled in the lobby of the campus library that depicted The Citadel's Civil War cadets and their attack on the abovementioned steamship by artist David Humphreys Miller ("New Mural Honors 'Citadel Cadet Company'" 1960). The March 1961 issue of the *Association of Citadel Men Alumni News* provided details on these and other events, including "The Confederate Ball." This particular festival required that cadets and their companions dress in period uniforms and dresses. At the start of the 1961 spring semester, historian Bruce Canton delivered a keynote address, concerning the firing on the *Star of the West* and declared: "It was not only, in a real sense, the opening paragraph in the story of the Civil War: it is eternally eloquent regarding the way in which that war came about" (Canton 1961, 7). Canton argued that, "what happened on January 9 is one of the most fascinating 'if's' in American history" and pondered what might have happened if the ship's captain had returned fire and a battle had taken place. Canton challenged his audience to think of what could have been if the North and South had taken the attack on the *Star of the West* as a harbinger of things to come and resolved the "so-called slave question," acknowledging that its days were numbered, and thus, avoiding this mid-nineteenth-century human tragedy of war and mass bloodshed.

Even though The Citadel's administration admitted the first African American student in 1966, cadet Charles D. Foster, white cadets continued to wave Confederate flags at athletic events and sing "Dixie" as the academy's unofficial fight song (Kytle and Roberts 2018). In the 1970s, Citadel recruits were exposed to an institutionally held belief that linked "the health of their school and their nation to the corps of cadets' ability to produce manly citizens" who could "save" the Union and preserve the "cultural distinctiveness" of the South (Macaulay 2009, 112). In 1983, the president of The Citadel, Maj. Gen. James Grimsley Jr., echoed these ideals: "The teachings of The Citadel for love of country, patriotism, honor, courage, loyalty, and devotion to duty have been hallmarks for its graduates in all major conflicts from Civil War days, beginning in 1861, through Vietnam" (Grimsley 1983, 12). Though The Citadel's administration has, in years past, decreased institutional references to the Civil War, the *Star of the West Scholarship* is still awarded. Like the above-mentioned mural and scholarship, other remnants of the Civil War are present at the military academy. Most notably, the "Big Red" South Carolina palmetto flag that was used by cadets when they fired the first shots in the American Civil War is on display at The Citadel's Holliday Alumni Center—a testament not only to the institution's military heritage, but also its ties to a period of extreme social divisiveness and postwar, Lost Cause ideology.

REFERENCES

Andrew, Rod., Jr. 2001. *Long Gray Lines: The Southern Military School Tradition, 1839–1915*. Chapel Hill: University of North Carolina Press.

Baker, Gary R. 1990. *Cadets in Gray: The Story of the Cadets of the South Carolina Military Academy and the Cadet Rangers in the Civil War*. Lexington, SC: Palmetto Bookworks.

Bartlette, Julius Lyman. 1863–1864. Julius Lyman Bartlette 1845–? Papers, 1863–1864. The Citadel Archives and Museum, Charleston, SC.

Blackwell, Michael D. 2003. *Remember Now Thy Creator in the Days of Thy Youth: The Religious Heritage of The Citadel*. Irmo, SC: Citadel Christian Heritage Foundation.

Board of Visitors Minutes. 1861–1865. The Citadel Archives and Museum, Charleston, SC.

Boinest, John E. Papers. Notebook, 1862. The Citadel Archives and Museum, Charleston, SC.

Bond, Oliver J. 1936. *The Story of The Citadel*. Greenville, SC: Southern Historical Press.

Buckley, William H. 2004. *The Citadel and the South Carolina Corps of Cadets*. Charleston, SC: Arcadia Publishing.

Canton, Bruce. 1961. "Citadel Cadets Fired First Shots." *Association of Citadel Men Alumni News* 18 (3): 6–9.

Civil War Engagements. "Citadel: Civil War Engagements." n.d. The Citadel Archives and Museum, Charleston, SC.

Citadel Cadets. "Civil War: Battalion of State Cadets." n.d. The Citadel Archives and Museum, Charleston, SC.

Conrad, James Lee. 2004. *The Young Lions: Confederate Cadets at War*. Columbia: University of South Carolina Press.

Coulter, John A. 2017. *Cadets on Campus: History of Military Schools of the United States*. College Station: Texas A&M University Press.

Durham, Frank. 1961. "A Symbolic Re-Enactment of The Citadel's Firing on *The Star of the West*: January 9, 1861." *Association of Citadel Men Alumni News* 18 (3): 10–13.

Edgar, Walter. 1998. *South Carolina: A History*. Columbia: University of South Carolina Press.

Fike, Claudius L. January 7, 1862. Letter to Parents. Claudius Lucian Fike Papers, 1862–1894. South Caroliniana Library. University of South Carolina.

Fike, Claudius L. January 9, 1862. Letter to Parents.

Fike, Claudius L. January 10, 1862. Letter to Parents.

Fike, Claudius L. April 20, 1862. Letter to Parents.

Government Printing Office. 1882. "A Compilation of the Activities of the Cadets of the South Carolina Military Academy During the War Between the States (1861–1865): Taken from 'War of Rebellion—Official Records of the Union and Confederate Armies.' Civil War: War of the Rebellion (Citadel)." The Citadel Archives and Museum, Charleston, SC.

Grimsley, James A., Jr. 1983. *The Citadel: Educating the Whole Man*. New York: Newcomen Society in North America.

Hall, Robert S. 1961. "Spiritual Values in the Confederacy." *Association of Citadel Men Alumni News* 18 (3):10–13.

Hollis, Daniel Walker. 1951. *University of South Carolina: South Carolina College*, vol. 1. Columbia: University of South Carolina Press.

Jefferies, Richard M. 1942. *The Citadel Completes A Century of Accomplishment: Address by the Governor R. M. Jefferies, The Citadel Centennial, December 18, 1942*. South Caroliniana Library. University of South Carolina.

Johnson, W. A. 1865. Diary. Transcribed by L. D. Wyly, 1935. The Citadel Archives and Museum, Charleston, SC.

Kytle, Ethan J. and Blain Roberts. 2018. *Denmark Vesey's Garden: Slavery and Memory in the Cradle of the Confederacy*. New York: The New Press.

Law, Thomas Hart, and John Adger Law. 1942. *Citadel Cadets: The Journal of Cadet Tom Law*. Clinton, SC: P. C. Press.

Macaulay, Alexander. 2009. *Marching in Step: Masculinity, Citizenship, and The Citadel in Post-World War II America*. Athens: University of Georgia Press.

Marshall, Richard. 1967. "The Firing on *The Star of The West*." *The Shako* (Corps Day Issue), June 1967, 6–8, 17.

Matalene, Carolyn B. and Katherine E. Chaddock. 2006. *College of Charleston Voices: Campus and Community Through the Centuries*. Charleston, SC: The History Press.

Matalene, Carolyn B. and Katherine E. Chaddock. 2009. *Vital Signs in Charleston: Voices Through the Centuries from the Medical University of South Carolina*. Charleston, SC: The History Press.

"New Mural Honors 'Citadel Cadet Company.'" 1960. *Association of Citadel Men Alumni News* 18 (2): 4.

Official Register, South Carolina Military Academy, 1860-1863. Columbia, SC: South Carolina Steam Printing Office. The Citadel Archives and Museum, Charleston, SC.

Patrick, John B. "A Journal by John B. Patrick, Mar. 23, 1861–Dec. 25, 1865." The Citadel Archives and Museum, Charleston, SC.

Sacher, John M. 2014. "Searching for 'Some Plain and Simple Method': Jefferson Davis and Confederate Conscription." In *The Enigmatic South: Towards Civil War and Its Legacies*, edited by Samuel C. Hyde, Jr. 133–49. Baton Rouge: Louisiana State University Press.

"Star of the West Scholarship Awarded." 1960. *Association of Citadel Men Alumni News* 18 (2): 3.

"Star of the West Centennial to be Observed." 1960. *Association of Citadel Men Alumni News* 18 (4): 3.

Thomas, Albert Sidney. 1964. *The Career and Character of Col. John Peyre Thomas, L.L.D.* Columbia, SC. N.p.

Thomas, John Peyre. 1874. *Address of Col. J. P. Thomas, Delivered at Cokesbury, S.C., September 1874. South Carolina—How Redeemed—Industrial Activity and Political Integrity—The Signs in Which we Conquer*. Charlotte, NC: Observer Print.

Thomas, John Peyre. 1879. *Historical Sketch of the South Carolina Military Academy*. Charleston, SC: Walker, Evans & Cogswell Co.

Thomas, John Peyre. 1883. *Col. J. P. Thomas' Oration. The Public Commemoration of the Re-establishment of the South Carolina Military Academy, 22d February 1883, Under the Auspices of the Washington Light Infantry, and pub. by Order of the Corps.* Charleston, SC: Walker, Evans & Cogswell Co.

Thomas, John Peyre. 1890. *True Citizenship and Rightful Legislation: Address Delivered at the Annual Commencement of the South Carolina Military Academy, July 2, 1890.* Charleston, SC: Walker, Evans & Cogswell Co.

Thomas, John Peyre. 1893. *The History of the South Carolina Military Academy.* Charleston, SC: Walker, Evans & Cogswell Co.

Thomas, John Peyre. 1899. "Calhoun's Theory of Government." *Southern Magazine* 1, no. 6 (November): 362–95.

Wiles, A. G. D. 1971. *The Boys Behind the Gun: The Citadel Cadets Who Fired the First Shot on the "Star of the West."* N.p.

CHAPTER TWO

"With the Pen of History, Write Carolina's Name"

Wofford College and the Challenges of War

Rhonda Kemp Webb

At the 1860 Wofford College commencement ceremony in Spartanburg, South Carolina, Taliaferro "Tally" Simpson addressed his graduating classmates. Tally, a member of the college's junior class, spoke the following words to the institution's seniors:

> For three long years we have been as a band of brothers—participating in those pleasures which a college life alone can afford. . . . Those hallowed associations endeared by many walks in these classic groves dedicated to the genius of literature and science must soon be considered as joys of the past. . . . Let your intellect be strengthened by the study of ancient lore and purified by the beautiful and chaste writings of modern times. . . . Obey the dictates of your consciences and make yourselves worthy of any position which duty or your country may assign you. (T. Simpson 1860)

Within months of Simpson's speech South Carolina belonged to a new country—the Confederate States of America. In his commencement address Tally encouraged his classmates to follow the duty assigned to them by their Southern country, and indeed, the region's young men were soon called to fight for the Confederacy. Many Wofford College students, alumni, and faculty served their new nation during the Civil War. At least 80 percent of the students enrolled at Wofford College during the 1860 academic year enlisted to fight for the Confederate army by November of 1861 (Wallace 1951). Tally and his brother, Richard "Dick" W. Simpson, were among those students who left campus to defend the Confederate South from the Union North.

Student perspectives, such as Tally's 1860 commencement speech, provide telling insights regarding Civil War-era student life at Wofford College. Tally and his older brother Dick wrote numerous speeches and letters over the course of their Wofford College years (1858 until they reported for Confederate service in 1861). Their letters to family members in Pendleton, South Carolina, illuminate not only day-to-day activities and curricular experiences but also their thoughts regarding the divisive political issues that gripped the United States during the late 1850s. Indeed, sectionalist strife and the Civil War itself deeply impacted both Simpson brothers and the entirety of Wofford College's enrolled and employed population.

WOFFORD COLLEGE'S PAROCHIAL FOUNDATION

In 1854, the South Carolina Methodist Church collaborated with the Spartanburg Town Boosters to found Wofford College. The organizers sought to promote the region's economic and societal development through the establishment of an academic institution (Wallace 1951; Felman 2004; Stone 2008). The college grew steadily until the outbreak of the American Civil War. The academy, like other Southern institutions of higher education, is an example of a regional college that experienced an academic transformation following the war, when once again the institution's administrators championed the institution's contribution to regional economic and social development.

Wofford College was named for its benefactor, Reverend Benjamin Wofford, who served the South Carolina Methodist Church as a traveling minister for sixteen years. Reverend Wofford engaged in business and banking interests while ministering to the people of his circuit and amassed substantial wealth by investing his wife's inheritance in successful business ventures. Reverend Wofford married twice during his lifetime, and both brides hailed from affluent families (Wallace 1951). Ministerial work during the mid-nineteenth century was not typically associated with significant financial reward as, on average, Southern Methodist ministers in 1855 were

"Taliaferro 'Tally' Simpson" c. 1862? Image courtesy of Bill Klugh, great grandson of R. W. "Dick" Simpson and grandnephew of Tally.

paid $150 per year (Holifield 1990). Reverend Wofford's upwardly mobile marriages were not uncommon in the South due to the high moral and social prominence ministers held in their communities. Ultimately, it was Benjamin Wofford's successful investment strategies that paved the way for the founding of Wofford College.

Benjamin Wofford died in December 1850 and willed that a portion of his wealth be used to create a regional college. The minister bequeathed

$100,000 "for the purpose of establishing and endowing a college for literary, classical and scientific education, to be located in . . . Spartanburg, and to be under the control and management of the Methodist Episcopal Church . . . of South Carolina" (Wofford College 1870, 20). The will made clear Wofford's commitment to the creation of an academic institution sustained by his endowment and operated by the Methodist Church in accordance with the denomination's parochial education principles. Members of the Methodist Church's General Conference promoted Christian education to enhance religious principles and intellectual development through the study of scriptural texts (Gross 1946). Methodist-affiliated colleges of the period were not typically seminaries intended to educate prospective ministers. Instead, church leadership established colleges primarily to educate the laity, including students of other faiths, to better understand Protestant theology (Geiger 2015). Methodist theologian Dr. William Wightman addressed a crowd of Methodist locals at the laying of Wofford College's cornerstone in 1851. He asserted that the institution's primary patron was the Methodist Church itself and that the college would be guided by Christian principles that "are abhorrent to sectarian bigotry, and breathe the true spirit of catholic liberty, of universal good will" (Wightman 1851). The Methodist college, with its strong reputation for morality, appealed to many community leaders in South Carolina's Upcountry region surrounding Spartanburg.

WOFFORD COLLEGE AND SOUTH CAROLINA'S SOCIOPOLITICAL LANDSCAPE

South Carolina, epicenter of a conflict that hurtled the nation into bitter civil war, was a state divided due to its own geography. The South Carolina Low Country along the Atlantic seaboard thrived on Charleston's lucrative commodity trade of plantation-grown rice and the area's Sea Island cotton. The Upcountry region of the state, while still immersed in agriculture, differed from the coastal region in terms of geography, demographic makeup, and economic pursuits (Ford 1986). The Upcountry lies closer to the Appalachian Mountains than the Carolina coastline, and the region's rivers do not provide navigable transportation routes to the state's port cities (Racine 2013). Given these significantly different geographic features, Upcountry agriculture afforded a more modest livelihood than the lucrative Low Country plantation system. The economic disparity between the Upcountry and Low Country also translated into political disparity within the state of South Carolina itself.

While South Carolina's coastal plantation elite spearheaded the state's political endeavors due to the region's larger population and economic influence, Upcountry representatives of the state's governing body did not always agree with their coastal counterparts. Many of Spartanburg's leaders were not tied to cotton or rice agriculture and listed their occupations as professionals and manufacturers. In the early 1850s, economic growth was the priority of Spartanburg's business organizers who helped establish Wofford College. Secession, as these mercantilists saw it, was not necessarily a benefit to their industries. Most of South Carolina's pro-Union sentiment was centered in the Upcountry region (Racine 2013). However, by the time of Abraham Lincoln's election in November 1860, most Upcountry people favored secession due to growing mistrust of Northern politicians, industrialists, and abolitionists.

Some of Spartanburg's influential textile manufacturers, including Simpson Bobo and E. C. Leitner, served on Wofford College's first Board of Trustees. Though the college was a parochial institution under the guidance of the South Carolina Methodist Church, the businessmen of Spartanburg were integral in the founding and initial operation of the institution. Bobo and Leitner's intentions were for the college to enhance the economic and political influence of the region by graduating men who would become state political leaders in addition to economic benefactors (Wallace 1951). In 1854, Wofford College opened with the support of both the South Carolina Methodists and Spartanburg's community leaders. Wofford College brought together the religious attitudes and broad educational goals of the more influential families of the Upcountry. They believed education was the key to securing greater prosperity and power for their geographic region. The Civil War quickly disrupted the new institution's momentum but destroyed neither the general development of Wofford College nor the growing trade center of Spartanburg.

WOFFORD CURRICULA PRIOR TO THE CIVIL WAR

The recorded minutes of the South Carolina Methodist Conference contain an annual report concerning its Committee of Education, which highlights the importance of Wofford College's opening and the committee's anticipation for a rapidly growing student body. Committee leaders also pledged that the Church "shall be prepared . . . to wield a decided religious influence over the rising generation entrusted to their charge" (South Carolina Conference of the Methodist Episcopal Church 1854, 34). Nine students enrolled in Wofford College's first term and twenty-four students enrolled in the second term. By the second academic year, enrollment grew to thirty-five. By 1860 the academy's enrollment increased to seventy-nine students (Board of Trustees 1860). Three men of distinguished credentials made up the inaugural faculty, and they remained at the college in various capacities throughout the war years. Their areas of expertise reflected the European, classical curricular tradition, which the college's governing board adopted. The first faculty members included Dr. William Wightman (president and professor of mental and moral science), Dr. David Duncan (treasurer and professor of ancient languages), and Dr. James Carlisle (secretary and professor of mathematics and astronomy). Wightman had previously taught at Virginia's Randolph-Macon College and was the editor of the *Southern Christian Advocate*, a prominent Methodist publication. Duncan was the chair of classical languages at Randolph-Macon College prior to joining the Wofford College faculty, and Carlisle had previously taught at Columbia Male Academy. Reverend A. M. Shipp soon joined the faculty as a professor of mental and moral philosophy, leaving his position as chair of history at the University of North Carolina. Dr. Warren DuPre became professor of natural sciences during the college's pre-Civil War years. DuPre had previously taught at South Carolina's Newberry College (Wallace 1951). These men established a solid foundation of scholarship and classical academic curriculum at the burgeoning upstate South Carolina institution.

The college's classical curriculum focused on Latin and Greek literature through analytical writing and oration. Classical higher education, it was believed, trained students to think, but did not necessarily structure coursework to prepare students for specific professions—commercial, scientific, or otherwise (Stetar 1985). Harvard College's colonial curriculum is one of the earliest examples of higher education's classical tradition in the United States, which remained popular in US educational institutions throughout the late nineteenth century (Kraus 1961). Wofford College followed such a classical curricular design from its inception forward. Members of the South Carolina Methodist Conference Committee on Education included in their 1854 report an explanation for employing the classical approach in their

Church-sponsored institutions. The committee wrote: "The careful training of the mind for clear thinking, correct judgment, steady self-reliance; the large-hearted, well-balanced character, fitted for enlightened usefulness in the living world of action—the product of this sort of culture, makes liberal education a boon of priceless worth" (South Carolina Conference of the Methodist Episcopal Church 1854, 33).

Classical coursework engaged students in the intensive study of Greek and Latin, literature, and rhetoric, though science and mathematics gradually became accepted components. Intense study was expected of students at classical institutions, including Wofford College. Subsequently, Dick and Tally Simpson experienced the demands of a classical education during the college's early years. The Simpson brothers' letters often reference their classical course of study as well as the high expectations set by the academy's faculty. Dick and Tally first enrolled at Wofford College in the fall of 1858 and remained at the Spartanburg institution until a few months prior to their graduation in the spring of 1861. The brothers left the campus before formal graduation, along with many of their peers, to join the Confederate army (Everson and Simpson Jr. 1994). Wofford College's professors awarded Dick and Tally (both seniors) their diplomas early in the semester since they had completed the bulk of the final term's coursework.

Tally and Dick's lettered descriptions of Wofford College curricular activities mirrors coursework offered at fellow Southern antebellum colleges and universities. Tally praised the wisdom of his professors and explained his curricular experiences to his father, Congressman Richard F. Simpson, on October 22, 1858. "This morning Prof. Carlisle gave us one of the best lectures that I ever heard. . . . I have learnt since I have been here the advantage of good teachers. If we had such teachers when we were going to [preparatory] school as these profs are, we could take first honor just as easy as we wanted to, but I think [with] a little training under Prof. Duncan we can catch [up] . . . in Greek. In Mathematics, History, and Antiquities I can say that I am as good as any of them in the class" (T. Simpson 1858). Though Tally claimed that both he and his brother were inadequately trained by the instructors at their hometown preparatory academy in Pendleton, South Carolina, he had hopes that he would excel given the ability of the Spartanburg college's faculty.

The dual purpose of Wofford College to foster morality and mentally train students is evident in the Simpson brothers' letters. Dick Simpson described to his aunt, Caroline Miller, the demanding Wofford schedule in an 1858 letter. "We have to go there every day in the week. Saturday not excepted and Sunday we have to go to the chapel" (R. W. Simpson 1858). He further explained the rigor of his daily college schedule and assignments to his mother. "We are now regularly installed in the line of College duties, without any spare moments to think or meditate on any other subject except our studies. And besides our studies we have to spend all our spare moments in writing compositions getting speeches to speak on the stage, and what is most of all I have to make an original speech once every week, in our society" (R. W. Simpson January 30, 1859). The brothers' academic experiences at Wofford College were certainly demanding, but, as was made clear in regular correspondence to their family, also edifying.

Tally and Dick's letters provide insight into the pre-Civil War college experience from the student perspective and are, at times, humorous. The brothers often tried to convince their parents to send more money. At other times, the brothers attempted to soften the shock of report cards that reflected grades below their father's expectations. Wofford College's faculty maintained high academic standards for Dick and Tally, even though their father was a US congressman. Their report cards do not indicate that favoritism was shown to the progeny of a prominent politician. In one comical letter from Dick to his sister Anna, he attempts to justify his poor grades. Dick complained, "The first thing I want to talk about is our reports. One thing I have to say, neither of them done us justice, for that satisfactory should have been highly satisfactory" (R. W. Simpson March 19, 1859). In addition to engaging in rigorous academic study, Wofford College students were also involved in various extracurricular activities.

COLLEGE LIFE AT WOFFORD

Although they spent considerable time studying, letters from Dick and Tally Simpson indicate that Wofford College attendees also engaged in Spartanburg community activities, looked forward to annual college functions, and took great interest in the young women who attended nearby Spartanburg Female College. The Simpson brothers often recounted their escapades involving fellow students in the city and surrounding community. For entertainment, Spartanburg hosted various traveling shows and religious revivals, which were often attended by students enrolled at local colleges and schools. One unique Spartanburg event documented by Tally and Dick in June 1859 was the weeklong exhibition of famed phrenologist, Dr. William H. Barker. Dick booked an individual session with Barker, which resulted in a nine-page report entitled, "A Delineation of the Character of Richard W. Simpson as Given by Dr. W. H. Barker" (Barker 1859). Phrenology was a popular nineteenth-century pseudoscientific study of cranial shape to determine character and personality traits, and Dr. Barker attracted large crowds to his lectures throughout the American South (Tomlinson 2005). Upon leaving a similar engagement at the University of North Carolina, it was written of Dr. Barker, "The Dr. took with him on his departing, considerable money, and in addition the good will of the students generally" ("College Record" 1885, 230).

According to their familial correspondence, Dick and Tally spent much of their free time entertaining young women from the aforementioned Spartanburg Female College. Tally was particularly concerned with affairs of the heart, and on many occasions wrote to his family about various love interests. Tally wrote to his aunt Caroline about a particular young woman he was interested in from the female college, "I want to get her card, daguerreotype, etcetera. . . . Look out for a new niece. . . . She may take possession of my heart. And if she does I am afraid I will study very little" (T. Simpson January 23, 1859). The young men of Wofford College sometimes serenaded the Spartanburg Female College students as Tally recounted in an 1859 letter to his aunt: "[My] brother, several more students, and myself went over to the Female College and serenaded the young ladies. We were showered with flowers some of which I now have in my room" (T. Simpson March 19, 1859). These nineteenth-century flirtations reflect the social dynamic of the Wofford College experience. The desire to court young women and retain keepsakes of their interactions was a regular happenstance in the American South.

Events in Spartanburg often brought Wofford College students together with local townspeople. One of the most celebrated events each spring was the three-day college commencement celebration. Tally wrote to his sister in 1859 predicting "Spartanburg will be literally crowded to death with people this commencement" (T. Simpson June 2, 1859). Dick also wrote to his sister about commencement. He described the elaborate plans for a large ticketed dinner in addition to several much-anticipated speeches (R. W. Simpson May 27, 1859). Though community events were important to Dick, Tally, and their fellow college pupils, some of the most significant gatherings involved campus organizations—literary societies in particular.

LITERARY SOCIETIES AS NURSERIES OF ELOQUENCE

A primary social and competitive activity in Southern antebellum colleges involved oratory and debate. Literary societies were highly regarded organizations, which elevated the best speakers and debaters to popular distinction on campus. Southern colleges and universities often housed literary societies as important extensions of classroom training. College students who honed their oratorical and debate skills became leaders among their literary society peers, and often went on to become political and business leaders later in life. Literary societies were not typically part of the formal college curriculum (Geiger 2015). Rather, they were unique and separate student-led organizations that reflected the prowess of academic life and mental fortitude. These societies provided an important training ground for students to practice, via public speaking, the reasoned thought cultivated via the classical educational model. Most courses in the classical tradition required students to recite compositions in Latin or Greek. Literary societies on these same campuses taught students to invent unique, self-authored arguments and deliver their own compositions (Westbrook 2002). Early nineteenth-century classrooms promoted passive learning through a reliance on recitation. Nineteenth-century literary societies, on the other hand, actuated a more critical pedagogy and were often considered "nurseries of eloquence" even though they functioned largely as extracurricular associations (La Borde 1859, 428).

Two literary societies sharpened the oratorical and debate skills of Wofford College students: the Calhoun Society (named for South Carolina political theorist and Democratic statesman, John C. Calhoun) and the Preston Society (dubbed in honor of South Carolina senator and Whig Party member, William C. Preston). Both societies maintained detailed records of membership, debate topics, and debate results. Many literary society topics dealt with general philosophical questions such as "Is genius innate?" (McElligott 1860, 220). However, some topics addressed contemporary political issues that divided the nation during the antebellum period, such as "Ought the blacks of the free states to have the privilege of voting[?]" (McElligott 1860, 216). Dick and Tally Simpson, like many Southern college men of the period, joined their institution's literary societies. Tally joined the Wofford College Calhoun Society and Dick joined the Preston Society. Tally wrote to his father in 1859 asking for money to join the Calhoun Society. He explained his urgent desire to become affiliated with this essential college organization: "I mention[ed] in one of my letters home a remark from one of the students to me—and now I repeat it 'that the Professors formed bad opinions of young men who did not commit themselves with the Society thinking that they wanted Saturday night to frolic. Therefore, if you desire us to be members send the money immediately—Ten Dollars apiece" (T. Simpson November 14, 1859). These student organizations, which provided not only scholastic benefits but also an element of fraternal secrecy and camaraderie, met every Saturday night in their respective club rooms on campus.

During their college years, the Simpson brothers rose in the ranks of their respective societies—each held the office of secretary. As members, both gave addresses imploring their classmates to develop their talents to the greater good of the neighboring community and state. Dick Simpson, in his speech at Wofford College's 1860 May exhibition, addressed the perilous political situation the United States was facing and urged students to use their mental abilities for the good of South Carolina. His words were borrowed from an 1851 poem written about North Carolina by University of North Carolina alumnus William Waightstill Avery. Quoting Avery, Dick spoke, "Ye youth of Carolina, I call upon you now, to add a single jewel to the crown upon her brow, you are entering from her College the battlefield of life, and her fostering care has armed you right and nobly for the strife. Walk onward then to glory. Seek literary fame, and with the pen of history write Carolina's name" (R. W. Simpson 1860). Like his brother, Tally urged his classmates to become political and community leaders even as regional sectionalism grew during the pivotal presidential election year of 1860 (T. Simpson July 10, 1860). Tally's words to Wofford College's graduating seniors were prophetic given that within a few short months, Lincoln was elected President. Thereafter, South Carolina seceded from the Union and the Civil War officially began with the siege at Fort Sumter.

Enrollment at Wofford College declined precipitously after the start of the war. Most students who remained consisted of younger boys in a newly organized preparatory department (Wallace 1951). Literary society minutes indicate that both organizations initially continued to function during the war, often debating topics related to contemporary wartime affairs. The debate topic entered in the Calhoun Society minutes for June 6, 1863 was, "Should Mr. Vallandigham be received into the Southern Confederacy and allowed to remain during the present war with the North and South?" (Calhoun Literary Society 1863, 154). Clement Laird Vallandigham was a political leader in Ohio. As a seminal figure in Ohio's Copperhead, antiwar faction of the Democratic Party, he had been convicted of supporting the Southern enemy through public sentiment and was exiled for violating General Order No. 38: treason for opposition to the war (Klement 1965). In addition to providing issues for debate, the Civil War also prompted greater activism on Wofford College's campus, including the formation of a student militia.

WOFFORD'S "SOUTHERN GUARD" STUDENT MILITIA

The notion of citizen-soldiers was popular in both the North and South even before the Civil War. Individuals on both sides believed personal sacrifice was a civic duty, an idea deeply embedded within the American psyche. The citizen-soldier ethos fueled greater white male participation in political and military matters to help shape national progress (Bledsoe 2015). White men on college campuses throughout the antebellum United States eagerly joined local volunteer militias. The Spartanburg community, as well as Wofford College, assembled volunteer units as the national political scene grew increasingly perilous. By 1860, twenty-seven known volunteer companies existed in the South Carolina Upcountry alone. Political differences persisted between the Low Country plantation elite who called for secession. Even so, citizen units drew widespread support across South Carolina. Upcountry units tended to attract members from more affluent families with at least some business ties to the state's slave economy, even if they did not own enslaved people themselves (West 2005).

One Upcountry unit, the Spartan Rifles, revived its membership in Spartanburg a few months before the Civil War began. The organization grew to approximately one hundred members under the leadership of Col. Joseph Walker (Landrum 1900). The original Spartan Rifles regiment was formed in 1776 and gained notoriety by winning the Battle of Cowpens during the American Revolution (Capace 2000). The Morgan Rifles, another area volunteer regiment, was formed nearly eighty years after the Spartan Rifles, in 1856. Both Spartanburg militia groups held community events, drilled regularly in town, and sent volunteer companies to join state-sponsored regiments. Wofford College students' interaction with these civic military groups heightened their awareness of local Confederate army preparation. Tally Simpson wrote to his mother about a target shooting competition hosted by the Morgan Rifles. The community event offered prizes such as a rifle, silver cup, and medals for winners (T. Simpson May 22, 1859). The Spartan Rifles eventually joined Company K, 5th Regiment of the South Carolina Volunteers after the fall of Fort Sumter (Landrum 1900). Over the course of the Civil War, approximately four thousand men from Spartanburg and surrounding communities served in various South Carolina military units (Racine 2013).

Wofford College students and faculty supported their community's efforts to prepare for war. The district's six elected delegates to South Carolina's December 1860 Secession Convention included Wofford College's mathematics professor James Carlisle and one of the institution's trustees, Simpson Bobo (Racine 2013). In addition, the college's enrolled students and faculty formed the Southern Guard militia on campus in February 1860, as resolution to the national conflict appeared unlikely. The Wofford College Southern Guard was a source of great pride for students. Dick and Tally Simpson participated in the unit's formation and reveled in their new military duties. Tally wrote to his father in 1860 about the new campus military group:

> I am now Lieutenant Taliaferro Simpson—quite an honorable title for an unworthy junior. . . . The Governor of South C. has approved of our course and intends to send us arms as speedily as possible. . . . We are about to bring before the College some resolutions . . . to wear nothing but homespun cloth for coat, pants, shirt during the winter seasons as long as we remain in college. . . . We intend to wear nothing coming from the North. Some of the fellows are going to find out from the Charleston merchants which of them imports foreign goods. (T. Simpson February 6, 1860)

In addition to Tally's letter discussing pro-Confederate student activism, a ledger page from a local Spartanburg store lists the military items both Simpson brothers purchased for their leadership positions in the new unit. Tally bought a sword, belt and clasp, sergeant's epaulettes, grey cloth, trimmings for a military coat, and a military cap for $27.85 (Ledger 1860). The divisive national political climate and resulting campus activism transformed the young men's academic college experience into a training ground for military activity.

Members of the Wofford College militia spent most of their time drilling and marching under the guidance of its student leaders. A letter from Tally to his sister Anna indicates the Southern Guard received military supplies from the South Carolina Military Academy's Citadel campus in Charleston

(T. Simpson April 7, 1860). The Southern Guard offered their services to South Carolina's Governor Francis Wilkinson Pickens following Lincoln's election, and again after the state's secession "to show the north what we are willing to do for the land of Fathers and Mothers—for the land of Calhoun" (T. Simpson April 7, 1860). Responding to both offers, Governor Pickens encouraged the students to remain at their college. Pickens wrote on January 28, 1861, "It would be a great injury to the State to have our literary institutions broken up, by the young men going into the active military service of the State" (F. Pickens 1861). A group of Wofford College students later met with Pickens, who again urged them to remain on campus. Governor Pickens believed the war would be short and the state would need statesmen more than soldiers after the Confederate victory was won.

Upon secession, Wofford College students wondered if they should abandon the college militia group and instead enlist in their respective hometown companies. Initially, most students remained committed to the Southern Guard. The student-led unit celebrated its first anniversary on February 22, 1861, amid much college and community fanfare (R. W. Simpson 1861). As part of the celebration, the Southern Guard invited the Spartan Rifles and Morgan Rifles to parade with them through Spartanburg. The local *Carolina Spartan* newspaper documented the military observance with a lengthy article proclaiming, "the military display was grand, imposing, and attractive. . . . As they passed before us, our thoughts involuntarily adverted to the present political crisis, and the ultimate destiny of each if required to vindicate Carolina's honor" ("Celebration" 1861, 2). As this salubrious activity and related campus events indicate, college students were not exempt from the emotional tug of wartime experiences.

ENDOWMENT LOST IN WAR INVESTMENTS

The Civil War consumed the South and lasted longer than many, including Governor Pickens, anticipated. Wofford College weathered the storm and remained open through the four years of fighting—due largely to enrollment in the recently established preparatory department. Financially, the college suffered capital losses due to limited enrollment and devastating monetary investments in Confederate currency. By October 1861, over forty students chose to enlist instead rather than reenroll. Enrollment numbers continued to dwindle as the war escalated. Faculty members relinquished most of their salaries and some, including Wofford College instructor Whiteford Smith, were reassigned to minister in regional churches. Some volunteered in the army, including professor of natural sciences, DuPre, who made salt for the Confederate army along South Carolina's seacoast (Wallace 1951).

Wofford College, like many other Southern institutions, faced economic strife because of the war. Confederate losses at Gettysburg, Pennsylvania, and Vicksburg, Mississippi, in 1863 brought greater economic uncertainty and inflation to the Confederate South. To curb inflation, the Confederate government passed financial legislation encouraging investors to convert regular currency into Confederate bonds. Removing money from circulation, it was hoped, would increase the remaining currency's value. One such funding law, passed in March 1863, set August 1, 1863, as the deadline to convert currency notes into bonds at higher rates of interest (Pecquet, Davis, and Kanago 2004). Wofford College's trustees believed their only option to save the value of their college's financial endowment was Confederate investment. As such, they invested the institution's endowment currency notes into the higher percentage rate bonds to preserve their value before the deadline. A letter from George Williams, a Wofford College trustee in Charleston, to Wofford College's treasurer, David Duncan, indicates the urgency to invest. Williams reported, "Ten Thousand Dollars to be invested in Confederate Bonds for Wofford College. If I cannot get the 8% bonds at reasonable rates, I will invest all of the funds of the College in 7% bonds" (G. Williams 1863). Williams, a Wofford College trustee himself, tried to get the best rate possible for the institution's investment. However, the bond rate dropped to 4 percent by 1864 (Davis and Pecquet 1990). Consequently, the college's leaders struggled to preserve the institution's economic resources. The institution's remaining securities included $85,897 in Confederate bonds and certificates, $1,297 in Confederate money, and bank stocks of $17,525 par value (Wallace 1951). Today, almost $90,000 of worthless Confederate currency and bonds remain in Wofford College's vault (Boggs, Brasington, and Stone 2005).

WOFFORD COLLEGE CURRICULUM REIMAGINED

Southern higher education leaders, faculty, and community members spent decades regaining economic stability following the war. Communities and individuals began to transform their economies by planting more diverse crops and increasing manufacturing pursuits. Wofford College administrators also diversified the institution's course offerings in order to address the region's changing academic needs. The college curriculum gradually evolved from the strictly classical approach to include more practical commercial and vocational training. Regional academic individuals and institutions also charted new paths following the Civil War. Dick and Tally Simpson's lives were changed forever when they left college to become soldiers. Tally Simpson, the spirited former Wofford College student and secretary for the Calhoun Literary Society, died in 1863 at the Battle of Chickamauga (Everson and Simpson Jr. 1994). The war experience also influenced Dick's future, as he became a progressive regional leader determined to rebuild South Carolina. The surviving brother also contributed to the post-Reconstruction shift in South Carolina's higher education philosophy towards a more practical curricular approach.

Higher education became even more important in the South as individuals tried to repair their lives and personal fortunes. Professor Whiteford Smith identified the war as a catalyst for new educational pursuits among those who had previously seen little need for formal learning. Smith described an illiterate neighbor whose husband, also illiterate, had entered the Confederate army. During the war, the couple learned to read and write so that they could correspond regularly (Racine 2013). The strain of the American Civil War promoted literacy for practical purposes, which Wofford College faculty recognized. When the war ended, new forms of practical, literacy-based education also developed to meet the demands for rebuilding a society left in ruin by the conflict.

Recollecting Wofford College's overtly classical curricula, Tally, while still attending college, questioned the wisdom of his institution's complete adherence to classical instruction. He delivered an address in 1861, in which he expressed these thoughts:

> It has been the practice in our educational institutions heretofore to ignore the science of government and to solicit a course of study which will extend the moral and mental capacity of the young. This practice was established when there existed no necessity for a different practice. . . . As Government is so essential to the happiness and civilization of men we can not see how our institutions of learning can any longer ignore it as a science and a science worthy

> of their most careful attention. Many no doubt can be found who would cry out in dismay at the mere suggestion that young men in our colleges should be taught the science of politics, but it is a necessity nonetheless. (T. Simpson 1861)

Following the war, Dick Simpson pursued a profession external to his classical training. He became a prominent lawyer, which required the garnering of a legal education that was not part of his Wofford College instruction. Through his work as the trusted estate lawyer and friend of Thomas Clemson, Dick Simpson promoted higher education reform in South Carolina. Conversations between Simpson and Clemson concerned the need for practical higher education in agriculture and business and resulted in a plan to establish Clemson University in Clemson, South Carolina. These academically progressive men recognized the practical, vocation-centric curricular approach would help their war-ravaged state and its citizenry (Everson and Simpson Jr. 1994). Dick Simpson assisted his client in writing the will that set in motion the founding of a new agricultural and business college by means of an endowment for the institution that still bears Clemson's name. Following the Civil War, Southern political and business leaders like Dick Simpson made critical changes to foster productivity and economic stability in South Carolina.

Indeed, South Carolina colleges established after the Civil War were largely focused on practical curricula. Even so, administrators at established academies, like Wofford College also sought to meet the demands of a changed Southern society. Administrators relaxed Wofford College's entrance requirements in 1867 due to the preparatory academic interruption most young men experienced during the war years (Board of Trustees 1866). The college's postwar catalog included new class offerings in bookkeeping, English, and history beyond the classical coursework. These classes made up a new curricular track for the pursuit of what was, at the time, considered an inferior bachelor of science degree (Wofford College 1876). The institution's faculty also abandoned the practice of rigidly dividing students into year-based class groups (i.e. freshman, sophomore, junior, senior) during the Reconstruction era. The new system created "schools" of academic study, in which students concentrated their coursework on areas of thought, such as accounting or business administration. When a student completed the required courses in a school, he received a diploma. Despite these changes, Wofford College administrators did not abandon the institution's classical foundation. Rather, they supplemented the curriculum with additional courses and a new academic structure designed to promote flexibility for students whose academic preparation and aspirations might have been negatively influenced by the war.

Wofford College's new system more appropriately met the specific needs of individual students and the surrounding community following the war's profound regional impact. An explanation as to why the faculty deemed it necessary to add English to the course of study appeared in the 1867 Wofford Course Catalog, which indicates the significance of the curricular change. "The Trustees and Faculty are profoundly convinced that . . . in doing this they are helping to solve the much-mooted question of practical education" (Wofford College 1876, 18). As a result, the South Carolina academy's "classic groves dedicated to the genius of literature and science," as described in Tally Simpson's 1860 commencement address, expanded to meet the needs of the Spartanburg community. Thus, while Wofford College leaders refused to abandon its classical roots entirely, regional leaders such as Dick Simpson helped the college reevaluate the purpose of Southern higher education, eventually settling on a more progressive and practical higher education experience for its postwar students.

REFERENCES

Barker, W. H. 1859. "A Delineation of the Character of Richard W. Simpson as Given by Dr. W. H. Barker." MSS-221, Box 1. Report. Richard F. Simpson Papers. Clemson University Special Collections Library.

Bledsoe, Andrew S. 2015. *Citizen-Officers: The Union and Confederate Volunteer Junior Officer Corps in the American Civil War*. Baton Rouge: Louisiana State University Press.

Board of Trustees. 1860. Records of the Board of Trustees Wofford College 1853–1894, 46. Sandor Teszler Library Archives and Special Collections. Wofford College.

Board of Trustees. 1866. Records of the Board of Trustees Wofford College 1853–1842, 63. Sando Teszler Library Archives and Special Collections. Wofford College.

Boggs, Doyle, Joann Mitchell Brasington, and Phillip Stone. 2005. *Wofford: Shining with Untarnished Honor, 1854–2004*. Spartanburg: Hub City Writers Project.

Calhoun Literary Society. Records. Sandor Teszler Library Archives and Special Collections. Wofford College.

Capace, Nancy. 2000. "Celebration of 1st Anniversary of Southern Guards." 1861. *Carolina Spartan*. February 28, 1861, 2. *Encyclopedia of South Carolina*. St. Clair Shores, MI: Somerset Publishers.

"College Record." 1885. *University Magazine* 9 (5): 229–32. Sando Teszler Library Archives and Special Collections. Wofford College.

Davis, George K. and Gary M. Pecquet. 1990. "Interest Rates in the Civil War South." *Journal of Economic History* 50 (1): 133–48.

Eelman, Bruce W. 2004. "Entrepreneurs in the Southern Upcountry: The Case of Spartanburg, South Carolina, 1815–1880." *Enterprise and Society* 5 (1): 77–106.

Everson, Guy R. and Edward W. Simpson Jr. 1994. *Far, Far from Home: The Wartime Letters of Dick and Tally Simpson, 3rd South Carolina Volunteers*. New York: Oxford University Press.

Ford, Lacy K. 1986. "Yeoman Farmers in the South Carolina Upcountry: Changing Production Patterns in the Late Antebellum Era." *Agricultural History* 60 (4): 17–37.

Geiger, Roger L. 2015. *The History of American Higher Education: Learning and Culture from the Founding to World War II*. Princeton, NJ: Princeton University Press.

Gross, John O. 1946. "Religious Work on Methodist College Campuses from Cokesbury to 1945." *Christian Education* 29 (3): 210–22.

Holifield, E. Brooks. 1990. "The Penurious Preacher: Nineteenth Century Clerical Wealth North and South." *Journal of the American Academy of Religion* 58 (1): 17–36.

Klement, Frank L. 1965. "Clement L. Vallandigham's Exile in the Confederacy, May 25–June 17, 1863." *Journal of Southern History* 31 (2): 149–63.

Kraus, Joe W. 1961 "The Development of a Curriculum in Early American Colleges." *History of Education Quarterly* 1 (2): 64–76.

La Borde, Maximilian. 1859. *South Carolina College: From Its Incorporation Dec 19, 1801 to Nov 25, 1857*. Carlisle, MA: Applewood Books.

Landrum, J. 1900. *History of Spartanburg County*. Atlanta: Franklin Printing and Publication Co.

Ledger. 1860. MSS-221, Box 1. Report. Richard F. Simpson Papers. Clemson University Special Collections Library.

McElligott, James N. 1860. *The American Debater*. New York: Ivison, Phinney & Co.

Pecquet, Gary, George Davis, and Bryce Kanago. 2004. "The Emancipation Proclamation, Confederate Expectations, and the Price of Southern Bank Notes." *Southern Economic Journal* 70 (3): 616–30.

Pickens, Governor F. 1861. Letter to Wofford College Southern Guard. January 28, 1861. Records of the Board of Trustees Wofford College 1853–1942. Sandor Teszler Library Archives and Special Collections. Wofford College.

Racine, Philip N. 2013. *Living a Big War in a Small Place: Spartanburg, South Carolina, During the Confederacy*. Columbia: University of South Carolina Press.

Simpson, Richard W. November 13, 1858. Letter to Caroline Miller. MSS-221, Box 1. Richard F. Simpson Papers. Clemson University Special Collections Library.

Simpson, Richard W. January 30, 1859. Letter to Mary Simpson.

Simpson, Richard W. March 19, 1859. Letter to Anna Simpson.

Simpson, Richard W. May 27, 1859. Letter to Anna Simpson.

Simpson, Richard W. May 28, 1860. Speech. Wofford College May Exhibition.

Simpson, Richard W. February 21, 1861. Letter to Anna Simpson.

Simpson, Richard W. October 22, 1858. Letter to Richard F. Simpson.

Simpson, Richard W. January 23, 1859. Letter to Caroline Miller.

Simpson, Richard W. March 19, 1859. Letter to Caroline Miller.

Simpson, Richard W. May 22, 1859. Letter to Mary Simpson.

Simpson, Richard W. June 2, 1859. Letter to Anna Simpson.

Simpson, Richard W. November 14, 1859. Letter to Richard F. Simpson.

Simpson, Richard W. February 6, 1860. Letter to Richard F. Simpson.

Simpson, Richard W. April 7, 1860. Letter to Anna Simpson.

Simpson, Richard W. July 10, 1860. Speech. Wofford College Commencement Address.

Simpson, Richard W. February 20, 1861. Speech. Wofford College.

South Carolina Conference of the Methodist Episcopal Church, South. 1854. Minutes. Charleston: Office of the Southern Christian Advocate.

Stetar, Joseph M. 1985. "In Search of a Direction: Southern Higher Education After the Civil War." *History of Education Quarterly* 25 (3): 341–67.

Stone, R. Phillip. 2008. Review of *Entrepreneurs in the Southern Upcountry: Commercial Culture in Spartanburg, South Carolina, 1845–1880*, by Bruce W. Eelman. *South Carolina Historical Magazine* 109 (3): 234–36.

Tomlinson, Stephen. *Head Masters: Phrenology, Secular Education, and Nineteenth-Century Social Thought.* Tuscaloosa: University of Alabama Press, 2005.

Wagoner, Jennings L. 1983. "Higher Education and Transitions in Southern Culture: An Exploratory Apologia." *Journal of Thought* 18 (3): 104–18.

Wallace, David Duncan. 1951. *History of Wofford College, 1854–1949*. Nashville: Vanderbilt University Press.

West, Stephen A. 2005. "Minute Men, Yeomen, and the Mobilization for Secession in the South Carolina Upcountry." *Journal of Southern History* 71 (1): 75–104.

Westbrook, B. Evelyn. 2002. "Debating Both Sides: What Nineteenth-Century College Literary Societies Can Teach Us About Critical Pedagogies." *Rhetoric Review* 21 (4): 339–56.

Wightman, William M. 1851. "Address of the Cornerstone Laying." July 4, 1851. Papers of William May Wightman. Archives. Sandor Teszler Library Archives and Special Collections. Wofford College.

Williams, George. 1863. Letter to David Duncan. July 13, 1863. Records of the Board of Trustees Wofford College 1853–1942. Sandor Teszler Library Archives and Special Collections. Wofford College.

Wofford College. 1870. "Office of Registrar: Catalog of Wofford College, 1870–1871." College Catalogs, Paper 9. Last modified October 8, 2015. https://digitalcommons.wofford.edu/catalogues/9.

Wofford College. 1872. "Office of Registrar: Catalog of Wofford College, 1872." College Catalogs, Paper 8. Last modified October 8, 2015. https://digitalcommons.wofford.edu/catalogues/8.

Wofford College. 1876. "Office of Registrar: Catalog of Wofford College, 1876–1877." College Catalogs, Paper 6. Last modified October 8, 2015. https://digitalcommons.wofford.edu/catalogues/6.

CHAPTER THREE

Mississippi College and the Mississippi College Rifles

A Campus at War and Death on the Battlefield

David E. Taylor, Holly A. Foster, and R. Eric Platt

The story of Mississippi College is almost as old as the state from which it derives its name. Mississippi gained statehood in 1817, and the Hampstead Academy, predecessor of Mississippi College, followed nine years later. The college sprang up along the only manmade thoroughfare venturing inland, the Natchez Trace (Busbee 2019; Finley 1995). The academy was neither located near the Mississippi River nor along the seacoast, where institutions, such as Jefferson Military College (Washington, Mississippi) and St. Stanislaus College (Bay St. Louis, Mississippi) had been founded (Blain 1976; Nolan 2002). But here, at a remote spring far removed from major waterways, early central Mississippi residents took it upon themselves to found first a college, then a town. After land was ceded to the United States from the Choctaw Tribe following the Treaty of Doak's Stand in 1820 (Stahr 2017), Raymond Robinson ventured to Mississippi from South Carolina in search of inexpensive land to grow cotton (Monette 1846). He was fortunate in that he found a prize spring near the Natchez Trace and bought it along with approximately 1,500 acres. Property surrounding the spring became known as Robinson's Spring, and today lies directly in the center of Clinton, Mississippi, then called Mount Salus (Monette 1846; Miller 1996).

The area was first named by then-governor of Mississippi, Walter Leake. Leake located his family home ten miles from the capital city of Jackson, preferring the clear air in Mount Salus to the malaria-infested swamps along the Pearl River near Jackson. Because of its healthy environment, Leake named the area Mount Salus, meaning "mountain of health" (McLemore 1979, 4; "Sketch of Gov. Walter Leake of Mississippi" 1904). In 1828, the Mount Salus community was renamed Clinton in honor of the New York governor who furthered the completion of the Erie Canal—DeWitt Clinton (Chisholm 2007). Two of Mississippi's early governors, as well as other prominent state officials, lived in or around Mount Salus. Thereafter, affluent businessmen, doctors, lawyers, land officials, and planters settled in the area. In the 1830s, construction on the Vicksburg-to-Clinton railroad was begun, which bolstered the region's cotton plantation economy. When the railroad was completed in 1840, it was estimated that the line's steam locomotives could ship over twenty thousand bales of cotton per year to the Mississippi River for sale abroad (Martin 2007). Plantation affluence in Clinton, Mississippi, was paramount to the region's economic and social success. While slave-stocked plantations enhanced the South's "cotton kingdom," medical practitioners and businessmen echoed the financial acumen of the latter. With the city's growth, a more diverse social structure evolved, inclusive of lower-class, cabin-dwelling yeomen. In time, the regional elite considered founding an academy to educate their children and, as a result, further demarcate Clinton's upper social class from the lower yeoman class. Instead of sending their children to Northern colleges or abroad to European institutions, Clinton's young men would receive a higher education in their home community (McLemore 1979).

BAPTIST AFFILIATION AND STUDENT LIFE

The earliest meetings regarding an academy in Clinton, Mississippi, took place in 1825. It is believed that the resultant Hampstead Academy was named for Hampstead Heath, a park just north of London, England. A state charter was granted on January 24, 1826. In 1827, the academy's name evolved to reflect the surrounding state—Mississippi Academy. The institution's title was changed once again to Mississippi College by an act of the Mississippi legislature on December 16, 1830 (Mayes 1899). In 1831, Mississippi College's curricular structure was expanded and the college became the first coeducational institution in the United States to grant baccalaureate degrees to women: Alice Robinson and Catherine Hall. In fact, the college did not grant a baccalaureate degree to a man until 1843 (Martin 2007).

The early history of Mississippi College was fraught with economic challenges. The institution was founded as a private, nonsectarian institute with strong Christian ties. Soon thereafter, college leaders realized the need for denominational support if the institution was to persist. First the Methodists and then the Presbyterians were asked to lend their financial support, but both soon realized the ongoing demands associated with such an endeavor were beyond their denomination's regional capacity. By 1850, the college was at the verge of closing due to a significant want for capital support. At that time, Mississippi College was offered to the Baptists who accepted (Rowe 1881). Mississippi's Baptist leaders had been in search of just such an institute to further their religious efforts in the Deep South via higher education. To support the new Baptist-affiliated college, a financial endowment expansion campaign set at $100,000 was initiated. Within a short period of time Mississippi's Baptists had rallied around the idea of a college undergirded by their denominational beliefs, and the needed monies were pledged. Despite regional denominational support, the Baptist population in Clinton was low. Local Baptists were so few that they did not have their own physical church facility but met on alternating Sundays with the Presbyterians in their facility. In fact, the local Baptist community did not have a separate church building until 1852 (Leavell and Bailey 1904; Howell 2014).

Though members of the denomination were prepared to accept the college property and pledge their financial support, they were ill-prepared to fill it with tuition-paying students. When the Baptist Convention accepted Mississippi College in 1850, convention members were immediately pressed to fill the campus with both faculty and students. When the 1851 academic semester began, Isaac Newton Urner had been selected as the intuition's president. First opening with only a preparatory department comprised of approximately 17 students, enrollment, over the course of the first academic year, increased to 66. The following years saw a steady increase in both students and faculty. By the 1860–1861 academic year, the college boasted 227 students and 8 faculty. By the end of that year, enrollment was listed at 229 (Mississippi College Catalog 1860–1861; "Prof. I. N. Urner" 1860; "Mississippi College" 1861).

With a growing number of students, a new chapel building (which stands to this day), and an increased financial endowment, the influence of Mississippi College reached as far as New Orleans, Louisiana, Richland, Arkansas, and Memphis, Tennessee. Still, most students hailed from Clinton, the surrounding Mississippi counties, and a handful of north Louisiana parishes (Mississippi College Catalog 1860–1861). Indeed, Mississippi College had become quite well known in Louisiana. The institution's administrators often advertised in New Orleans newspapers. The August 6, 1859, edition of the *Daily Picayune* ran the following advertisement: "This college was established in 1850 by the Baptists of the State of Mississippi. Over $100,000 have been subscribed as an endowment fund, and the college is in a flourishing condition. The course of studies is thorough" ("Mississippi College" 1859, 2).

Surpassing newspaper ads, Mississippi's Baptist ministers were perhaps the best salesmen for the college. Baptist ministers appealed to members of their local parishes for students to populate the Clinton-based academy. Though Mississippi College, its faculty, and administrators, opened the 1860 fall semester with a bevy of students, the faculty could not dismiss the national upheaval surrounding the presidential election of Abraham Lincoln and the looming threat of Civil War. This concern was mentioned in the college's 1860–1861 academic catalog. Even so, the college's leaders were more concerned with the institution's pecuniary growth and believed the war would be short-lived. As stated in the college's 1860–1861 academic catalog: "as soon as the present war ends, it is proposed to raise another hundred thousand dollars endowment" (Mississippi College Catalog 1860–1861, 15). This statement reflected the popular Southern belief that the war would be short and conclusive with the Confederate states as victors.

Students arriving in the fall of 1860 were accompanied by their fathers, whose responsibility it was to see them properly housed at the campus before returning to their homes. Parents secured housing for their sons with one of Clinton's many families, as the college had no boarding facilities at that time (Mississippi College Catalog 1860–1861). However, the institution's leaders provided the names of approved families who had been vetted, deemed propitious, and were willing to house said students. The college's leaders believed this housing arrangement provided students with "the advantage of family influences while away from home" (Mississippi College Catalog 1860–1861, 29). The practice of pairing students with host families, coupled with a strict code of conduct, left little room for students to err, even though temptations abounded. Antebellum Clinton had grown to become a hotbed of promiscuity, especially at local resorts and hotels. Amusement in the forms of "dance bands, billiard tables, ten-pen allies, choice liquors and wines, and every amusement usual at watering places" (Howell 2014, 65) were available to those with money. However, detailed governance was dictated through the college catalogs expressly forbidding the playing of billiards, cards, or raffling, and such illicit practices as "visiting groceries, or other places, where intoxicating liquors are sold" or "going to the depot at [train] car time" (Mississippi College Catalog 1860–1861, 29).

Mississippi College students were given "friendly" warnings by faculty members for minor rule infractions, public admonition in front of other students, suspension, or even expulsion if the infraction was perceived by the faculty as more serious. Such punishments were described as "Just and Proper" in the college catalogs and were further supported by the institution's "Laws for the Government of Students." In addition to penalties, class structures and academic expectations were also harsh. From the beginning of the fall term through March, students were expected to study from morning prayers until 12:30 p.m. After a brief lunch and short break period, students recommenced their studies from two o'clock until four in the afternoon, and again from seven until nine each evening. If students were not engaged in recitations or classes, they were expected to be in their rooms studying. Even the weekends lacked freedom. "On Friday night students must prepare for Monday" (Mississippi College Catalog 1860–1861, 33–34). Simply put, Mississippi College students were to take their studies seriously, leave the temptations of the world outside the realms of academia, and become the young men God intended them to be. Sabbath school (an early form of the modern "Sunday school"), daily scripture reading, and campus Bible society participation were mandatory for all attending Mississippi College. Upon arriving at the institution students were expected to sign a matriculation pledge, swearing to keep the rules of the academy and to give up all firearms that might be in their possession (Mississippi College Catalog 1860–1861). By placing their students under the authority of a household and the college's faculty, Mississippi College's administration expressed their belief that the young men entrusted to their care would not fall by the wayside, but would become the educated, Christian leaders Mississippi would need in the future.

Given the college's strict code of conduct and the intense hours committed to study, it might appear that Mississippi College was a place of totalitarianism with little room for enjoyment. This was not entirely the case. Any forms of "enjoyment" fostered by the college were, however, rooted in religion. According to historian Walter Howell, at one point there was "a Lyceum that provided programs of cultural enrichment for town and gown," and "faculty members also started the Clinton Bible Society to offer programs on biblical and non-biblical subjects" (2014, 63). Traveling speakers, revival evangelists, and political orations also added to the general fanfare of Clinton social life. Regardless of the nature of said events, Mississippi College students could only attend if the activity was approved by the college's administration. At times, social interactions were allowed between Mississippi College's male students and the attendees of nearby Central Female Institute (founded in 1853). Occasionally, female wards from the aforementioned women's academy could take courses at Mississippi College, while the male students of Mississippi College were, at times, permitted to take courses at Central Female Institute (Central Female Institute was later renamed Hillman College, which closed and merged with Mississippi College in 1942) (Standifer 1988; Balmer 2004).

In addition to sporadic coed classes, both student populations, male and female, were required to attend a common Sabbath meeting, segregated by sex. To further Biblical and literary studies, a Philomathean Literary Society was begun at Mississippi College in 1846. A Hermenian Literary Society was later formed in 1854. Both societies met on Saturdays, "the day for preparation of Declamations and Essays," in preparation for presentations on Mondays. "For more than a century these two organizations—in cooperation and in competition—were a major part of the educational program and student life at Mississippi College" (Martin 2007, 88). The Hermenian and Philomathean Literary Societies furnished a principal form of extracurricular activity on the campus during the latter 1840s and throughout the 1850s. "Their members were the student leaders on the campus" (McLemore 1979, 199). As the antebellum era came to a close and Civil War permeated the interior of Mississippi, student life at Mississippi College significantly changed.

CIVIL WAR AND THE MISSISSIPPI COLLEGE RIFLES

Unlike other Southern colleges and universities, Mississippi College did not close during the war, due in large part to a well-stocked preparatory department comprised of students too young to enlist (Fox-Clark 1990). To further support the institution's wartime existence, faculty wages were diminished.

This was especially costly to President Urner as, at times, he received no financial compensation (McLemore 1979). "Though a large number of other colleges have suspended, we have deemed it best to continue the exercises of our College. Our country does not require the services of all of her young men in the field, and many boys are too young to enter the army. All these should continue their studies, and thus fit themselves better for the weighty responsibilities that will be theirs in a few years" (Mississippi College Catalog 1860–1861, 38). While several of the preparatory students remained enrolled instead of leaving for the supposed protection of their family homes, many older Mississippi College students were swept up in a wave of Confederate fervor and subsequent military enlistment.

Mississippi College, like several of its regional academic peers, responded to the call for Confederate soldiers. At the start of the Civil War, thirty-two students and three members of the faculty formed their own volunteer regiment, titled the Mississippi College Rifles. In time, this college-affiliate corps was reorganized as the 18th Mississippi Regiment. Student cadet drilling began on the grounds of Mississippi College under the leadership of John York, E. G. Banks, and M. Judson Thigpen. The Mississippi College Rifles was formed in February of 1861 for the purpose of preparing young men for military service in the Confederate army. Johnson Welborn, a thirty-six-year-old Clinton merchant and Mississippi College trustee, was elected the company's commander. While some students' families paid for their sons' uniforms and arms, Welborn was reported to have paid the cost of any student unable to finance himself in the military company (Fox-Clark 1990; Howell 2014; McLemore 1979).

Such patriotic zeal and support for the Confederacy continued throughout the early years of the war. On April 18, 1861, Silas Talbert White, a senior in the college's preparatory department and a member of the Mississippi College Rifles, wrote to his family:

> Dear Father, I seat myself tonight to give you as long Patriotic a letter as I can (not calling myself a Patriot) but I feel a Spirit of resistance to Northern oppression and I intend to stand to Southern rights as long as I have a drop of blood and a single bullet to shoot. Truly we have the Spirit of '76 raise[d] among us and there is a general determination to stand to Southern rights or die in the attempt. We the Students of Mississippi [College] have formed a military company and are going to offer our service to the Governor as soon as possible. (White 1861)

Spirits soared in the initial days of the Confederacy, and Mississippi College students, like students enrolled in a host of other regional colleges and universities, supported secession and the chance to fight in the Confederate armies. However, as the harsh realities of military life and war sullied the concept of "battlefield honor," student zeal decreased. "Drilling is warm work," wrote a private in the Mississippi College Rifles. "We would get pretty tired before our day's work ended. We were, however, learning our lessons in soldiering, and the drill was an important part of them. It is this mainly that make[s] the difference between trained soldiers and a mob" (Davis, 1977, 23).

During the initial months of the Civil War, the student cadets associated with the Mississippi College Rifles enjoyed the gaiety and excitement that permeated pro-Confederate Clinton, Mississippi. Mrs. Ulysses Moffett, a Clinton resident, hosted a social gathering for the college's military company at her nearby home before they departed campus for the warfront (Fox-Clark 1990). Not long thereafter, "During the month of May the company basked in the sweet smiles of lovely women and indulged itself with the Luxuries abundantly showered upon it by the good people of Clinton and Hinds [County]" (Parish 1865, 1). Area female denizens stitched together a company flag that was presented to the Mississippi College Rifles before their departure for the battlefield. In response, M. Judson Thigpen, a professor at Mississippi College and elected lieutenant of the college's rifle company, responded with gratitude: "Ladies of Clinton and vicinity—With high beating hearts and breasts full of emotion, we receive from your hands this handsome flag; proud emblem of our young Republic . . . we prize this flag, ladies, not so much for its intrinsic worth, but for the sake of those who gave it" (Gragg 1989, 22). On May 27, 1861, the college rifles departed campus while the institution's brass band played, "The Girl I Left Behind Me"—a military tune that accompanied military and navel units when they set out for battle (McLemore 1979, 76; Ralph 1964).

Leaving Mississippi College behind, the college rifles boarded a train headed to Corinth, Mississippi. Members of the rifles joined the Confederate army first as members of Company E of the 18th Mississippi Infantry. The 18th Mississippi Infantry was thereafter transferred to Camp Pickens near Manassas Junction in Virginia to serve under Confederate general Pierre Gustave Toutant-Beauregard. The college students experienced their first episode of conflict at the First Battle of Manassas on July 21, 1861. By war's end, only eight of the college students-turned-military men of the

Mississippi College Rifles were present at the Confederate surrender at Appomattox Courthouse. Most of the College Rifles were eventually affixed to the Southern Army of the Potomac, which had been absorbed into the Army of Northern Virginia. Of the 139 students who joined in the College Rifles, fifteen were killed in battle or succumbed to war-related wounds. Nine others died of disease, three resigned, eleven transferred to other military units, fourteen deserted, fifty-two were discharged for various reasons, two were dropped from rolls, and thirty-three were unaccounted for (Fox-Clark 1990).

Despite the egress of the Mississippi College Rifles, the institution remained open. In addition to the loss of the student cadets, three instructors left to join the Confederate forces and, as the war progressed, several other students exited the college to support the Southern cause. Even so, eight students graduated in the summer of 1861. The next year only two graduated. By the end of 1862, most of the faculty had resigned due to reductions in pay (Howell 2014).

The burden to maintain the academy fell predominantly to President Urner. He continued in his post despite a 25 percent reduction in pay (Martin 2007). During the war, the college's preparatory department averaged thirty students per year under Urner's administration. However, during the final years of the conflict, the outlook for the college was bleak. By this time, the war had come close to campus. While the Mississippi College Rifles were busily engaged as a part of the conflict in Virginia, Union general Ulysses S. Grant invaded Jackson, Mississippi, and surrounding communities (Wynne 2006). Alice Shirley, a student at the Central Female Institute (also located in Clinton) documented the arrival of Union soldiers in her journal.

> The terrified people cried out 'the Yankees are coming, the Yankees are coming' . . . the usually quiet town of Clinton was now all confusion. The soldiers were bent on destruction, stables were torn down, smoke houses invaded and emptied of their bacon and hams, chicken houses were depopulated, vehicles of all kinds were taken or destroyed, barrels of sugar and molasses . . . were emptied . . . the dry goods stores were broken into, the beautiful goods given to negroes or destroyed. . . . The best store in town was owned by Mr. William Dunton, a union man. . . . At last all the soldiers were gone and Clinton was left to take a long breath, pick up the remains of everything and go on with life again. (as quoted in Winschel 1993, 16)

It was reported that President Urner urged Union forces to leave the campus and its facilities unharmed. The Union soldiers complied. However, both sides did make use of campus buildings during the war. In 1862, Confederate officers used the campus chapel as a hospital. Later, Union forces used the upper floors of the chapel as a hospital while stabling their horses on the ground level. In July of 1864, Confederate Capt. W. A. Montgomery, accompanied by one hundred Confederate troops, attempted to capture the Federal troops at the college campus. Despite Montgomery's efforts, Union soldiers retreated into the chapel and repulsed the attack. The Confederate soldiers were said to have "liberated" only two of the Union horses for their efforts before they fled (Howell 2014, 127).

A MISSISSIPPI COLLEGE CADET AT WAR

While Urner and the remainder of Mississippi College's students persisted in maintaining academic activities, members of the college rifles were separated, mustered into separate military companies, and sent to support the Confederacy. Silas Talbert White was one of the college rifle members that had been transferred to another company. Prior to leaving Mississippi College with his fellow cadets, White was a senior in the institution's preparatory department when the War began (Mississippi College Catalog 1860–1861). White (eighteen years old at the time) and his fellow students were cautioned by Capt. J. W. Welborn of Clinton to receive permission from their parents before formally signing with the Mississippi College Rifles. On April 18, 1861, White wrote to his parents, "our Captain an honorable gentleman and a true patriot requests us to inform our parents of our noble and spirited undertaking. Father and Mother brothers and all it is with tears in my eyes that I think of leaving you to go to the battlefield and I now ask your assents to the great and glorious cause which we have undertaken. Please write immediately I shall not leave before I get an answer and if I don't go with this Company I am going to come home." White also requested that his brother George join him as an enlisted member of the college rifles. However, George White joined Company I of the 3rd Louisiana Cavalry (Lloyd 2018).

Born January 5, 1843, Silas White was the son of Andrew Jackson White and Tullia Talbert White of East Feliciana Parish, Louisiana (MacKillican 2002). White's grandfather, John T. White, had migrated from Timmonsville,

"Silas Talbert White," c. 1861. Image courtesy of the Center for Southeast Louisiana Studies and Archives, Sims Memorial Library, Southeastern Louisiana University, Hammond, Louisiana.

South Carolina, to Louisiana in 1806. John White established a seed company and gristmill that was later recognized as part of Louisiana's "Egypt" plantation (Lloyd 2018). It was amidst this family of yeoman farmers that Silas White was born and raised. Farming, faith, and the Baptist denomination were integral to the White family. Silas White's grandmother, Lydia, was baptized at the Ebenezer Baptist Church of East Feliciana Parish in November of 1813. That same month she left Ebenezer Baptist Church and joined the Hephzibah Baptist Church congregation, which her husband helped organize. A first cousin to Silas White, Jared White later became a Baptist preacher. The family's strong connection to the Baptist denomination perhaps explains why they sent Silas to the Baptist-affiliated Mississippi College despite the close proximity of the Methodist-affiliated Centenary College of Louisiana. It is possible that members of the White family learned of Mississippi College via the various traveling Baptist preachers and denominational agents who canvassed both Mississippi and Louisiana in search of students to enroll (Mississippi Baptist State Convention Minutes 1860; Morgan 2008). White was unlike most of the students at Mississippi College in that he had traveled more than 130 miles to get there. Most of the students traveled less than 50 miles and many of them were either citizens of Clinton or natives of surrounding Hinds County (Mississippi College Catalog 1860–1861).

After leaving Mississippi College with his fellow cadets, White requested a formal release from the college rifles. White wrote to Mississippi governor John J. Pettus for permission to transfer to a military division representing his home state of Louisiana (Fox-Clark 1990). His request was granted, and White joined Company K of the 4th Louisiana Regimental Infantry on July 9, 1861 (Wynne 2006). The following day White wrote a letter to his father and explained that he and his fellow soldiers were being sent to Camp Neafus near Biloxi, Mississippi (July 10, 1861). White was stationed at Camp Neafus for one week before being transferred to Ship Island, a Mississippi barrier island in the Gulf of Mexico, to aid in the construction of brick fortifications. In a July 28, 1861 letter from White to his family, the former Mississippi College Rifle member proffered his account of life on the island: "I will try to give you a description of Ship Island or 'Second Hell' as some of the boys call it. It is about 25 miles long and one wide. The eastern end is finely timbered and a little elevated but the western part for the space of five miles is a barren tract with a few patches of salt water grass. There is the place the camp and post is situated. One of the hottest places I ever saw." The complaints about camp life on Ship Island and its untenable position were ubiquitous among Confederate soldiers stationed there. The island, and its incomplete brick fortification, Fort Twiggs, named for Confederate general David E. Twiggs, were so irksome to soldiers that Confederate forces could not properly garrison it. As a result, Southern soldiers withdrew within two months. Not long after Silas' stint on Ship Island, Union forces arrived by means of the steamer USS *Massachusetts*. The island was secured by Union troops, and the fort was renamed Fort Massachusetts, eventually becoming the site of a war prisoner camp (Winters 1991; Wynne 2006; Arnold-Scriber and Scriber 2008).

Those Confederate soldiers who withdrew from Ship Island in 1861 hastened to the lower Atchafalaya River and Bayou Teche in Louisiana to impede

Federal penetration via those viaducts. While on the Atchafalaya River, on July 28, 1861, White wrote about his surroundings:

> We have been divided into four different parts and stationed at different points on the Atchafalaya. . . . [We are] stationed at a very beautiful place surrounded by sugar plantations and mills which adds a great deal to the appearance of the scenery. The people are generally very hospitable to us. They have sent us at different times all kinds of vegetables, potatoes, and one or two [barrels] of molasses since we have been here. We are stationed in a dark part of the state and therefore hardly ever get any papers which has almost rendered us perfectly ignorant of what is going on among the Federals as well as among the Confederates but there is one thing I can assure you of and that is we will never get in a fight as long as we stay in this part of the country. By right, I think we ought to be sent where we could do some good for we are about the best drilled Regiment in the Confederate Service everything well organized but we will have to let things go as they are now and when this campaign is over all those that wish to get a rattle can go VA direct and jack some company that is in active service. (White 1861)

Almost five months later, White was still stationed in Louisiana. Christmas Eve of 1861 found White returning to Camp Lovell in Berwick, Louisiana for a twenty-four day work detail. On December 24, 1861, White wrote to his family: "I have for the last 24 days been working off from camp on detached service helping to blockade the channel that leads from the mouth of the Atchafalaya river through bay into the Gulf [of Mexico] and I think we will be ten days longer. I would not care if we were sixty days longer for I enjoy myself fine. We stay on the boats which carries the blockading timbers down for us. We have comfortable quarters to stay in. Father, I am sorry to tell you I cannot come home during Christmas holidays."

Although the enlisted men were relatively comfortable in their winter accommodations, White's next letter depicts a young man ready to come home or, at the very least, return to Mississippi College, which, by this point, was still open with only a handful of students too young to enlist. White, on the other hand, was confronted with the prospect of reenlistment and prolonged military service—most of which, up until this point, had been spent laboring rather than fighting. White wrote to his father on January

17, 1862 and explained that "I have tried to comply with your requests until I see it is no use to try. . . . I have come to the conclusion to stay until my time is out it being only a little more than three months [April]. . . . Great deal is being said now in camp about re-enlisting at the expiration of our time and taking sixty days furlough, but I don't think I shall reenlist without the time getting mighty hard." White's overall desperation to enter the fight while cooling his heels in the remote swamps of Louisiana seemed to be taking its toll. It is clear that he felt himself removed from action and perhaps even his fellow Mississippi College Rifle fellows. Other members of the college rifles had seen action in the First battle of Bull Run while others had served under the command of such Confederate generals Robert E. Lee and Thomas Jonathan "Stonewall" Jackson (Howell 2014; "Mississippi 18th Regiment" 1861). Regardless of his college peers' involvement in the fray, the zeal for war and heroic thoughts of dying for the Confederacy and secessionist cause, had faded. Sadly, Silas White, like other members of the Mississippi College Rifles, never returned to either his family or the Clinton-based college.

DEATH ON THE BATTLEFIELD AND POSTBELLUM MISSISSIPPI COLLEGE

Following Confederate defeats at the Battle of Fort Henry on February 6, 1862, and the fall of Fort Donelson on February 16, Union forces intended to make use of river passage to further invade the Confederate South. Confederate troops moved to defend the Southern interior and relocated Silas White and other Confederate troops to New Orleans. From there, they would be deployed to stave off further Union invasion. White wrote again to his family on February 22, 1862: "We have been here [New Orleans] two days and how much longer we are to stay I can't tell but it is rumored that the right wing of our Reg. will be here today and that we will leave on Monday, Feb 20th. I will write as soon as I get to my destination which is either Nashville or Columbus where we are to have a bully fight."

White was indeed sent North, but instead of Nashville, he found himself in Corinth, Mississippi, after a brief stay in Jackson, Tennessee. In March of 1862, White wrote a detailed letter to his father in East Feliciana Parish:

> Dear Father, I seat myself this evening to pencil you a few lines to let you know I am still in the land of the living and soldiering in due style. When I wrote you last, I was in Jackson, Tenn but necessity has caused us to be removed. We were first ordered to Bettell on the Mobile and Ohio R.R. to meet the yankees but their movements proved to be a faint one in order to draw our troops to that place. . . . General Beauregard . . . immediately sent us to this place where we expect to have a bully fight in a few days. One that will settle the fate of Tenn . . . and one in which the Yankees will be (according to my notion) cut entirely to pieces. We are fortifying ourselves at this point and have an army of 70 or 80 thousand. Our pickets can plainly hear the drum of the Yankees who are about fifteen miles from this point. It is said the Yankees have their baggage marked "Corinth or Hell" and according to my opinion they will see the latter place long before they will Corinth. I am proud to hear that East Feliciana has nobly responded to the call . . . and sent another company of veterans whom I have hope for their motto, "Liberty or Death." We have met with several defeats lately, it is true, but that ought not to keep any back. Our people are fit to come out and all put their shoulders to the wheel which would make it turn much more easier and slide us on faster to the day when our independence is to be declared . . . [This] would raise us higher in the estimation of other nations who would look upon us any longer as a rebel party but would . . . finally acknowledge our independence. . . . Father I have been through within the last few days and weeks what I never thought of before. I have had to sleep out two nights lately without any tents in the rain, and cold rain too but I am willing to sleep in the rain and even do worse so it is to the advancement of our cause, the holy cause of Liberty. But we are comfortably camped at this time about one-mile East of Corinth on the Charleston and Memphis R.R. . . . I am well and hearty, in fine spirits and as fat as ever. I weigh 155 (nineteen more) [pounds]. Give my best respects to all enquiring friends. . . . Nothing more but my love to all. (White 1862)

This letter, penned just weeks before the Battle of Shiloh in southwestern Tennessee, was the last correspondence White sent to his family. White's Confederate patriotism, his zeal for the battlefield, and his connections to the Mississippi College Rifles were blown away by a cannonball in early April of 1862. Almost one year prior to his death, White wrote the following to his father: "to die for one's country is sweet" (April 18, 1861). Those words, for White, were prophetic. For this college student-turned-solider, Civil War-era college life and military involvement ended in death at Shiloh. Like so many students formerly enrolled in Southern institutions of higher education, White never saw his college campus again.

While this Mississippi College student represented his institution as a Confederate soldier, the college itself suffered financial burdens due to lost enrollments, as well as general wartime hardships, such as loss of instructors and temporary military occupation. Still, the college remained open with President Urner at the helm. When the war came to a close in 1865, Urner requested back pay from Mississippi College's governing board. During the war, the president's salary was reduced by 25 percent to further support the weakened academy. In total, the governing board owed Urner $6,681.55. The administrative board, however, was unable to pay the sum. As a result, Urner sued the college trustees and settled for the sum of $6,000. He then left Mississippi and returned to South Carolina (Martin 2007). Sans Urner and with several unpaid debts (not to mention the former president's legal suit earnings), Mississippi College was in financial straits. Most of the college's prewar endowment had existed almost entirely on paper, thus was gone by the close of the Civil War. Mrs. Adelia Hillman made a fundraising trip to New England and raised enough money to provide Mississippi College a $7,000 loan in the name of her husband Walter Hillman, president of nearby Central Female Institute. The agreement stipulated that in exchange for paying Mississippi College's postwar debt, the college would become the property of Hillman if the trustees failed to repay him by 1869. The college almost became the property of Hillman had it not been for a young Mississippi College mathematics instructor, M. T. Martin, who raised the necessary funds to repay Hillman (Martin 2007).

Though the debt to Hillman had been paid, Mississippi College was left without a president. Although President Urner had kept the college open during the war, the institution needed a new leader to guide campus rebuilding, lead enrollment efforts, and enhance the college's curricular structure. Hillman, the successful president of Central Female Institute who was regionally lauded for keeping the women's academy open throughout the war was asked to replace Urner (Standifer 1988; Balmer 2004). In the fall of 1867, and under the direction of Hillman as president, the college enrolled two students in the freshman class. These new pupils joined nine preparatory students who were already enrolled. As time passed, enrollment grew and Hillman's reputation as Mississippi College's lead administrator further enhanced the academy. Thereafter, positive reports of Mississippi College began to circulate in regional newspapers and enrollment jumped to 153 in 1870 and climbed to 190 by the end of Hillman's tenure. Under the new presidential administration of Warren Sheldon Web (1873–1891), support from Mississippi's Baptists intensified as the college maintained strong ties with the denomination throughout the latter half of the nineteenth century ("The State Fair" 1870; "The Schools at Clinton" 1875; McLemore 1979; "Presidents" 2020a).

By the end of Southern Reconstruction, state newspapers announced that, at Mississippi College, "young men may acquire as complete and thorough an education here as at any College in the South" ("Mississippi College, Clinton, Hinds County, Mississippi" 1875, 1). Not only had enrollment grown, the college had several stable academic departments that mirrored popular, antebellum liberal arts academies: Greek, Latin, Mathematics, Natural Sciences, English, Literature, French, German, Mental and Moral Sciences, and a well-stocked preparatory department. At the same time, the college's curricular structure had been modified to include practical, job-specific courses such as commercial science and commercial law ("Mississippi College, Clinton, Hinds County, Mississippi" 1875). As the college progressed into the twentieth-century, enrollment rose to four hundred, and the institution's endowment had not only recovered from its post-Civil War state but climbed to over $500,000, thanks in part to regional Baptists as well as Mississippi College alumni ("Early 20th Century" 2020b). Mississippi College remains in existence as the longest-lasting college in the state of Mississippi, the second oldest Baptist institution of higher education in the nation, and one of the few Southern colleges and universities to remain open throughout the Civil War.

REFERENCES

Arnold-Scriber, Theresa and Terry G. Scriber. 2008. *Rosters and History of the Civil War Prison Ship Island, Mississippi*. Jefferson, NC: McFarland & Company, Inc.

Balmer, Randall H. 2004. *The Encyclopedia of Evangelism*. 2nd ed. Waco, TX: Baylor University Press.

Blaine, William T. 1976. *Education in the Old Southwest: A History of Jefferson College Washington, Mississippi*. Natchez, MS: Judson Printing Company.

Busbee, Westley F. Jr. 2015. *Mississippi: A History*. 2nd ed. Hoboken, NJ: Wiley-Blackwell.

Chisholm, Chad. 2007. *Clinton: Images of American*. Charleston, SC: Arcadia Publishing.

Cormier, Steven A. 2000. "Compendium of C. S. Armies: Louisiana 73–75." Last modified June 28, 2020. http://www.acadiansingray.com/.

Davis, William C. 2020. *Battle at Bull Run*. Garden City, NY: Doubleday and Company, 1977.

Finley, Lori. 1995. *Tracing the Natchez Trace*. Durham, NC: John F Blair Publishers.

Fox-Clark, Carrie A. 1990. "The Mississippi College Rifles: From War to Recovery." BA Honors Paper, Mississippi College.

Gragg, Ronald W. 1989. *The Illustrated Confederate Reader.* New York: Harper & Row.

Howell, Walter. 2014. *Town and Gown: The Saga of Clinton and Mississippi College.* Clinton, MS: Walter Howell Books.

Leavell, Zachery Taylor and Thomas Jefferson Bailey. 1904. *A Complete History of Mississippi Baptists from the Earliest Times*, vol. 2. Jackson: Mississippi Baptist Publishing Co.

Lloyd, Bettiann W. 2018. "Descendants of John White." Accessed December 5, 2018. http://www.genealogy.com/ftm/1/1/0/Bettiann-W-Lloyd/GENE5-0002.html.

MacKillican, Stuart. 2002. "My Southern Family: Solomon and Batson Morgan." Last modified May 26, 2002. http://freepages.rootsweb.com/~mySouthernfamily/genealogy/myff/sources/sou0021.html.

Martin, Charles E. 2007. *Mississippi College with Pride: A History of Mississippi College, 1826–2004.* Clinton, MS: Mississippi College.

Mayes, Edward. 1899. *History of Education in Mississippi.* Washington: Government Printing Office.

McLemore, Richard Aubrey. 1979. *The History of Mississippi College.* Jackson, MS: Hederman Bros.

Miller, Mary Carol. 1996. *Lost Mansions of Mississippi.* Jackson: University Press of Mississippi.

Mississippi Baptist State Convention Minutes. 1860. Mississippi Baptist Historical Archives, Mississippi College.

"Mississippi College." *The Daily Picayune.* August 6, 1859, 2.

"Mississippi College." *Copiah County News.* August 21, 1861.

Mississippi College Catalog. 1860–1861. Mississippi Baptist Historical Archives, Mississippi College.

"Mississippi College, Clinton, Hinds County, Mississippi." *The Daily Clarion.* October 5, 1875.

Mississippi College. 2020b. "Early 20th Century." Mississippi College History. Last modified September 20, 2020. https://www.mc.edu/about/history/early-20th-century.

Mississippi College. 2020a. "Presidents." Mississippi College History. Last modified September 28, 2020. https://www.mc.edu/about/history/presidents.

"Mississippi 18th Regiment." 1861. *Memphis Daily Appeal.* August 7, 1861.

Monette, John Wesley. 1846. *History of the Discovery and Settlement of the Mississippi Valley by the Three Great European Powers, Spain, France, and Great Britain, and the Subsequent Occupation, Settlement, and Extension of Civil Government by the United States Until the Year 1846*, vol. 2. New York: Harper & Brothers Publishers.

Morgan, Lee. 2008. *Centenary College of Louisiana, 1825–2000: The Biography of An American Academy.* Shreveport: Centenary College of Louisiana Press.

Nolan, Charles. *The Catholic Church in Mississippi, 1865–1911.* Lafayette: University of Louisiana at Lafayette Press, 2002.

Parish, Robert P. "Report of Company History, written outside of Richmond, Virginia, March 3, 1865." Record Group 9, Container V9B. Mississippi Department of Archives and History.

"Prof. I. N. Urner." 1860. *Weekly Mississippian.* June 27, 1860.

Ralph, Theodore. 1964. *The Songs We Sang: A Treasury of American Popular Music.* New York: Dover Publications.

Rowe, A. V. 1881. *History of Mississippi College: An Address Delivered Before the Alumni Society at Clinton, Hinds County, June 28, 1881.* Jackson, MS: Charles Winkley.

"The Schools at Clinton." *Weekly Clarion.* July 7, 1875.

"Sketch of Gov. Walter Leake of Mississippi." 1904. *Virginia Magazine of History and Biography* 11 (4): 417–19.

Smith, Timothy B. 2010. *Mississippi in the Civil War: The Home Front*. Jackson: University Press of Mississippi.

Stahr, Beth A. 2017. "Treaties of Doak's Stand, Dancing Rabbit Creek and Pontotoc Creek." *Mississippi Encyclopedia*. Last modified April 19, 2018. http://mississippiencyclopedia.org/entries/doaks-stand-dancing-rabbit-creek-and-pontotoc-creek-treaties-of/.

Standifer, Leon C. 1992. *A Rifleman Remembers World War II*. Baton Rouge: Louisiana State University Press.

"The State Fair." 1870. *Daily Clarion*. October 28, 1870.

White, Silas Talbert. April 18, 1861. Letter to Parents. Silas T. White Papers. Leland Speed College, Mississippi College.

White, Silas Talbert. July 28, 1861. Letter to Parents.

White, Silas Talbert. December 24, 1861. Letter to Parents.

White, Silas Talbert. January 17, 1862. Letter to Parents.

White, Silas Talbert. February 22, 1862. Letter to Parents.

White, Silas Talbert. March 23, 1862. Letter to Parents.

Winschel, Terrence J. 1993. *Alice Shirley and the Story of Wexford Lodge*. Fort Washington, PA: Eastern National Park and Monument Association.

Winters, John D. 1991. *The Civil War in Louisiana*. Baton Rouge: Louisiana State University Press.

Wynne, Ben. 2006. *Mississippi's Civil War: A Narrative History*. Macon, GA: Mercer University Press.

CHAPTER FOUR

"Rise Southerners, Rise! 'Tis the Voice of War!"

Confederate Patriotism and the Society of Jesus at Spring Hill College

R. Eric Platt and Donavan L. Johnson

Spring Hill College, one of the first institutions of higher education in Alabama and the fifth oldest Catholic college in the United States, was founded in 1830 by Mobile's first bishop, Michael Portier. During the nineteenth century, the institution was well known throughout Alabama as well as Louisiana, Mexico, Cuba, and Central and South America due to its connection with the Catholic Church and, later, the Society of Jesus (Jesuits) (Clark 1889; Kenny 1931; Thomason 2001). To establish the college, Portier purchased three hundred acres from local landowner William Robertson. The campus, approximately six miles northwest of Mobile Bay and affixed atop a hill, "afforded panoramic views of the town [Mobile] and its harbor" (Padgett 2007, para. 2). Portier recruited priests from European seminaries to staff the burgeoning institution, specifically members of religious orders who had taken vows of poverty, chastity, and obedience. The bishop's advertisement was clear: "We offer you: no salary: no recompense: no holidays: no pension. But: much hard work: a poor dwelling: few consolations: many disappointments: frequent sickness: a violent or lonely death: an unknown grave" (Smith 1957, 5). Ultimately, two priests and four seminarians were employed to teach at and govern Spring Hill College alongside Portier, who taught Greek to lay students and theology to the newly arrived seminarians (Power 1958; Padgett 2007).

ANTEBELLUM SPRING HILL COLLEGE

When Spring Hill College first opened, 30 students enrolled. In the fall of 1832, this number rose to 60, and by the end of the second academic year enrollment swelled to 132. In 1836, "the college was incorporated by the Alabama legislature, and on Aug. 20, 1840, it received from [Pope] Gregory XVI, the title and privilege of a university [seminary], with the right to confer degrees in divinity and canon law" (Widman 1898, 269–70). The campus, set apart from the urban sprawl of nearby Mobile, was renowned for being free of disease—particularly yellow fever. Yellow fever was a common and deadly occurrence in highly populated cities in the American South. Mobile, like its sister Gulf South city, New Orleans, experienced this seasonal plague during the hot months of summer and early fall (Humphreys 1992). Consequently, local parents enrolled their sons at the rural campus to keep them away from the dreaded illness. Despite the college's popularity with regional residents, early institutional leadership was inconsistent. First led by the Fathers of Mercy, the college's early presidents included such names as Father Mathias Loras (later Bishop of Dubuque, Iowa) and Father John Stephen Bazin (later Bishop of Vincennes, Indiana). The quick transition in presidential management (the average presidential tenure at Spring Hill College prior to 1846 was two years) made one scholar critique the Vatican's role as a hindrance to the Catholic academy's development: "The Holy See was no help . . . the Pope increased the difficulty by apparently making a practice of taking the early presidents of Spring Hill to make them bishops" (Smith 1957, 6).

The college's third president, Father Pierre Mauvernay (a former military officer in Napoleon Bonaparte's armies), created curricular offerings that made the college more attractive to new students. In the latter half of the 1830s, Mauvernay initiated a student cadet corps (Platt, McGee, and King 2016). First armed with wooden rifles, then lances, and finally functioning firearms, the student organization progressed to become a noted fixture at both the college and in Mobile. The cadets marched in city parades, stood at attention for religious services, and trained daily on the college campus (Boyle 1993). Despite the successful implementation of military curricula, Mauvernay's administration was short lived: he passed away in 1839. Following Mauvernay's death, the Fathers of Mercy relinquished control in the early 1840s. In 1845, the Eudist Fathers took charge of the institution and, for a few months, the future Archbishop of New Orleans (1883–1887), Francis

Xavier Leray, taught at Spring Hill College (Baudier 1939). Eudist governance, however, lasted less than one year. With their exit, the college was suspended until another religious order assumed command. In 1846, the Society of Jesus was petitioned to take over the Catholic college and, the following year, Jesuit Father Francis de Sales Gautrelet arrived to oversee the academy (Platt 2014; Jeffrey 2020). Gautrelet reinstated courses and, thereafter, the institution was closely wedded to the Society of Jesus, the organization's pedagogical practices (as prescribed by the 1599 publication, *Ratio Atque Institutio Studiorum Societatis Iesu*— "Official Plan for Jesuit Education"), and its religious motto *Ad Majorem Dei Gloriam* —"For the Greater Glory of God" (Widman 1898). Regardless of the college's overt Catholic affiliation, it was well patronized by regional Protestant families due to the pedagogical renown of its Jesuit faculty (Stern 2012).

Unfortunately, the constant turnover in college leadership influenced the institution's reputation and enrollment had decreased as a result. Regardless of Gautrelet's efforts to recruit local Catholic, Protestant, and Jewish students, Spring Hill College began the 1848–1849 academic year with only seventeen boys and young men in attendance (Widman 1898). The subsequent antebellum years passed with few interruptions save annual occurrences of yellow and scarlet fever that affected the surrounding community but left the college untouched. With Gautrelet at the helm enrollment steadily increased (Sherry 1898). His disciplinary style (founded on compassion rather than fear) and promotion of scientific curricula in addition to the college's already robust liberal arts course of study (religion, Greek, Latin, English, etc.), enhanced the institution's reputation. As a result, enrollment increased to 250 with students ranging in age from 10 to 23. Soon thereafter, additional buildings were constructed to house classes and serve as dormitories (Boyle 2004). Prior to the start of the 1850s, the campus had expanded to include an infirmary, chapel, refectory, and a central building complex that contained general classrooms, science laboratories, a drawing classroom, college library, museum, and a domestic chapel. Faculty rooms were located in the main building, near the chapel, while students resided on the third floor. The campus grounds were divided into separate recreation spaces for junior preparatory students and senior "college level" students. Additionally, there was a freshwater spring that fed a nearby lake. Students not only bathed in the lake; they also swam in it during the warmer months to cool off (Portier 1861).

"Jesuit Father Francis Gautrelet," n.d. Image courtesy of the Jesuit Archives and Research Center, US Central and Southern Province, Society of Jesus, St. Louis, Missouri.

As the campus grew, curricular offerings improved. In 1843, the cadet corps was given over to the instruction of Capt. Robert Sands, a Spring Hill College graduate, military officer, and cotton farmer (Busey and Busey 2017). Jesuits were well known for their pedagogical practicality. When curricular expertise was needed for subjects unfamiliar to the order's fathers and brothers, knowledgeable lay faculty were employed (Platt 2014). Such was the case with the Spring Hill College cadets. To enhance this popular student group, instructional leadership was handed over to Sands and Lt. G. M. Parker. Sands divided the student corps into two companies—junior and college level. Sands drilled the senior division while Parker instructed the junior cadets (Kenny 1931, "Spring Hill Cadets, Spring Hill Junior Cadets" 1859). Both cadet groups practiced drilling on campus, which by then included a small cemetery where Jesuit priests and brothers who died while serving at the Mobile college were laid to rest (Semple 1925). The cemetery not only functioned as the final resting place for several Spring Hill College Jesuits, it also served as a site, at least on one occasion, for student frustrations. As enrollment grew, disciplinary issues became apparent. Though military training had dampened some attitudinal and behavioral problems, student fights were not unheard of, which forced college administrators to be creative in how they dealt with such issues. To make friends of two student adversaries, Father René Holaind took the two pupils to the Jesuit cemetery where he allowed them to whip each other with a "cat o' nine tails" made from corded rope. The whipping, it seems, caused little physical damage but resulted in laughter on the part of Holaind whose "cackling laugh, from his joy in each whack, soon became contagious, and finally the two deadly enemies marched arm-in-arm back into the classroom as sworn friends for life" (Semple 1925, n.p.).

Antebellum student life and curricular activities at Spring Hill College progressed in much the same way as other Southern academies. Classes included "classical and modern languages, mathematics, history, belles lettres, and the sciences" (Padgett 2007, para. 3). Before long, the college boasted a small brass band, which accompanied the Spring Hill College cadets during the 1850s. Prior to the Civil War, cadets and band members were often seen carrying blue and red cloth pennants in local parades and community events. Though the student military group championed national patriotism during the antebellum period, by 1860 zealous Southern patriotism had replaced American nationalism. Indeed, as historian Michael Kenney explains, "Southern Patriotism" had become "the dominant note" of the campus population (1931, 212). Similarly, campus student dress changed to reflect enhanced Southern nationalism. Originally, the students wore dark blue uniforms, with pantaloons the same dark blue for winter and white for the warmer spring months. As talk of disunion and war increased, however, many of the older students traded their blue garments for similar outfits dyed gray, the color of the burgeoning Confederate army. As the 1850s ended, Spring Hill College was a source of academic pride for south Alabama residents despite the growth and popularity of the University of Alabama in Tuscaloosa. Having secured the college's success, Gautrelet was called to serve the Society of Jesus in Europe. His replacement, Father Anthony Jourdant, was installed as president in 1859 (Boyle 2004, Curioz 1859–1962).

Jourdant was born in Lyons, France, in 1809. Before his priestly life he served as a French military officer and fought in the 1832 Siege of Antwerp following the Belgian Revolution. After his return to France, Jourdant exchanged his officer's livery for a priest's cassock and studied theology. He briefly served as president of the Lyceum of Lyons before entering the Society of Jesus in 1844. In 1847 Jourdant was sent to teach at Spring Hill College and was ordained a priest the following year. He was then appointed rector of St. Charles College, a Jesuit institution in Grand Coteau, Louisiana. In 1852 he acted as superior for members of the Society of Jesus who taught and preached in south Louisiana. However, after tending to yellow fever victims in Baton Rouge he contracted the disease. Jourdant survived and was sent to France to preside over the College of Mongré, but by the end of his first academic term he requested to return to the United States. Responding to his request, Jourdant's Jesuit superiors assigned him the presidency of Spring Hill College amidst a backdrop of heightened Southern nationalism and outcry for Civil War (Kenny 1931).

SOUTHERN PATRIOTISM ON CAMPUS

Following in Gautrelet's footsteps, Jourdant attempted to further modernize the college's curricular structure by splitting coursework into two separate areas of study: liberal and commercial. Until this point, curricula had overlapped to the point that students applying for a degree could only receive the bachelor of arts, regardless of their scholarly concentration (Kenny 1931). Despite his efforts, Jourdant's pedagogical plans were delayed due to Alabama's secession from the Union on January 11, 1861. When news of disunion reached Mobile, city residents and Spring Hill College students alike rejoiced (Boyle 2004; Curioz 1859–1862). Soon after, student numbers decreased due to military enlistment, and plans to operate dual curricular tracts were dismissed (Kenny 1931). To offset the loss of tuition due to decreased enrollment and the sudden increase in provisional costs resultant from the war itself, both tuition and fees for services rendered were increased. In the 1861 academic catalog, the $200 charge for tuition, boarding, washing, stationery, and medical fees was scratched out with quill and ink. On the same printed page, in clear handwriting, the explanation for increasing prices was stated as follows: "Owing to the high price of provisions, the costs of tuition have been raised" ("Terms" 1861, 28).

Regardless of rising costs, student support for the Confederacy increased. When news reached the college that Confederate forces had fired upon Union-occupied Fort Sumter, students celebrated. The cadet corps drilled and fired salutes to honor the occasion (Schmandt and Schulte 1982). Even though Jourdant's curricular plans were abandoned, he and his fellow Jesuits were in accord with their wards and supported the Confederacy. As the issue of slavery became intertwined with Southern arguments for "states' rights" and decreased federal oversight, many immigrant newcomers to the American South, including the Jesuits at Spring Hill College, rallied around the concept of a "Southern" government that would champion reduced legislative oversight and the maintenance of chattel servitude (Kenny 1931; Manning 2007). To immigrant Jesuits at the Catholic Mobile academy, disunion seemed a positive phenomenon, and they rewarded their wards for Confederate victories. For example, after Virginia seceded on May 17, 1861, students were given an extra thirty minutes of recreation to celebrate. Likewise, on July 23, Spring Hill College pupils enjoyed a full day of recreation for the Confederate victory at the First Battle of Bull Run two days prior ("Vice President's Diary" May 18, 1861 and July 23, 1861).

Students not only celebrated the Confederacy via recreation and camaraderie, they also commemorated the secessionist cause in spoken and written verse. Prior to the war, three literary societies were established at Spring Hill College: the Philomathic Society, the Eurodelphian Society, and the Calliope Society. These organizations encouraged students to compose speeches, poetry, and other forms of written narrative to enhance composition and speaking skills. "Every month members are chosen from each Society to speak before the Professors and Students assembled. Four times a year, at Public Exhibitions, they deliver speeches and other compositions" ("Literary Societies" 1860, 2). With the South embroiled in war, students spoke about the merits of secession and the Confederacy in general. Students not only presented their literary work to fellow classmates and instructors, they published selected pieces in a short-lived student-edited periodical, the *College Album*. This monthly campus publication, one of the first student-organized publications at Spring Hill College, was started by twelve students in 1861.

Governed by a member of the faculty, student editors and authors representing all previously mentioned literary societies invited their college peers to submit their work. Any student could submit manuscripts to be reviewed and, if deemed worthy, printed. This new publishing club was, however, not without its critics. Not long after its founding, the organization acquired the reputation of being a secret society due to the student editors' use of pseudonyms. These aliases included "Messers. Fashion, Parson, Plump, Bluster, Mute, Fidget, Busybody, Goblin, Homer, Juvenile, Grave, [and] Spoonbill" ("Preface" 1861). Secret societies, particularly those that did not profess allegiance to dogma reflected in the Catholic Catechism, had been banned by the Church since the mid-1700s. In 1738 Pope Clement XII condemned any organization, such as the Freemasons, which bound its members to organizational silence via oaths and pacts. Subsequent popes including Benedict XIV, Pius VII, and Leo XII heaped further infamy on such secret societies by denouncing them as deist organizations that did not necessarily align with the Church's conception of the Judeo-centric iteration of God. When fraternal organizations and other secret clubs began to appear on college campuses the Vatican took note. In 1829, Pope Pius VIII indicated that college organizations with secretive backgrounds were just as problematic as Freemasonry (Fanning 1912).

To "repeal the accusation of secret society," each student editor provided lighthearted descriptions of themselves in the *College Album* so that readers could "guess" who each might have been. "Mr. Fashion," for example, was described as "a young man of great parts . . . universally esteemed for his highly polished manners and is in fact the very prototype of good breeding, a regular carpet knight . . . He is the life of all of the company and one never regrets the time spent in his society." Mr. Bluster, on the other hand, was described as a great lover of debate, heated discussion, and never willing to acknowledge discursive defeat. Another member, Mr. Goblin, was chronicled as deeply learned, whimsical, and a lover of books, "yet stranger to say, where there is a question of ghosts, hobgoblins and night walkers, he becomes childish in his views. He is a firm believer in spiritual rapping's, and dreams and speaks of nothing but enchanted castles and the like" (Morgan 1861, 7).

While some students submitted essays on the joys of grammar, the creation of Adam as detailed in the biblical book of Genesis, and fictional narratives of hunters lost in dark woods, other students submitted poems and treaties on the Civil War itself, the need for Southern citizens to fight, and memorials to Confederate soldiers killed in battle. In 1861, Gibbs Morgan, a native of Baton Rouge, Louisiana, published several poems that recounted aspects of the war. One poem penned by Morgan honored the death of Louisiana Lt. Col. Charles Didier Dreux of the Louisiana Guard Battalion, one of the first Confederate field officers killed in the Civil War (Héman 2012). Shot in Warwick, Virginia, Dreux's final words were reported to be "Steady, boys! Steady!" His New Orleans funeral was attended by more than thirty thousand mourners (Ward 2004, 112). Lamenting the loss of his fellow Louisianan, Morgan wrote: "Weep Crescent city, weep for him / Who now is lost to you, / The young, the gallant, and the brave, / The noble Colonel Dreux. / Oh! Louisiana, thou hast lost / In him a valiant son / And one who had his life been spared / Had many a battle won" (Morgan 1861, 36).

Yet another student, L. Claiborn, in a poetic attempt to honor the newly minted Confederate flag, its symbolic creation, and the freedom it represented for all Southerners (sans any acknowledgment of the South's enslaved population), wrote the following:

When freedom from her lofty home,
Looked down on Lincoln's throng;
She plumed her wing to leave the dome
On which she sat so long

We Southerners called her to our aid,
And on our knees we swore,
As at her sacred shrine we prayed:
"We'll leave you never more."

She heard our oft repeated calls,
And came from Northern crag
Amidst the raving storm of balls,
To perch upon our flag.

That flag was once as purely white
As the untrodden snow,
Which on Mount Blanco's dizzy height
The skies forever strow.

But midst the roaring cannonade,
'Twas dipped in tyrant's gore;
And two such crimson bars were made
As ne'er were seen before.

We plucked the azure from the sky,
And gaily set it there:
And now whole to beautiful
The brilliant stars appear.

Oh! Children of the South behold
That banner with respect:
When to the breeze we it unfold
With all its glories decked.

'Twill be the emblem of the free
In every land and clime;
And it will wave on every sea
Throughout the length of time (Claiborn 1861, 40).

Mirroring Claiborn's Southern patriotic zeal, Morgan published another poem, this one concerning the First Battle of Bull Run. In his epic, Morgan depicted the fight as one of stark Confederate bravery in the midst of a cannonball-decimated landscape. Morgan described Southern military men battling with "lightning speed" and standing as firm as "adamantine rock" against the onslaught of Union soldiers. Representing the Southern cause as a holy struggle to triumph over Northern tyranny, Morgan wrote "In vain they [Union soldiers] come with thirsty blades, the Southern cause Jehovah aids" (Morgan 1861, 31).

Following the above quoted poem, Morgan also published a fictionalized tale of a skirmish between the noble, radiant, and graceful Confederate president, Jefferson Davis, and the knavish, ugly, Union president, Abraham Lincoln. In Morgan's tale, Lincoln and Davis draw blades and engage in a flashy duel where Lincoln is subdued and killed by Davis. The student story, written as a recollected dream, concluded thusly: "Down down they went in deadly strife when Davis drawing forth his knife, held high in air the thirsty blade and speaking thus to Abe he said: 'Now yield thee knave or by my head another word, and thou art dead.' Urged on by hatred or by hell the fallen tyrant, strange to tell, bade full defiance to the brave who unto him the death blow gave" (Morgan 1861, 35).

In 1862, Morgan left Spring Hill College to enlist as a private in the Confederate army. He fought at the Battle of Baton Rouge (August 5, 1862) and was later assigned to Fenner's Battery of the Louisiana Artillery. Morgan survived the war, studied and practiced law in New Orleans, managed a sugarcane plantation in St. Charles Parish, and was twice president of the Audubon Park Commission—an organization founded in 1886 to promote the development of the titular New Orleans-based botanic garden. Morgan passed away in 1925 ("H. Gibbs Morgan Succumbs at 82" 1925). Just before he left Spring Hill College to enlist, Morgan penned a farewell verse to his fellow students, closing with: "And now to you, good old Springhill [*sic*], we bid a last adieu, it may be long, if ere again, your classic halls we view" (Morgan 1861, 45).

In the same spirit as Morgan and Claiborn, another Spring Hill College student, A. Baillio, called on all loyal Southerners to fight for the Confederacy in a poem titled "An Appeal to Southern Patriots."

Hark ye braves! Hear ye not the booming gun
That breaks like thunderbolt upon the deep,
That echoes from the heights of Charleston,
That wakes you from your silent midnight sleep?

Rise Southerners, rise! 'tis the voice of war!
Your rights demand your presence in the field.
God sides with you. Look to the Southern star
And mount your steeds: haste there your arms to wield.

Will ye, the palm of cherished liberty
Our common boast, a high-souled nation's pride,
Yield to oppression and vile tyranny?
No! scorn your foe, and fight like friends allied.

Haste! Break the clanking chains they've forged for you,
Go tell your foe how foolish his attempt.
Stand Spartan like; and though ye be but few,
He'll know the freeman breathe for death contempt.

The roaring cannons nor the whizzing balls
Shall ne'er our Southern hearts with fear inspire;
They may sweep our ranks, they may beat our walls,
But liberty revives her sacred fire.

And now, go, stranger, go! All nations tell
How Southern foes a foreign foe despise,
How Southern braves their country's fears dispel,
How Southern men smile when death dims their eyes. (Morgan 1861, 21–22)

Not only was the Confederate spirit alive and well at Spring Hill College, nearby Mobile was replete with Confederate activity as male residents eagerly enlisted for active duty. Similarly, Spring Hill College students were eager to join the fray. Though many students were too young to enlist, those who were of age found that their parents refused to give their blessing. Parents believed that their sons were safer remaining at college than serving the South as a soldier. Even so, some students fled and enlisted without familial or clerical approval. Runaways were a recurring concern for the college's administration throughout the war and did nothing to relieve ongoing enrollment woes (Biever n.d.). Indeed, as one Louisiana-based reporter extoled in the *Carrolton Sun*, Spring Hill College's administration could do little to keep some students on campus: "Some thirty of the students of Spring Hill College have left with a view of joining the volunteer services of the States to which they belong. The fraternal discipline and well-ordered regulations of this college are unable to restrain the headlong fighting pluck of the Young American" ("Enlistment of College Boys" 1861, 1).

RAVAGES OF WAR

As the war progressed, enrollment decreased to one hundred students and Jourdant was required to vacate the college presidency in 1862. Superiors in the Society of Jesus transferred him to New Orleans to oversee the well-attended Jesuit College and Church of the Immaculate Conception in the bustling commercial district of the Crescent City (Leveque 1900). Though no specific reason was uncovered to justify this transfer, members of the religious order may have felt that Spring Hill College needed an administrator better able to recruit and retain students during this trying period of US history. Though New Orleans fell to Union troops in April of 1862, it appears that Jourdant arrived in the port city mere months before its capture. That same year, Father Gautrelet returned to serve as Spring Hill College's president. As Gautrelet had ably developed and bolstered Spring Hill College previously, it was assumed that he would successfully guide the institution through the remainder of the war (Boyle 2004).

Following Gautrelet's return to south Alabama, he addressed the college's most pressing concern: student runaways. Retaining students was essential if the institution was to remain open. Gautrelet sent Jesuit priests, brothers, and college students to search for wayward pupils, despite inconsistent success. If runaways returned, they were verbally chastised, forced to apologize on bended knee, and given religious counsel. Student "rescuers," on the other hand, were rewarded with picnics. In addition to runaways, the college's administration was forced to face both detrimental parental reactions and penitential religious observations in response to Confederate losses. On February 23, 1862, six students were withdrawn following reports of military raids near the campus. These student departures caused other pupils to long for the comfort and safety of home. On February 28, a day of fasting was imposed in observance of Southern military defeats at the Battles of Forts Donelson and Henry. Less than two months later, on April 11, students attended a solemn Mass for Southern soldiers who died at the Battle of Shiloh ("Vice President's Diary" February 23, 1862; February 28, 1862; and April 11, 1862).

While student numbers decreased, fears of losing able faculty, in addition to college wards, became all too real. In 1863, the college and surrounding communities were placed under draft orders. All able-bodied men were to enlist in the 89th Alabama Infantry. On January 1, it was recorded in the vice president's diary that the Jesuit fathers and brothers experienced a "testy" day when a military recruiting officer arrived to conscript the academy's Jesuit brothers. Gautrelet stood firm and denied the officer his recruits. Twenty days later, the officer returned and insisted that the brothers enlist ("Vice President's Diary" January 1, 1863 and January 21, 1863). Though clerics and students were exempt from conscription, Jesuit brothers did not meet the qualifications of pupil or priest. Despite being members of the Society of Jesus, brothers were not ordained and were, therefore, eligible for conscription. As several Spring Hill College Jesuits had left the classroom to serve as Confederate chaplains, all remaining personnel were needed. Efforts to conscript Jesuit brothers were soon put to rest when Gautrelet secured a forty-five day exemption from Gen. Simon Bolivar Buckner and the Confederate assistant secretary of war, John Archibald Campbell. Thereafter, Gautrelet traveled to meet with Confederate president Jefferson Davis and requested the cessation of military conscription at the college ("Annals of Spring Hill College" 1914).

As previously mentioned, various Jesuit priests served as spiritual directors in the Confederate armies throughout the American South. Father Louis-Hippolyte Gache served as a chaplain in both Florida and Virginia. Father Darius Hubert also served in Virginia. Father Francis Nachon served at fortifications below New Orleans, while Father Anselm Usannaz served souls in a Georgia military prison. Father Anthony de Chaignon functioned as chaplain to the 18th Louisiana Regiment. Fathers Francis Lespes and David McKiniry visited military men throughout Alabama. As for the Spring Hill College Jesuits, Father Gautrelet was sent as an army chaplain throughout the South prior to returning to Spring Hill College. Father Andrew Cornette, Spring Hill College's chemist, left to provide spiritual aid to military men in Georgia. Father Isadore Turgis, a diocesan priest, and Jesuit Father Andrew Cornette were remembered for rowing a boat across Mobile Bay to provide religious services to Confederate soldiers at Spanish Fort prior to Federal troops laying siege to and burning the site (Neyray and Clancy 2015; Buckley 1981; Schmandt and Schulte 1962; Widman 1898). Similarly, several lay faculty left to fight. For example, both instructors of Spring Hill College's cadets resigned in order to fight. Sands went on to command the Mobile Guards of the 3rd Alabama Infantry, while Parker served as provost marshal in Mobile (Beck 2000; Radley 1989). In 1863, Sands was promoted to lieutenant colonel (Beck 2000). He was shot in the knee at the Battle of Gettysburg on July 3, 1863, and left military service in 1864 (Busey and Busey 2017). Regardless of these faculty losses, student numbers remained steady at one hundred (Smith 1957).

Despite diminished enrollments, Gautrelet and his fellow Jesuits managed to keep numbers relativity steady, and academic courses continued. Unfortunately, Spring Hill College's food and clothing supplies were running low due to the Federal occupation of New Orleans and the establishment of Confederate harbor blockades in Mobile Bay. These events also encumbered student transportation. At the start of the war, Spring Hill College priests traveled to New Orleans by railroad and, on occasion, by steamship to retrieve enrollees destined to study at the Mobile academy ("Spring Hill College" 1861). Cut off from additional students and supplies, the Jesuits and their wards had no choice but to "fast for the cause of the Confederacy" (Kenny 1931, 213). In time, the religious faculty noted that students' clothing had become tattered and worn. Shoes, hats, and clothes were ragged and in desperate need of replacement or repair (Kenny 1931). Likewise, food rations ran low.

To bolster reduced supplies, the faculty relied on available resources near campus. For example, wild grapes (otherwise known as scuppernongs) were gathered and used to make sacramental wine for religious services. The Jesuit brothers, now safe from conscription, crystallized salt via evaporation techniques on Mon Louis Island in Mobile Bay. The brothers grew vegetables, raised livestock, and donated additional food and salt supplies to Mobile residents and hospitals in the wake of crippling citywide ration reductions ("Vice President's Diary" September 1, 1864; Kenny 1931). Like food, medical supplies were scarce. There was a shortage of the ipeca plant (*Carapichea ipecacuanha*), which was used to make the purgative syrup, ipecac. Like other mid-nineteenth-century pharmaceuticals, the herbal syrup was a mainstay in army medical tents along with other such drugs as calomel, lead acetate, and chloroform (Gilchrist 1998). Though not all of these medicines were useful—in fact some were quite dangerous—Civil War doctors treated wounded soldiers with the "ignorance of the day, with little more than . . . painkiller and purgative" (Winchester 2005, 66). Dr. F. J. B. Rohmer, a Mobile physician, Confederate surgeon, and Spring Hill College's campus doctor, identified a regional alternative, *Richardia scabra* (also known as rough Mexican clover) that could be used in lieu of ipeca. As a result, the chemical laboratories at the Jesuit college temporarily manufactured an ipecac substitute for Confederate military doctors serving in Alabama (Vasey, Collier, and Le Duc 1879).

In the face of food shortages and military defeats, Jesuits and students alike continued to support the Confederacy. They regularly attended Mass and said prayers for the Southern cause. In accordance with the Confederate Congress's wishes that Southern citizens prayerfully remember Confederate troops on Thanksgiving, students, faculty, and priests attended Mass celebrations dedicated to the Southern military cause followed by parade drill performed by the college's cadet corps. The priest's homily referenced the book of Exodus and the throng of pharaoh's soldiers sent to recapture the Israelites. The priest compared Federal armies marching on the South to this biblical tale and stated, "The Northern hordes abandoning their ice-clad hills and frozen ponds, [march] to spread ruin and devastation among the peaceful and industrious inhabitants of the sunny South" (Meridienalis 1861, 37).

The cleric also compared the Union to Goliath and the Confederacy to the underestimated, yet ultimately victorious, David. Just as God had guided David's deadly slingshot, He would guide the South to victory. Following the homily, a "Te Deum" was sung for the repose of Confederate soldiers slain in battle (Meridienalis 1861). As more news of Southern losses arrived, priests and students prayed for supernatural intervention to restore depleted armies (Kenny 1931). With the 1863 passage of the Emancipation Proclamation and the Union victory at Gettysburg, anxieties increased. Food supplies were further depleted, and, on March 10, it was reported that college livestock were no longer secure. According to the Spring Hill College vice president's diary, "A pig was taken and upon this news, the brothers will remain on the farm for watch of all properties" ("Vice President's Diary" March 10, 1863). Indeed, the college's administration feared "that robbers [were] all around." After two calves were stolen, the Jesuits moved all livestock from surrounding fields onto the college campus. Jesuit brothers took nightly shifts to guard the remaining livestock in case raiding soldiers tried to pilfer a pig or cow (Kenny 1931).

In the shadow of livestock theft and food shortages, students once more left the campus in hopes of enlisting or reaching their families. On March 16, "Two boys [ran] away," but returned that afternoon and were "punished for many days." Shortly thereafter, three additional students left. It was later reported that they had safely arrived at their family homes. While some students returned to campus or were reunited with their parents and siblings, others successfully enlisted. Those students who left to join the Southern armies sometimes returned as "sworn in" soldiers to visit their former classmates. These visits were short lived, however, as students-turned-soldiers were ultimately called away to battle. It was clear that not all students found war appealing. In May 1863, a few former Spring Hill College students-turned-soldiers returned to the academy as refugees. In less than a month, the number of refugees rose to fourteen. Father Gautrelet welcomed these expatriates, but when a recruiting officer visited the campus in search of deserters, the refugees were reenlisted ("Vice President's Diary" March 16, 1863; June 16, 1863; February 21, 1864; February 24, 1864).

HUMBLING OF CONFEDERATE PRIDE

On August 5, 1864, the Spring Hill College community burst into a frenzy of apprehension when it was announced that Federal steamships were approaching nearby Mobile Bay forts, Gaines and Morgan. Led by Rear Adm. David Glasgow Farragut, the Union fleet advanced into the bay inlet. However, when the ironclad USS *Tecumseh* was sunk by an underwater mine (then referred to as a "torpedo"), ship captains looked to Farragut for alternative orders. Undaunted, Farragut allegedly shouted "Damn the torpedoes, full speed ahead!" (Duffy 2006) Other sources indicate that Farragut ordered the ships under his command to disregard the *Tecumseh's* fate and speedily advance using the following naval directive: "Damn the torpedoes, four bells!" (Symonds 2009; Lewis 1943) Naval cannon shot was so loud that Spring Hill College students easily heard it on campus. Pupils counted the number of cannons fired per minute and reported that, in one particular minute, they counted no less than one hundred shots (Semple 1925).

The Battle of Mobile Bay resulted in victory for the Union. Mobile was the Confederacy's fourth largest city and was a considerable supplier of Southern warships. Indeed, Alabama's port city produced numerous naval vessels including the gunboat CSS *Selma* and the *H. L. Hunley* submarine. The Federal fleet's maritime success resulted in the bay's closure to all hostile vessels and the cessation of Confederate shipbuilding in south Alabama (Pickett 1900; Duffy 2006; Chaffin 2008). Soon after, older Spring Hill College students left en masse, and enrollment dropped to fifty. Students, stirred by the naval siege, left for Mobile to help bolster remaining Confederate troops ("Vice President's Diary" September 1, 1864, and September 12, 1864). Other students, particularly those from Caribbean countries or South America, left the United States altogether. In 1864, Spring Hill College students and brothers Ernesto and Nemesio Guilló returned to Havana, Cuba. While in Mobile, both developed a love for that most-American sport: baseball. After returning to their home country, they started a Cuban team, later known as the Havana Baseball Club. This organization flourished and eventually became the Cuban National Baseball Team (Thorn 2016). Despite decreased enrollment following the Mobile Bay skirmish, more students soon arrived, as local families feared that, due to the Confederate naval defeat, their sons would be conscripted unless enrolled in a college or university (Biever n.d.).

Regardless of their parents' efforts, a handful of students managed to escape campus and enlist. Father Gautrelet imposed harsher student-leave restrictions, and, in response, one student wrote to Confederate general Dabney Herndon Maury claiming that forty students wished to join the armies of the South but were prevented from doing so by the college's administration. The letter was published in the *Advertiser* per Gen. Maury's request. After reading the publication, Gautrelet spoke out against the student's claims. The next day, students were called to the president's office and asked if they wanted to enlist and if they had given authorization for their names to be published alongside the letter. All replied in the negative and a report was sent to the newspaper's editor. Three days later, the letter's author was uncovered and expelled but was reinstated after Gen. Maury requested that he be forgiven and readmitted ("Vice President's Diary" March 31, 1865; April 1, 1865; April 4, 1865; and April 5, 1865). Despite this altercation, student numbers steadily increased as parents believed the college safe from Union capture and Confederate draft. Likewise, several high-ranking Confederate generals such as P. G. T. Beauregard, Robert Bullocks, Dabney Maury, Nelson Miles, and Richard Taylor enrolled their sons at Spring Hill College. Even Rear Adm. Raphael Semmes deposited his sons at the Jesuit college. Regional families also implored the Jesuit faculty to safeguard personal valuables (jewelry, cutlery, dishes, etc.) in case Federal troops raided their homes ("Names and Residences of Scholars" 1865; Kenny 1931; Smith 1957; Ward 2011). With the fall of Mobile, citizens and students alike dealt with the repercussions of Union occupation. Three days after Confederate general Robert E. Lee surrender at Appomattox Courthouse, Spring Hill College's faculty and students were inundated with Federal soldiers.

On April 12, 1865, two thousand Union soldiers marched to the campus and camped on the surrounding lawns. Spring Hill College students were both frustrated by their presence and humiliated, as Union military musicians would "play Northern airs beneath the windows of the dormitories." (Biever n.d., 169). Southern students were proud of their regional heritage, but they demurred as the Jesuit faculty warned all pupils "not to show exteriorly any opposition to the Federal government" (Schmandt and Schulte 1982, 5). Similarly, when newspapers reported Lincoln's assassination, Father Gautrelet ordered students not to celebrate despite the fact that they had often been heard chanting phrases like "Jeff Davis. He's a gentleman. Abe Lincoln, he's a fool. Jeff Davis rides a big white horse; Abe Lincoln rides a mule" and "Here's to the health of old Abe, for I wish he was in the grave." Students were also fond of saying "We'll hang Abe Lincoln on a sour apple tree" (Boyle 2004, 29). Regardless of students' Confederate patriotism, the college's cadet corps, by order of the Jesuit administration, fired a salute for the Union president's peaceful repose. The Jesuit administration, by this point, had been made aware of the recent burning of the University of Alabama by Federal forces. Consequently, they did not want ill-placed pro-Confederacy sentiment to result in the sacking of their south Alabama academy (Schmandt and Schulte 1982).

By the war's end, Southern patriotism had waned as students had grown tired of cheering for a dying military cause. Though the war terminated in April of 1865, blue-garbed military men remained at the college until May 25, when they were recalled to Mobile due to the explosion of a large powder magazine. The blast destroyed a third of the city, killing 1,200 ("Vice President's Diary" May 21, 1865, and May 25, 1865). As the city recovered from the devastating detonation (the exact cause was never discovered) Father Gautrelet left Mobile to serve the Society of Jesus in New Orleans (Kenny 1946; Leveque 1900). He was replaced by Father Aloysius Curioz as Spring Hill College's president. At the same time, several students left to visit family members they had not seen in years. As a result, enrollment once again decreased, but not for long, as Jesuit fathers and brothers recruited additional students from Central America, Latin America, and Cuba (Smith 1957).

Despite nearby battles, conscription attempts, and the presence of Union troops, Jesuit father Conrad M. Widman wrote, "all through the war, the college was protected with equal kindness and efficacy by the federal and confederate authorities. After the war, it gradually resumed its former prosperity . . . [despite] the financial decline of the country [the South]" (1898, 273). Though the college emerged from the conflict with an 1865 enrollment of three hundred, it faced financial hardships related to political and physical reconstruction (Platt 2014). In addition, Spring Hill College students had to contend with a new standard of living as family fortunes had been destroyed, slavery had been abolished, and Reconstruction-era politics brought the first waves of postwar civil rights legislation into the Deep South. Not only had Confederate pride diminished, student hopes for inherited wealth had been dashed. As Father Widman explained, "It took the 'late unpleasantness' to humble our young generation and force them to work, if they wished to live" (1898, 272). As a result, postbellum students were encouraged to academically excel beyond their parents, who had accrued their fortunes by means of slave labor. Per their Jesuit instructors, Reconstruction-era students would have to rely on their mental faculties and the sweat of their brows to prosper in the New South.

Even though the war had ended, vestiges of Southern patriotism remained. Like other Southern Catholic institutions, Spring Hill College, its priests, lay faculty, and students often participated in activities that venerated the Lost Cause (Pasquire 2003; Woods 2011). For example, the college brass band was known to play "Dixie," the Confederate anthem, whenever Southern officials like Alabama senator John Tyler Morgan visited the campus. In 1903, Morgan and three officers: Maj. Hannon, Col. Rapier, and Capt. Quill toured the campus with members of the brass band playing in the background ("Annals of Spring Hill College" 1914). Similarly, in 1919, "A touching incident recalling other war memories was the visit of the Raphael Semmes Chapter of the United Confederate Veterans. An honor guard of Spring Hill Cadets met the grizzled warriors of the [eighteen] sixties at the front entrance [of the college] and escorted them to the Senior campus; and Capt. Daly, having recalled the College of Admiral Semmes and of his descendants for three generations, pinned the commemorative medallion on young Raphael Semmes, great-grandson of the Admiral and then a student at Spring Hill" (Kenny 1931, 351).

Though the college suffered from the Civil War, the institution remained open and continued to provide intellectual training (Moore 1927). After a postwar fire devastated the campus in 1869, Father Gautrelet (now serving as president of the Jesuit-administered College of the Immaculate Conception in New Orleans) returned to Mobile for a brief period to assist Spring Hill College's new president, Father John Montillot (installed as president in 1868), in rebuilding and improving the institution (Boyle 1993; Leveque 1900). After the campus chapel was rebuilt, the Jesuits remarked on its physical superiority to the old one. Because of his assistance, Gautrelet was counted as a loyal "Springhillian" until his death in 1894 (Semple 1925). His body was interred in the campus cemetery alongside several of his Jesuit peers (Clancey 1998). Though several Spring Hill College students gave their lives to the failed Confederacy, those who lived and graduated from the Jesuit college returned to their homes to help rebuild south Alabama as community leaders, lawyers, priests, educators, etc. Today, Spring Hill College is one of twenty-seven US Jesuit colleges and universities, and was, at one time, part of a larger network of Southern Jesuit colleges and universities. Presently, only two colleges associated with the Society of Jesus remain in the American South: Loyola University New Orleans (founded 1912) and Spring Hill College.

REFERENCES

"Annals of Spring Hill College: Mobile, Alabama, 1839–1914." 1914. Spring Hill College, Burke Library, Spring Hill College Archives and Special Collections.

Baillio, A. 1861. "An Appeal to Southern Patriots." *The College Album*. Mobile, AL: Printed at the Office of the Mobile Daily Register and Advertiser. Spring Hill College, Burke Library, Spring Hill College Archives and Special Collections.

Baudier, Roger. 1939. *The Catholic Church in Louisiana*. New Orleans: A. W. Hyatt Stationary Mfg. Co. Ltd.

Beck, Brandon H. Editor. 2000. *Third Alabama! The Civil War Memoir of Brigadier General Cullen Andrews Battle, CSA*. Tuscaloosa: University of Alabama Press.

Biever, Albert Hubert. "Diary and Notes on Spring Hill College, Mobile, 1878–1885." New Orleans Province Archives. Jesuit Archives & Research Center, St. Louis.

Boyle, C. J. 1993. *Twice Remembered: Moments in the History of Spring Hill College*. Mobile, AL: Friends of the Spring Hill College Library.

Boyle, C. J. 2004. *Gleanings from the Spring Hill College Archives*. Mobile, AL: Friends of Spring Hill College Library.

Buckley, Cornelius M. 1981. *A Frenchman, A Chaplain, A Rebel: The War Letters of Pere Louis-Hippolyte Gache, S. J.* Chicago, IL: Loyola University Press.

Busey John W. and Travis W. Busey. 2017. *Confederate Casualties at Gettysburg: A Comprehensive Record*. Jefferson, NC: McFarland & Company, Inc.

Chaffin, Tom. 2008. *The H. L. Hunley: The Secret Hope of the Confederacy*. New York: Hill and Wang.

Claiborne, L. 1861. "The Confederate Flag." *The College Album*. Mobile, AL: Printed at the Office of the Mobile Daily Register and Advertiser. Spring Hill College, Burke Library, Spring Hill College Archives and Special Collections.

Clancey, Thomas. 1998. *Our Friends*. 3rd ed. New Orleans: Jesuit Provincial Residence.

Clark, Willis G. 1889. *History of Education in Alabama*. Washington: Government Printing Office.

Curioz, Louis. "Superior's correspondence, New Orleans Mission, 1859–1862." New Orleans Province Archives. Jesuit Archives & Research Center, St. Louis.

Duffy, James P. 2006. *Lincoln's Admiral: The Civil War Campaigns of David Farragut*. Edison, NJ: Castle Books.

"Enlistment of College Boys." 1861. *Carrolton Sun*. January 26, 1861.

Fanning, William. 1912. "Secret Societies." *The Catholic Encyclopedia*, vol. 14. New York: Robert Appleton Company.

Gilchrist, Michael R. 1998. "Disease and Infection in the American Civil War." *The American Biology Teacher* 60, no. 4 (April): 258–62.

"H. Gibbs Morgan Succumbs at 82." 1925. *Times Picayune*. July 4, 1925.

Hémard, Ned. 2012. "Two Fallen Soldiers." In *New Orleans Nostalgia: Remembering New Orleans History, Culture and Traditions*, edited by Ned Hémard. New Orleans: Ned Hémard. Last modified March 26, 2018. http://www.neworleansbar.org/uploads/files/TwoFallenSoldiers.6-6.pdf.

Humphreys, Margaret. 1992. *Yellow Fever and the South*. New Brunswick, NJ: Rutgers University Press.

Jeffrey, Katherine Bentley. *First Chaplain of the Confederacy: Father Darius Hubert, S.J.* Baton Rouge: Louisiana State University Press, 2020.

Kenny, Michael. 1946. *Jesuits in Our Southland, 1566–1946: Origins and Growth of New Orleans Province*. Kenny Papers. New Orleans Province Archives. Jesuit Archives & Research Center, St. Louis.

Kenny, Michael. 1931. *The Torch on the Hill: Centenary Story of Spring Hill College, 1830–1930*. New York, NY: The American Press.

Leveque, J. M. 1900. "The Churches." In *Standard History of New Orleans, Louisiana: Giving a Description of the Natural History in Regard to Flora and Birds, Settlement, Indians, Creoles,*

Municipal and Military History, Mercantile and Commercial Interests, Banking, Transportation, Struggles Against High Water, the Press, Educational, Literature and Art, the Churches, Old Burying Grounds, Bench and Bar, Medical, Public and Charitable Institutions, the Carnival, Amusements, Clubs, Societies, Associations, Etc., edited by Henry Righter, 480–511. Chicago, IL: The Lewis Publishing Company.

Lewis, Charles Lee. 1943. *David Glasgow Farragut: Our First Admiral.* Annapolis: US Naval Institute.

"Literary Societies." 1860. *Catalog of the Officers and Students of Spring Hill College (St. Joseph's) Near Mobile, Alabama, for the Academic Year 1859–60.* Mobile, AL: Printed at the Offices of the Mobile Daily Register. Spring Hill College, Burke Library, Spring Hill College Archives and Special Collections.

Manning, Chandra. 2007. *What This Cruel War Was Over: Soldiers, Slavery, and the Civil War.* New York: Random House, Inc.

Meridienalis. 1861. "Thanksgiving at College." *The College Album.* Mobile, AL: Printed at the Office of the Mobile Daily Register and Advertiser. Spring Hill College, Burke Library, Spring Hill College Archives and Special Collections.

Moore, Albert Burton. 1927. *History of Alabama and Her People.* Chicago: American Historical Society.

Morgan, Gibbs. 1861. "A Combat Between Jeff Davis and Abe Lincoln—A Dream." *The College Album.* Mobile, AL: Printed at the Office of the Mobile Daily Register and Advertiser. Spring Hill College, Burke Library, Spring Hill College Archives and Special Collections.

Morgan, Gibbs. 1861. "The Battle of Manassas." *The College Album.* Mobile, AL: Printed at the Office of the Mobile Daily Register and Advertiser. Spring Hill College, Burke Library, Spring Hill College Archives and Special Collections.

Morgan, Gibbs. 1861. "The Editors of the Album." *The College Album.* Mobile, AL: Printed at the Office of the Mobile Daily Register and Advertiser. Spring Hill College, Burke Library, Spring Hill College Archives and Special Collections.

Morgan, Gibbs. 1861. "Our Farewell." *The College Album.* Mobile, AL: Printed at the Office of the Mobile Daily Register and Advertiser. Spring Hill College, Burke Library, Spring Hill College Archives and Special Collections.

Morgan, Gibbs. 1861. "To the Memory of Col. Charles Dreux." *The College Album.* Mobile, AL: Printed at the Office of the Mobile Daily Register and Advertiser. Spring Hill College, Burke Library, Spring Hill College Archives and Special Collections.

"Names and Residences of Scholars." 1865. *Catalog of the Officers and Students of Spring Hill College (St. Joseph's) Near Mobile, Alabama, for the Academic Year 1865–1866.* Mobile, AL: Printed at the Office of the Daily Register and Advertiser. Spring Hill College, Burke Library, Spring Hill College Archives and Special Collections.

Nayrey, Jerome and Thomas Clancey. 2015. *Southern Jesuit Biographies: Pastors and Preachers, Builders and Teachers of the New Orleans Province.* Lafayette, LA: Acadian House Publishing.

Padgett, Charles Stephen. 2007. "Spring Hill College." *Encyclopedia of Alabama.* Last modified October 26, 2020. http://www.encyclopediaofalabama.org/article/h-1029.

Pasquire, Michael. 2003 "Catholic Southerners, Catholic Soldiers: White Creoles, the Civil War, and the Lost Cause in New Orleans." Master's thesis. Florida State University.

Pickett, Albert James. 1900. *History of Alabama and Incidentally of Georgia and Mississippi from the Earliest Period: Annals of Alabama, 1819–1900.* Birmingham: The Webb Book Company, Publishers.

Platt, R. Eric. 2014. *Sacrifice and Survival: Identity, Mission, and Jesuit Higher Education in the American South*. Tuscaloosa: University of Alabama Press.

Platt, R. Eric, Melandie McGee, and Amanda King. 2016. "Marching in Step: Patriotism and the Southern Catholic Cadet Movement." *The Catholic Historical Review* 102, no. 3 (Summer): 517–44.

Portier, Michael. 1861 reprint. "Foundation of Spring Hill College." *The College Album*, 7–9. Burke Library, Spring Hill College Archives and Special Collections.

Power, Edward John. 1958. *A History of Catholic Higher Education in the United States*. Milwaukee: The Bruce Publishing Company.

"Preface." 1861. *The College Album*. Mobile, AL: Printed at the Office of the Mobile Daily Register and Advertiser. Spring Hill College, Burke Library, Spring Hill College Archives and Special Collections.

Radley, Kenneth. 1989. *Rebel Watchdog: The Confederate States Army Provost Guard*. Baton Rouge: Louisiana State University Press.

Schmandt, Raymond H. and Josephine H. Schulte. 1962. "Civil War Chaplains—A Document from A Jesuit Community." *Records of the American Catholic Historical Society of Philadelphia* 73, no. 1/2 (March–June): 58–64.

Schmandt, Raymond H. and Josephine H. Schulte, eds. 1982. *A Civil War Diary: The Diary of Spring Hill College between the Years 1860–1856*. Mobile, AL. Spring Hill College, Burke Library, Spring Hill College Archives and Special Collections.

Semple, Henry C. 1925. "Spring Hill Sixty Years." *The Springhillian* 1, no. 4 (March). Spring Hill College, Burke Library, Spring Hill College Archives and Special Collections.

Sherry, John. 1898. "Our Southern Houses during the Yellow Fever." *Woodstock Letters* 27 (1): 61–62.

"Spring Hill Cadets, Spring Hill Junior Cadets." 1860. *Catalog of the Officers and Students of Spring Hill College, (St. Joseph's) Near Mobile, Alabama, for the Academic Year 1859–60*. Mobile, AL: Printed at the Offices of the Mobile Daily Register and Advertiser. Spring Hill College, Burke Library, Spring Hill College Archives and Special Collections.

Smith, Andrew C. 1957. *The Phoenix and the Turtle: Some Highlights on the History of Spring Hill College*. Mobile, AL: Spring Hill College Press.

"Spring Hill College." 1861. *Daily Picayune*. October 3, 1861.

Stern, Henry Andrew. 2012. *Southern Crucifix, Southern Cross: Catholic-Protestant Relations in the Old South*. Tuscaloosa: University of Alabama Press.

Symonds, Craig L. 2009. *The Civil War at Sea*. Santa Barbra, CA: Preger.

"Terms." Catalog of the Officers and Students of Spring Hill College (St. Joseph's), Near Mobile, Alabama, for the Academic Year 1860–61. Mobile, AL: Printed at the Offices of the Mobile Daily Register and Advertiser, 1861. Spring Hill College, Burke Library, Spring Hill College Archives and Special Collections.

Thomason, Michael. 2001. *Mobile: The New History of Alabama's First City*. Tuscaloosa: University of Alabama Press.

Thorn, John. 2016. "Cuba, U.S., and Baseball: A Long if Interrupted Romance." *Our Game: MLBlogs*. Last modified March 21, 2016. https://ourgame.mlblogs.com/cuba-the-u-s-and-baseball-a-long-if-interrupted-romance-7a20d217e90d.

Vasey, George, Peter Collier, and William G. Le Duc. 1879. "Report of the Botanist and Chemist on Grasses and Forage Plants." In *Annual Report of the Commissioner of Agriculture for the Year 1878*, edited by George C. Gorham, 157–94. Washington, DC: Government Printing Office.

"Vice President's Diary, 1859–1887." Spring Hill College, Burke Library, Spring Hill College Archives and Special Collections.

Ward, Laura. 2004. *Famous Last Words: The Ultimate Collection of Finales and Farewells*. London: PRC Publishing Limited.

Ward, Thomas J. Jr. 2011. "Spring Hill College." In *The New Encyclopedia of Southern Culture, Volume 17: Education*, edited by Clarence L. Mohr. 306–7. Chapel Hill: University of North Carolina Press.

Widman, Conrad M. 1898. "Spring Hill College." *Woodstock Letters* 27 (3): 268–76.

Winchester, Simon. 2005. *The Professor and the Madman: A Tale of Murder, Insanity, and the Making of the Oxford English Dictionary*. New York: Harper Perennial.

Woods, James M. 2011. *A History of the Catholic Church in the American South, 1513–1900*. Gainesville: University Press of Florida.

CHAPTER FIVE

Tuskegee Female College and the Confederacy

"Yankees! Yankees! Yankees! Every Way You Turn"

Courtney L. Robinson and Zachary A. Turner

The antebellum city of Tuskegee, a hotbed rife with anti-Union sentiment forty miles east of Montgomery, Alabama, was the original location of Tuskegee Female College—the institution that would later become Huntingdon College (renamed in 1935). The desire for a local women's college was championed by the wife of a probate judge (Farnham 1995), which was further supported by Methodist Reverend Clayton Crawford Gillespie. In addition, $26,000 was allocated to support the college's construction by the Alabama Methodist Episcopal Conference (Lazenby 1960). Officially chartered on February 2, 1854, the college opened to much fanfare, as reporters for the *Alabama Weekly Journal* called it "the grand emporium of female education in Alabama," despite the previously established, Baptist-affiliated East Alabama Female College, which was also located in Tuskegee (Lazenby 1960, 1049). The academy opened in a single four-story building that newspapers called "the finest college building in the state." In addition, the college's chapel was reported to be the largest concert hall in Alabama at the time ("Tuskegee Female College Later Becomes Huntingdon" 1965, n.p.).

PREWAR DAYS

The college's cornerstone was laid on April 9, 1855, accompanied by a dedication speech from Henry Washington Hilliard, who would later go on to

"Tuskegee Female College, Ala.," n.d. Image courtesy of the Library of Congress Prints and Photographs Division, LC-DIG-pga-01123, Washington, DC.

become a Confederate army general. A year later, on February 11, 1856, the college's doors officially opened under the leadership of Methodist minister Andrew A. Lipscomb, who previously served as Chancellor of the University of Georgia and taught at Vanderbilt University in Tennessee. A prolific writer, Lipscomb composed thirty-nine articles for *Harper's Bazaar* during his Tuskegee presidency, several of which focused on issues pertaining to young women as college students and graduates (Ellison 1954). Carrie Hunter, a Tuskegee Female College student and a student in Lipscomb's philosophy courses, spoke highly of him in her diary, writing "How often have I strove against my habitual reluctance to rising early in the morning &, fault remaining, I came down too late for breakfast thereby encountering Dr. Lipscomb's inquiries as to the state of my health (which was never better) & of course I had to put down my late-rising to the score of laziness. What a blessing it is to have such a good & learned man as he is constantly with you in the freedom of daily intercourse, to lead family prayer, instruct in his conversations, & by his affability winning the regard of everyone" (Hunter 1857, n.p.).

Despite Lipscomb's position as the leader of a women's college, he maintained a traditional view of women at the time. Indeed, he wrote of his belief that appropriate responsibilities for women included "disciplining the home, dressing well, speaking 'low and not much,' caring for the poor and sick near her home and lecturing drunkards, attending preparatory school committees and clothing clubs, 'organizing ragged schools,' reading books and discussing them with her husband, doing copy work for her husband and perhaps—if he were a minister—correcting his sermon" (Lipscomb 1854). Hunter's diary also included several detailed depictions of social activities at prewar Tuskegee Female College, including sporting tournaments, horse shows known as "Fantastics," and a New Year's Eve party complete with cake and eggnog provided by the faculty (Hunter 1857, n.p.). Outside of the college, the community offered many attractions as well. A September 10, 1857, edition of the *Tuskegee Republican* reported the town had a population of around three thousand with two female colleges, one male high school, and two mixed schools. The town boasted two hotels six dry goods stores, three drugs stores, three furniture stores, three printing offices, fifteen physicians, seventeen lawyers, and one steam mill (Editor Republican 1857).

Upon becoming Tuskegee Female College's first president, it was Lipscomb's duty to oversee the hiring of faculty members. Among them was George Price, a science instructor who would himself later ascend to the college's presidency, and his brother W. H. C. Price, a science professor who would later be appointed by Confederate president Jefferson Davis to lead the Nitre and Mining Bureau of the Confederate government (Lazenby 1960). While faculty were hired and taught classes, students progressed in their studies. The college's first graduating class consisted of four students (Alabama Conference Female College 1908). Despite the small size of the first graduating cohort, prewar college enrollment boomed, and the college graduated 16 students two years later. One of those graduates was Mary Bettie Lathrop. According to records later donated to Huntingdon College by her family, Lathrop was monumental in fundraising efforts to establish a United Daughters of the Confederacy monument on Alabama's capitol grounds (Vickers 1962). In 1859, Tuskegee enrolled 216 students and had a graduating class of 29 (Alabama Conference Female College 1908). One of the graduates was Sarah Fitzpatrick Baldwin Bethea, who reportedly attended the Confederate presidential inauguration of Jefferson Davis as well as his inaugural ball. Several years later, Bethea's family informed the college's administration that she remained committed to the prewar Southern mindset, as a member of the Daughters of the American Revolution and president of a chapter of the United Daughters of the Confederacy (Huntingdon College n.d.).

PREWAR CAMPUS ENVIRONMENT

By 1861, the Civil War had begun, and there were many skirmishes fought close to the Tuskegee Female College campus. The war years brought various challenges to the academy, but the institution continued to offer coursework throughout the duration of the fighting. Despite the fanfare over booming prewar enrollment, the college community experienced heightened awareness of the churning political climate, especially after Alabama's secession in 1861. Not long after the Montgomery-based inauguration of Jefferson Davis, Tuskegee Female College students found themselves within earshot of rocket blasts and cannon fire. Soon, the entirely female student body found their traditional daily life subsumed by war, which forced changes to their collegiate routines. In fact, student Carrie Hunter designed and made a flag for the regional cavalry while other students sewed clothing for Confederate soldiers. Though the college's enrollment waned during the war, it did not completely evaporate. Despite limited access to concrete student statistics during the Civil War, records indicate that although the institution never closed, Tuskegee Female College experienced a few years with a handful of graduates (Alabama Conference Female College 1908). Even while serving the Confederate army, instructors still educated students in English poetry, Latin, Greek, philosophy, and oil painting, seemingly unaware—or in direct rebellion—to the raging war just beyond their doorstep. To fully comprehend the challenges faced by the Tuskegee Female College campus during the war years, it is imperative to analyze the college's formal opening, in 1856, just five years prior to the war.

When the college first opened, the institution focused on the education of Southern women in many areas, specifically subjects focused on knowledge deemed societally acceptable across the American South, like music and embroidery. The vast wealth from a thriving cotton industry created many wealthy Southern men who desired sophisticated, well-bred women as wives and equally affluent families who sought formal education for their daughters. As president, Lipscomb insisted that higher education for women include courses in the arts and sciences to foster intellectual prowess in addition to the development of domestic skills. In 1859, following the abolitionist John Brown's attempted raid on Harper's Ferry, George Price ascended to the presidency of Tuskegee Female College amidst significant political discontent that was enveloping the surrounding city. Price, only twenty-six years old at the time, had already proven his success as an educator. He was a skilled musician and spoke five languages fluently, including Greek and Latin. A July 14, 1859, issue of the *Tuskegee Republican* summarized Price's qualifications for the position of college president: "He brings to his new position that ripe scholarship, great energy and long experience which, with the deep affection entertained for him by the pupils of the school, give an earnest of his full success, and of the maintenance of the high position which the College occupies" (Ellison 1954, 39). At the beginning of his tenure at Tuskegee Female College, Price, with the assistance of a $5,000 gift from the estate of a young Methodist woman, Sarah Altona Thompson, enhanced the academy's curriculum by adding a resident graduate course focused on philosophical readings, criticism, and reflection, for women who had already completed their coursework at another institution. It is likely that the "Thompson Fund," as the estate was named, would have resolved any financial challenges the college was facing, had the Civil War not begun (Massey 1916, 281).

Price's decision to add a resident graduate course was generally well-received, and a similar course was added at Alabama Central Female College in Tuscaloosa the following year. In 1860, Tuskegee Female College celebrated a momentous occasion with the enrollment of more than two hundred students. That same year, ten graduated. The graduating class presented gifts to Price, including a silver tea service. The commencement ceremony spanned four days, and included sermons, art exhibits, and musical concerts, in addition to the graduation exercises (1857, n.p.). Antebellum student life at Tuskegee Female College was busy but also pleasant. In a letter to her brother, Hunter (1857, n.p.) acknowledged she found little time to write, as "I am taking drawing, embroidery, music, [and] all of the rest of the time is occupied teaching," adding "[s]ituated as I am, it is a delightful employment [and] I am more in love with it than ever." In her letter, Hunter noted the institution was prospering, stating that the college's enrollment "exceeds the number by 25 or 30 with which [former Tuskegee Female College president] Lipscomb would be satisfied." Hunter also referred to Price as a "fine president," noting "everything goes on as easily as if Lipscomb were here" (Hunter 1857, n.p.). At that time, standard tuition at the Alabama-based academy was $50 for a nine-month scholastic year, with additional charges of $50 for music instruction, $30 for French instruction, $50 for oil painting, and $30 for embroidery. Boarding costs were set at $12.50 per month, which covered fireplace fuel, lighting, and washing services (Hunter 1857).

Compared to the challenges they would soon face, Tuskegee Female College students focused on far more trivial concerns prior to the war, including their dissatisfaction with campus food, as referenced by a diary entry by student Margaret Ann Ulmer, class of 1859. In her diary, Ulmer and her roommate admitted to purchasing a dozen eggs to avoid eating college-provided meals. However, this hoarding of food sometimes led to rat infestations within dormitories. To consume sufficient meals without procuring their own food, students often sought nourishment from local families. In her diary, Ulmer described an instance where she and four friends ate pork roast, rice, tomatoes, potatoes, biscuits, pickles, stewed apples, and hash made from pig's heads, along with boiled custard, almonds, raisins, and potato pie for dessert, courtesy of a local family. Ulmer complained that she suffered from a headache following this tremendous meal (Farham 1995).

The prewar merriment was short-lived, however. When students returned to Tuskegee Female College in September of 1860 they were met with defiant speeches and torch-lit processions, culminating with the election of Abraham Lincoln two months later. Political interest at Tuskegee reached new heights during an 1860 Southern Rights Leap Year party on New Year's Eve, when female partygoers donned homespun dresses alongside young men in coarse jerseys—apparel commonly worn by slaves. Commenting on the attire, a visitor remarked that he wanted to ask the student partygoers for passes, which were required of slaves when traveling away from plantations. A few days later, the city of Tuskegee's infantry was sent to south Alabama and were charged garrison forts that protected Mobile Bay. By February of 1861, Jefferson Davis was inaugurated as the first president of the Confederacy. That April, college students heard seven cannon shots, and witnessed locals setting light to roman candles and rocket flares, signifying the start of the war. Despite the onset of Civil War, nineteen students graduated from the college that spring (Ellison 1954).

THE EARLY DAYS OF WAR

In the initial days of the Civil War, Confederate military efforts were witnessed firsthand by Tuskegee Female College students, as members of the Macon Cavalry drilled in front of the campus. On campus, Hunter worked with her fellow wards to design a flag for the cavalrymen. She wrote that other students watched her work on the project daily, including her hand-embroidering the flag's stars (Hunter 1857). This gesture was noted in the proceedings of the Confederate congress during the twenty-fifth day of its session. William Parish Chilton, a senator from Macon County, remarked on Hunter and her peers' support of the Confederacy:

> They are but school girls, sir, yet they have early imbibed the spirit which animated the matrons of the Revolution. These models have been produced by them in the prosecution of their studies in the art department of the Tuskegee Female College, and I submit, sir, that several of them for originality of design and the artistic skill displayed in their execution reflect great credit upon the excellent institution in which they are members. . . . Our fair artists assure us that their efforts at originality were rendered difficult by constantly recurring visions of the "Stars and Stripes" which floated so proudly over the late United States. (Chilton 1861, n.p.)

The hand-sewn flag was presented to the cavalry group on March 20 in front of a group of students and local residents (Hunter 1857).

In subsequent months, students at Civil War-era Tuskegee Female College sewed uniforms for two Confederate military companies. Hunter was one of the students who sewed for the two companies. Pertaining to this experience, she wrote "[t]wo of my brothers have gone to fight the fanatical horde that would crush us. They have enlisted in a noble cause. God grant that they may be successful. Last Sunday was a strange sad day. Some went to church, and some went up to the Hall to finish the remaining suits that had to go off that night" (Hunter 1857, n.p.). The ties between the Southern war effort and the Alabama college ran deep, as one of the companies, referred to as the Macon Confederates, was commanded by Capt. Robert F. Ligon, a member of the Tuskegee Female College Board of Trustees and a state senator (Ellison 1954). After the war, Ligon successfully campaigned for the post of Alabama's lieutenant governor. His political platform, like other post-Civil War Southern politicians, bolstered regional white supremacy (Owen 1921).

As the women of Tuskegee Female College soon learned, war was an expensive endeavor. In June of 1861, they hosted a benefit concert that raised $216 for Confederate uniforms. In those early war days, Tuskegee Female College students not only crafted uniforms, they attended church with surrounding community members to pray for Confederate troops and fasted in religious support of the Southern secessionist cause (Ellison 1954). On June 13, Hunter declared "[this] has been one of the most solemn days I ever spent in my life," adding "[a]s we all know it was the day set apart for fasting and prayer by Pres. Davis. I never fasted before. We had Divine Services in the Methodist Church" (Hunter, 1861). As if in response to their prayers of support and protection, the college's students received gifts and affectionate notes from soldiers stationed in the Virginia. In response to such emotionally laced correspondence, students sought etiquette guidance from Madame Colvert's *Book of Politeness*—particularly as concerned communicating with servicemen. According to Colvert's text, "[i]f we are acquainted with military men, in addressing we only call them *General* or *Captain*, for it would be uncivil to give them titles of inferior grade; thus we shall not say Lieutenant" (Ellison 1954, 47). As the war continued, female students encountered more battle-associated challenges than situations that required proper etiquette. At the start of the Civil War, Tuskegee Female College students often romanticized the glory of battle. Many such students received small trinkets from their brothers and significant others on the warfront. As the war continued, however, enrollment and spirits dropped. In June of 1861, only five students graduated from the college. By 1862, war had become a mainstay of the Tuskegee student experience. Students noticed in particular when the Battle of Sharpsburg drew many young local soldiers to the battleground. Even past and current Tuskegee Female College professors joined the Southern military, including Thomas Goulding Pond, a former math professor who became an officer in the Confederate army (MacKethan 1998).

It was during this time that the college accepted war refugees (families and daughters) from across the state of Alabama. Among these refugees was a student who entered Tuskegee Female College in fall of 1862. She remained at the academy and graduated at the end of the war. This student, Maria Howard Weeden, became a well-known watercolor artist most noted for her paintings of former slaves. Weeden and her family, driven from their Huntsville home by Union soldiers, established residency at a Tuskegee plantation. As a war refugee she befriended Tuskegee Female College president Price, a friendship that continued after the war, when the Price family relocated to Huntsville after he assumed the presidency of the Huntsville Female Academy. Weeden, one of ten graduates in the class of 1865, returned to Huntsville with her family after the war (Ellison 1954). Finding her home looted and in need of significant financial assistance, Weeden sold her paintings, taught art classes, and wrote poetry and essays for print publications such as the *Christian Observer* newspaper, under the pseudonym "Flake White." In 1893, Weeden attended the World's Columbian Exposition in Chicago, Illinois where she was deeply affected by the caricatured portrayals of "freedpeople." Subsequently, she spent several years painting realistic images of the South's emancipated population. In time, her art and writings were put on display in Paris and Berlin, bringing her international notoriety for her Southern poetry and paintings (Timberlake 2013).

During 1862, while Weeden sought refuge from Union troops as a college student, Tuskegee Female College attendees experienced one of the most challenging periods of the war. In her diary, Hunter refers to a shortage of linen or cotton to make clothing. She also wrote about a lack of wheat to make biscuits and high-quality pens, paper, and lighting. In contrast to prior years with elongated, fanciful commencements, Hunter described the 1862 ceremony as "a quiet pleasant hour spent in hearing the essays read, a short baccalaureate address very appropriate, then we all came home" (Hunter 1857, n.p.). Due to a lack of college records from 1863, there is no evidence to indicate who served as president in Price's absence, and why no graduates were recorded for that year. It was previously hypothesized that the college temporarily closed in the spring of 1863 due to a combination of economic wartime and prewar debt incurred by the college's administration. Even so, evidence exists in the form of minutes from the 1863 Alabama Conference, which indicate that the state's educational institutions were reported as being "in a healthy and prosperous condition notwithstanding the war" (Ellison 1954, 52). Despite the indication from the Alabama Conference regarding the viability of the state's institutions during those tumultuous years, leaders at Tuskegee Female College did find themselves in financial straits. John Massey, who would become Tuskegee's president in 1896, stated "on account of the embarrassment caused by the war the Board sold the property to Reverend Jesse Wood, who had inherited some money with which it was hoped he could relieve the critical situation" (Massey 1916, 282). Thereafter, Wood served as the college's acting lead administrator.

WARTIME CHALLENGES ON CAMPUS

As expected, students faced abundant challenges on the Tuskegee Female College campus throughout the war. In addition to the lack of resources needed to produce goods, rampant financial inflation across the South caused tuition to jump from $200 in 1860 to $390 four years later. Increased tuition was not the only financial challenge. The demands of war increased the cost of calico fabric to $400 per yard, when it was available, which forced students to wear homespun dresses and hats made from palmetto fronds harvested from local swamps (Ellison 1954). Julia Spear, a former art and drawing teacher at Tuskegee Female College, wrote to Hunter in February 1863 of the deprivations that had become commonplace across Alabama:

> Your pine knot fires I should enjoy at night. One great privation of the war to us is the absence of good light. . . . We have bidden goodbye to buscuit [*sic*] until new wheat shall come, and Lizzy paid $15 for a pair of shoes the other day, the soles are a half inch thick and they (the shoes) are the admiration of everyone. The usual topic among ladies aside from the war is to catalogue their possessions. With what gusto people tell of their toilet soap, pins, shoes &c, [*sic*] where they have the good luck to possess such things. . . . When the blockade is over I will write on better paper with I hope a better pen. (Ellison 1954, 51)

In her letter, Spear also wrote in favor of young women's higher education, especially during war:

> The importance of female culture never impressed me so strongly as now. The standing in civilization which our new country takes during the next quarter of a century will depend on our young women. The general effect of war is demoralizing upon man, then the education of young men is to a great degree arrested. Even if we have peace soon the two years spent in service will have given them a distaste for school books and restraints. It would be like going back to a state of juvenility. To the cause of education that time is lost

> irretrievably. The more need then that ladies should be cultivated to supply this deficiency—but I need not write you a lecture. (Ellison 1954, 51)

In addition to maintaining classes, the college's administrators faced increased operational problems. Feeding students became difficult. Shortages made coffee and sugar exclusive and expensive commodities, which compelled college leaders to purchase less expensive food stocks such as peas, molasses, and sweet potatoes. A local soldier recommended that sweet potatoes be cut into small pieces and browned in an oven, then ground to a milled pulp. These sweet potato grounds were blended with coffee grounds to stretch the limited supply of the popular caffeinated beverage. During wartime winters, the price of fuel and timber escalated rapidly. Reportedly, wood sold at $40 per load in Montgomery during the winter of 1863–1864, while it was sold for $150 per load in nearby Augusta, Georgia (Ellison 1954).

In 1864, Tuskegee, both community and college, faced direct peril when a Union raid passed within five miles of the campus. Confederate infantry arrived to protect the college and forced the Federal cavalrymen to retreat. Ten Southern soldiers were killed in the skirmish, and several others were wounded. Without an area hospital to service the troops, the injured men were cared for in private residences. By the end of 1864, the regional death and injury toll nearly forced the college to close. That year the college only graduated two students. Though the war continued, and the recent graduating class was small, the Alabama institution hosted its June commencement as planned (Tuskegee College 1864). One of those two graduates was Elmyra Chisholm. Chisholm was, and remained, an active member of the Daughters of the American Revolution for the rest of her life (Vickers 1962).

Post-commencement, Reverend Jesse Wood made several financial changes to the academy. To attract additional students, Wood included the cost of fuel and laundry services in boarding charges and tuition was cut in half, payable with money or a provisional equivalent. Despite those discounts, students were required to provide their own bedding, quilts, and candles (Ellison 1954). Unfortunately, these financial adjustments to ensure institutional viability were unsustainable. Rhoda Coleman Ellison, author of *History of Huntingdon College 1854–1954*, wrote "[a]fter Mr. Wood had made such carefully calculated moves to appeal to war-impoverished Alabamians and continue to publicize them over his name through September, it is surprising to read exactly a month after the scheduled opening of the College that his place had been taken by another" (Ellison 1954, 56). In fact, later that year, after he sold the college to Collins D. Elliott, Wood returned to a religious position (West 1893). At the onset of the Civil War, Elliott administered the Nashville Female Academy and continued to do so even after the central Tennessee city fell to Union forces. While in Nashville, Elliott was incarcerated for ten months for persistently supporting the Confederacy. The *Montgomery Advertiser* called Elliott "the right sort of man to conduct a Southern College," even post-incarceration (Lazenby 1960, 1051).

By 1864, colleges and universities across the South had closed or were in the process of shutting down, yet Elliott and Price kept Tuskegee Female College open. During the war, the town of Tuskegee became a footpath for Union battalions, including one military unit led by James H. Wilson, a Union army major general known for destroying manufacturing facilities in Alabama and Georgia. During the war, Wilson and his troops traveled through Tuskegee and the surrounding area, and reportedly found the town awe-inspiring. Maj. Shipman, an architect, wrote of Tuskegee "it is one of the finest towns I have ever met with in the South. The most exquisite taste is manifested in the ornamentation of the ample grounds around each dwelling. There is the greatest variety of evergreens and the magnolia is in great abundance. The evergreen arches through the hedges were finer than I ever saw before. The architecture of the public and private residences was quite as good if not better than at Montgomery" (Jones 1976, 119). Even though Wilson's army spoke highly of the city and spared it from burning, Hunter recorded that the troops looted the town and stole jewels from some of her friends in what she called a display of "yankified yankeeism" (Ellison 1954, 59).

In the spring of 1865, Union general William Tecumseh Sherman spared the city of Tuskegee in his march south. Although the city and college remained undamaged by Sherman and his troops, Union general James H. Wilson quickly marched upon the city to cut off Confederate general Nathan Bedford Forrest in his defense of the city of Mobile. After Wilson's capture of the arsenal in Selma, Alabama, he and his infantry of thirteen thousand men sought to raid central Alabama in passing through Tuskegee on their way to Georgia (Ellison 1954). On April 14, one day before Wilson and his troops reached Tuskegee, Hunter wrote "A dread hour has arrived, the hour in which we are to meet that foe face to face. The murderers of our martyred brothers, 15,000 strong, are now camped either on the upper edge of Tuskegee or within a mile of town. They will sweep over our fair little town with a besom of destruction and lay low the stately public buildings that have so long been our pride and pleasure. What will become of us the Lord only knows. May he be our shield of protection in the coming storm for vain is the help of man" (Hunter 1857, n.p.).

Hunter's fears arose from the knowledge that Wilson's troops had burned the University of Alabama in Tuscaloosa on April 4 due to its operation as a military academy. Despite her concerns, the Union infantry spared Tuskegee Female College and departed the city three days later. Hunter wrote of her shock and excitement that Union officers burned no homes in the city, and that the college remained undamaged, writing "Well! the Yanks have come and gone and left us safe and sound with our house standing over our heads—a piece of clemency quite extraordinary" (1857, n.p.). Despite Hunter's excitement that the city and college remained unscathed, she was displeased with the residual presence of the Federal soldiers, writing "[t]he sights of blue coats daily, hourly, and minutely offends the eye, and the sounds of oaths hourly sicken the heart" (Lazenby 1960, 1051).

During Wilson's procession through town, Elliott and Price ordered an increase in campus security that continued even after the surrender of Confederate general Robert E. Lee and the assassination of Abraham Lincoln in 1865. Relatively cut off from outside communication, community speculation about the Confederate surrender worried Tuskegee Female College students. Hunter referred to speculations of Lee's defeat with sadness: "Rumors, for we are cut off from all communication . . . are dark, gloomy and foreboding. Advice of those who are prepared to be the judges is: Hope for the best but prepare your minds and hearts for the worst." Although classes continued, the Union victory march through the Tuskegee city streets disrupted classes and disturbed students. Hunter bemoaned the presence of the blue-coated soldiers who were a part of a Federal garrison stationed in Tuskegee. In response to their presence, she wrote "Yankees! Yankees! Yankees! Every way you turn. It is a sickening, humiliating subject" (Hunter 1857, n.p.).

Tuskegee hosted its annual commencement that spring with ten graduates, amidst Union troops and newly freed men, women, and children. The event was tame compared to similar prewar celebrations, especially as the destruction of the nearby railroad prevented several visitors from reaching the campus. Employment opportunities were sparse for the graduating class, as were prospects for marriage. A member of the 1865 graduating class stated "[f]or those young ladies who have lived single during the war the young men whose society was pleasant and suitable have been swept away. . . . The young men are going astray with dissipation and the evil consequences of army association" (Hunter 1865, n.p.). Later that year, despite their admitted disdain for the city's Federal occupation, townspeople and college students celebrated the Fourth of July with the Union troops as a show of goodwill. The students even conducted concerts for the community to raise funds for the benefit of war orphans and widows (Ellison 1954). Despite the contextual background of physical and political Reconstruction, Tuskegee Female College forged on. In 1866 two students graduated from the institution. Katherine Edmond, one of the two graduates, continued her academic career by enrolling in post-graduate coursework at Harvard College. She later became a teacher in Selma (Vickers 1962).

POSTWAR LIFE AT TUSKEGEE FEMALE COLLEGE

The American South faced various challenges during Reconstruction, and institutions of higher education were not exempt from these hardships. In the days and weeks after the war, Tuskegee Female College sought to start anew. The college, which had been spared burning and looting, existed in a city racked by postwar dilapidation and financial destitution. While many Confederate soldiers heralding from prominent regional families returned to Tuskegee, the destruction of war left some—often suffering from battle injuries—without homes or employment. With the war's end, president Elliott vacated his post, leaving the institution saddled with debt. Following Elliott's departure, the Board of Trustees promoted Price to the college presidency. To fund the ailing college, Price sold his home and relocated to the campus to assist in rejuvenating the college's boarding practices. In addition to attracting students whose families could afford tuition, Price was also tasked with hiring a bevy of new faculty. To Price's chagrin, it proved difficult to locate and employ qualified Southern educators as the new president wished to retain an air of Southern heritage at the college.

Despite challenges faced by the college's leadership, the women of Tuskegee Female College exhibited relatively standard academic and social behaviors compared to other women at Southern colleges and universities at that time, including their commitment to modern fashion. Indeed, there is evidence to suggest that the college wards attempted to remain in vogue despite limited resources to purchase and/or craft dresses in keeping with modern trends. In addition to postwar dress and related accoutrement, Tuskegee Female College students also sought local entertainment, social engagements, and parties—all in the attempt drown out the regional melancholy associated with Reconstruction. One such soiree, a masquerade ball, caused a Tuskegee newspaper reporter to respond negatively, as he believed such an event did little to bolster the moral perception of Tuskegee. The reporter angrily wrote: "[t]he prosperity of Tuskegee is dependent upon a high toned moral sentiment and action. If the Colleges and Schools flourish, the town prospers; if not it goes down. Now we ask, if a Masquerade Ball, which only appears on the surface of the cauldron of depravity in large cities, will be of any benefit to Tuskegee in public estimation?" (Ellison 1954, 69).

By 1870, the Tuskegee Female College tradition of vibrant commencement celebrations resumed. This grandiose, five-day affair may have helped hide the college's economic situation from the public. Even though the war was over and enrollment and tuition revenue had increased, the institution still had considerable financial debt. Indeed, financial troubles lasted well beyond the end of the Reconstruction period until the late 1870s, when creditors sued the institution for outstanding debts (Ellison 1954). During the tumultuous postwar years, the college's financial struggles and the defeat of the Confederacy remained at forefront of the thoughts of its students. At the 1880 commencement ceremony, an unnamed student delivered a speech titled "Character," that referenced the defeat of the Confederacy:

> It is also doubtless [*sic*] true that some lives are robbed of success and good name by "the fearful concentration of circumstances" as Daniel Webster has expressed it. But character is never snatched from a moral being by any concatenation of circumstances, however fearful. The same circumstances, that raised Gen. Grant to fame and to the presidency and made him the trumpeted and toasted hero of the Civil War, furnished the dark background from which have shone out in immoral splendor, "the greatness and the goodness, the magnanimity and the modesty, the consecration and the courage, the example, and the incentive, which were personified in Robert E. Lee on the field of war and in the still air of collegiate shades and which will be a benediction and a transforming influence, not only in Virginia, not only in the Republic, but across the seas and around the world. (Character 1880, n.p.)

A NEW LOCATION AND A NEW BEGINNING

By 1906, Tuskegee Female College leaders decided to relocate the academy to a more populous city—Montgomery—a plan spearheaded by college president John Massey. Massey sought—but failed—to acquire a land donation for the campus's new location. Thereafter, John Sellers, William Moore, and C. G. Zirkle purchased a parcel of land from a local resident and then donated the land to the college. In 1908, a landscape design for the campus was commissioned from Frederick Law Olmsted Jr., who was well regarded for his land conservation efforts in the Florida Everglades and Yosemite National Park and his garden design for the Biltmore estate in Ashford, North Carolina.

By August of 1909, the college's administration had moved the institution's books, equipment, records, and students into a rented facility while the first building on the new Montgomery campus, Flowers Hall, was constructed. Unfortunately, Hammer Hall, as the rented building was dubbed, was destroyed by fire not long after it was occupied by the college's wards. After the fire, students were moved by railway cars to Sullins College, a junior college, in Bristol, Virginia, for one year before relocating to the new campus (Bettersworth 1955). In the Fall of 1910, Tuskegee Female College reopened, but with a new name—the Women's College of Alabama. President Massey was credited for the college's relocation and postwar success and was even praised in a letter from Booker T. Washington. On January 8, 1908, Washington wrote, "I feel constantly indebted to you for your help and influence, which has always been exerted in wise and conservative directions. During all the years now more than twenty-five, that it has been my privilege to live in Tuskegee, I have never heard a single individual, white or colored, utter a single sentence that was not in your praise" (n.p.).

The Civil War was indeed a watershed for the United States and forced the reconfiguration of Southern life. While many men's colleges shut their doors during the war years due to a loss of students and faculty, women's institutions closed as a result of local battles and loss of resources. Tuskegee Female College, on the other hand, remained open and faced the arduous task of providing higher education to regional female students sans shuttering. This Civil War narrative of Tuskegee Female College (present-day Huntington College) relies on precious few documents that survived a violent war, postwar Reconstruction, financial difficulties, campus relocation, fire, and various organizational reconfigurations. Despite the tumultuous challenges experienced during and after the Civil War, Huntingdon College persists today as a highly regarded liberal arts academy that maintains a strong association with the United Methodist Church. Its faculty, staff, students, and administrators maintain a modern scholastic mission undergirded by a decisive academic motto: "Enter to grow in wisdom, go forth to apply wisdom in service."

REFERENCES

Alabama Conference Female College. 1908. *Alumnae of Alabama Conference Female College 1856–1908*. Montgomery, AL: Paragon Press. Houghton Memorial Library. Huntingdon College Archives and Special Collections, Montgomery.

Bettersworth, John. K. 1955. "Review: History of Huntingdon College, 1854–1954 by Rhoda Coleman Ellison." *The Journal of Southern History* 21 (2): 261–63.

Character. 1880. Commencement Speech. Houghton Memorial Library. Huntingdon College Archives and Special Collections, Montgomery.

Chilton, W. P. 1896. "Twenty-Fifth Day." *Montgomery Weekly Advertiser.* March 6, 1896.

Editor Republican. 1857. "Tuskegee in 1857." *Tuskegee Republican*. September 10, 1857.

Ellison, Rhonda. Coleman. 1954. *History of Huntingdon College 1854–1954*. Tuscaloosa: University of Alabama Press.

Farnham, Christie Anne. 1995. *The Education of the Southern Belle: Higher Education and Student Socialization in the Antebellum South*. New York: New York University Press.

Hunter, C. N.d. Personal Diary. Houghton Memorial Library. Huntingdon College Archives and Special Collections, Montgomery.

Huntingdon College. "Huntingdon History." 2018. http://www.huntingdon.edu/about/history/.

Jones, James Pickett. 1976. *Yankee Blitzkrieg: Wilson's Raid through Alabama and Georgia*. Lexington: University Press of Kentucky.

Lazenby, Marion Elias. 1960. *History of Methodism in Alabama and West Florida: Being an Account of the Amazing March of Methodism through Alabama and West Florida*. Nashville: North Alabama Conference and Alabama-West Florida Conference of the Methodist Church.

Lipscomb, Andrew A. 1854. "Rights and Wrongs of Women," *Harper's Bazaar* 9 (June), 123.

MacKethan, Lucinda H., ed. 1988. *Recollections of a Southern Daughter: A Memoir by Cornelia Jones Pond of Liberty County*. Athens: University of Georgia Press.

Massey, John. 1916. *Reminiscences*. Internet Archive. Last modified April 3, 2017, https://archive.org/details/ReminiscencesByJohnMassey/page/n151/mode/2up/search/wood.

Owen, Mary Bankhead and Thomas McAdory Owen. 1921 *History of Alabama and Dictionary of Alabama Biography*. Chicago: S. J. Clarke Publishing Company.

Timberlake, Steven. 2013. "Maria Howard Weeden." In *Encyclopedia of Alabama*. August 15, 2013. http://www.encyclopediaofalabama.org/article/h-3060.

Tuskegee College. 1864. "Tuskegee College—The Commencement Exercises." *Montgomery Advertiser*. June 27, 1864.

"Tuskegee Female College Later Became Huntingdon." 1965. *Tuskegee News*. November 11, 1965. Houghton Memorial Library. Huntingdon College Archives and Special Collections, Montgomery.

Tuskegee Female College Meeting Minutes. n.d. Houghton Memorial Library. Huntingdon College Archives and Special Collections, Montgomery.

Vickers, A. *Alumnae Data Sheets Alabama Conference Female College 1856–1909 N–Z.* 1962. Box 62. Houghton Memorial Library. Huntingdon College Archives and Special Collections, Montgomery.

Washington, Booker T. Letter to John Massey. June 8, 1908. Booker T. Washington Papers. Houghton Memorial Library. Huntingdon College Archives and Special Collections, Montgomery.

West, Anson. 1893 *A History of Methodism in Alabama.* Nashville: Methodist Episcopal Church South.

CHAPTER SIX

Mercer University, the Georgia Baptist Convention, and the American Civil War

Sarah Mangrum, Tiffany Greer, and Holly A. Foster

The first records pertaining to the Baptist denomination in the state of Georgia appear in 1757, though the denomination's leaders did not officially organize as the General Association of Georgia Baptists until 1822. In 1828, the religious organization's name was changed to the Georgia Baptist Convention (Ragsdale 1932). Despite an early aversion toward higher education development, these Georgia-based Baptists, in time, came to be regarded for their educational endeavors (Geiger 2015). Indeed, the organization's constitution charged its members with providing higher educational opportunities for "pious young men, who may be called by the Spirit and their churches to the Christian ministry" by way of establishing a fund for a regional college (Campbell 1874, 20). Even though Baptist-affiliated higher education was supported by the convention's leaders, lay members of state churches resisted the idea of a denominationally supported college due to the financial demands such an institution might have placed on church communities. Members of the Georgia Baptist Convention revisited the issue of formal education each year at their annual meeting but did not always agree on the need for higher education as they preferred ministers who had engaged in informal apprenticeships with seasoned pastors rather than newly minted, seminary trained clergymen (Geiger 2015). However, in time, support for the creation of a Georgia-based Baptist academy grew as convention leaders worked to foster an appreciation for formal education within community throughout the state.

In 1827, a fund was established to support the convention's mission to provide higher education for men seeking to enter a lifelong vocation of religious ministry within the Baptist denomination. Adiel Sherwood, the convention's treasurer, addressed his fellow convention members in an 1829 meeting and directly addressed the issue of crafting a formal educational institute for young men who wished to become Baptist preachers. In 1833, while serving on the Georgia Baptist Convention's Executive Committee along with fellow convention member Jesse Mercer, Sherwood authored a resolution "that as soon as the funds will justify it, this Convention will establish, in some central part of the state, a classical and theological school, which will unite agricultural labor with study, and be opened for those only preparing for the ministry" (Ragsdale 1932, 23). Sherwood later assumed the department chair of theology at Mercer University. He remained in Georgia until William Tecumseh Sherman's army raided his personal farm and burned most of his possessions (Burch 2003).

In 1829, Sherwood gave an oration at the Georgia Baptist Convention regarding the need for Baptist-affiliated higher education in the state of Georgia. He addressed, what he felt, was regional young men's desire to pursue formal education as well as attempted to assuage any trepidations they may have felt concerning the undertaking of a lengthy course of study. Sherwood went on to reveal that an educational fund had been established to foster the creation of a formal institute of higher learning. The establishment of this educational fund originated with money willed to the convention by Deacon Josiah Penfield, a prominent Georgian Baptist, merchant, and silversmith (Boykin 1881). Penfield's gift of $2,500 set a precedent for regional philanthropy that ultimately led to the establishment of Mercer Institute in 1833. At that same meeting, convention members voted to match Penfield's gift through individual contributions. Jesse Mercer and attorney Cullen Battle contributed the largest individual donations at $250 each (Ragsdale 1932).

Adiel Sherwood was not alone in his pursuit of Baptist-affiliated education that would support the ministry. Jesse Mercer was also a proponent. Mercer was a prominent, regional Baptist leader who later became "the first chair of the Mercer [Institute] Board of Trustees" (Mercer University 2009, 29). The son of Baptist minister Silas Mercer, Jesse was born December 16, 1769 in North Carolina. The junior Mercer did not have many educational opportunities as a child but studied theology alongside his father. Silas Mercer baptized his son at the age of 17 and, two years later, Jesse married a Wilkes County, Georgia, resident, Sabrina Chivers. When he turned 20, Jesse Mercer was ordained a Baptist minister and preached at churches in Powelton and Eatonton, Georgia (Boykin 1881). *Georgia Baptists: Historical and Biographical* describes Mercer as "the most influential minister of his day, and perhaps the most distinguished minister of the denomination ever reared up in the State" (Campbell 1874, 311). After Mercer's first wife died in 1826, the Baptist preacher relocated to Washington, Georgia, where he met and married Nancy Simons in 1827. Simons was a widow who had inherited a substantial sum from her former husband. As a result, her new husband, Mercer, was able to contribute the abovementioned $250 for what would become Mercer Institute. Upon Mercer's death in 1841, a substantial sum of money was willed to the academy (Rice and Williams 1979, 73). Ultimately, "Mr. Mercer gave 225 shares in Georgia Railroad and State Bank, his library, and the residuary of his estate" to the burgeoning Baptist college. Owing to Jesse Mercer's gift, it was decided that the new academy would bear his name (Sherwood 1860, 144).

Prior to the opening of Mercer Institute in 1833, the Georgia Baptist Convention dictated that the early college's curricular structure should be both "classical and theological." The organization's members also agreed that the college should be centrally located in the state so as to enhance access to all of Georgia's white male, Baptist residents. (Campbell 1874, 23). The convention members' initial intent was to limit enrollment to those preparing for ministerial work. This mission was soon amended to admit additional students desirous of liberal arts and manual careers external to religious life. On January 14, 1833, Mercer Institute opened as a manual labor academy with thirty-nine students in attendance— seven of whom were housed in the new college's theology department. Along with this first cadre of students, the institution housed the college's first president, Rev. Billington McCarthy Sanders (Campbell 1874). Sanders and his wife were dedicated to establishing the college's religious reputation and allowed twenty-six of the thirty-nine students to live in the Sanders home, where the college president and his wife acted as a surrogate family (Bryant 2005).

Mercer Institute opened "on a red clay farm" with two log cabins in Penfield, Georgia—named for the aforementioned Josiah Penfield who bequeathed funds for Baptist-affiliated higher education in the state of Georgia (Mercer University 2009, 30). Located seven miles north of Greensboro, Georgia, the city of Penfield has a rich history—much of which is associated with the Georgia Baptist Convention (Rice and Williams 1979). At the time of its founding, the campus of Mercer Institute was described in rather spartan terms. In the 1859–1860 university catalog, the college's original campus was said to be a physical location "such as to command itself to the judgement and good sense of all who may have sons or wards to send to college. It is situated seven miles from the Georgia Railroad, in a small, unassuming village, from which are debarred, by law, the most fruitful sources of temptation to dissipation, whilst the moral and religious influences are eminently conservative of the character of young men, and promotive of good order and industrious habits of study" (Ragsdale 1932, 21).

In 1837, the institution was officially incorporated and granted a state charter by an Act of the Georgia Legislature. The next year, the academy's name was changed to Mercer University (Mercer University Catalog 1859–1860). Three years later, in 1841, the institution hosted its first commencement ceremony consisting of three graduates. Described as an institution "affording facilities for instruction surpassing those of most institutions of the same age," (Mercer University Catalog 1859–1860, 21) the university campus continued to expand to include "buildings consist[ing] of the President's house and office, chapel, a large building occupied by the family of one of the professors and by students, library and apparatus building, building for recitations, and two society halls—all spacious, and most of them brick. They are situated in a beautiful campus of about four acres, which is well shaded by venerable oaks" (Campbell 1874, 147). Indeed, the college campus had grown from its log-cabin roots to encompass a much larger expanse dotted with Greek Revival red-brick buildings fronted by white-washed columns. With the support of city and community residents, the campus outgrew its log-cabin origins to encompass a much larger set of ornate buildings. One visitor to the newly renamed Mercer University described the campus in rhapsodic terms: "We take a leisurely stroll about the old campus. How refreshing the shade of its majestic oaks. How delightful the fragrance of the old-time pinks and roses. We gaze with hushed reverence upon the old buildings that remain, unique and antique in their architecture" (Ragsdale 1932, 27).

MERCER BEFORE THE CIVIL WAR

In their 1860 annual report, the institution's governing board boasted that Mercer University was more prosperous than it had been in the previous two years, with enrollment larger than ever before. The minutes from the 1861 Georgia Baptist Convention meeting concurred with the positive view, stating that, "Notwithstanding the pecuniary embarrassments of our State, and the political revolution through which we have been passing, resulting recently in actual war, it is a matter of gratitude . . . that we are enabled to report . . . that Mercer University has not merely sustained during the past year, but has been highly prosperous" (1861, 14). There were twenty graduates in 1860, the year before the American Civil War began. Of those, two graduated from the theological arm of the college, while the other graduates received a degree in either a collegiate course of study or a scientific course of study (Mercer University Catalog 1860–1861). Students applying for admittance to the freshman class were expected to have completed fourteen years of preparatory education and were required to undergo exams in a variety of subject areas prior to their collegiate matriculation. In contrast, students pursuing ministerial education in the college's theology department were expected to have obtained a formal liberal education, but no particular "scholastic terms of admission" were required, only "satisfactory evidence of piety and of a call to the Ministry" were necessary for admission (Mercer University Catalog 1860–1861, 32). The Georgia Baptist Convention's efforts to frame Mercer University as a religious seminary is reflected not only in the lack of academic prerequisites for students interested in theological studies, but also in the cost of tuition. In 1861, tuition for the theological seminary was listed as "Nothing" while tuition for the collegiate course of study was set at $15 for the fall term and $25 for the spring term (Mercer University Catalog 1860–1861, 34).

Despite the push for theology instruction, Mercer University's literary department overshadowed the institution's theology department, despite the latter's importance to the college's founders and members of the Georgia Baptist Convention (Campbell 1874). Further evidence of the importance placed in the formal education of ministers at Mercer University can be found in the report presented at the Georgia Baptist Convention meeting in 1861. In addition to a brief overview of Mercer University's financial condition, the report includes a statement about how many students were enrolled in theology—twelve: the highest theology enrollment thus far in the institution's history. The report's authors referenced the twelve theology students as "source of great encouragement." The report closed with a statement that encouraged members of the Georgia Baptist Convention to continue to pray for the ongoing success of the Penfield-based university (Georgia Baptist Convention 1861, 15).

Mercer University prospered in the years leading up to the American Civil War with a financial endowment approximated at $130,000 in 1860 and a small, but highly astute senior class comprising thirty-one young men in 1861—the largest senior class thus far (Mondy 1956). While the 1860–1861 Mercer University catalog mentions the academy's endowment in passing, the previous year's academic catalog dedicates an entire section to the endowment. The financial reserve was described as one "which probably exceeds that of any other denominational school in the Southern states, is of such an amount, and is so securely and profitably invested, that the proceeds are sufficient to support the existing organization, independent of other resources" (Mercer University Catalog 1859–1860, 22).

The 1861 Georgia Baptist Convention meeting minutes indicate that Mercer University's income was larger than ever before. The endowment's growth was attributed to "first, by an increase in receipts for tuition and room rent, amounting to $825.30; and secondly, by the large dividends received on the Stock of the Central Rail Road and Banking Company of 27 1/2 percent." A report was provided to convention's members that detailed the institution's financial growth. The report provided details regarding a significant philanthropic gift in the form of annual income derived from shares of stock in the Atlanta & West Point Rail Company. These stock shares were bequeathed to the university by Mrs. Jane Posey, wife of the late Rev. Humphrey Posey, for the express purpose of enhancing theological instruction (Campbell 1874). The 1861 dividend from said stock was $1,440.60 (Georgia Baptist Convention 1862). In recognition of her monetary gift, Mercer University's Board of Trustees planned to have a likeness of Mrs. Posey crafted and installed on the campus as a memorial to her life and donation. Posey, it was claimed, was one of the first women in the American South to make such a large financial donation to an institution of higher education ("Some of Mercer's Benefactors" 1920). Despite these financial accolades, the report's authors warned that, given the country's increasingly divisive political and social situation, it "would be very unsafe to rely in future upon a larger annual income than $16,380.00. And to what extent this amount may be diminished by the troubled state of the country it is impossible to predict" (Georgia Baptist Convention 1861–1863, 14).

THE UNIVERSITY AT WAR

From the opening months of the American Civil War, Baptist denominational and Confederate leaders both requested that religious congregations vocalize their support of the Southern secessionist cause. Four months after the Georgia legislature voted to secede from the Union (January 19, 1861), members of the Georgia Baptist Convention in May of 1861 called upon all Baptist churches in the state of Georgia to pass resolutions in support of the new, Confederate nation and the armed conflict that would protect "Southern rights" from Northern invaders. In 1862, "denominational leaders further called upon Baptist churches to evangelize Southern soldiers" (Gourley 2008, 218). These same passionate secessionist feelings were demonstrated at Mercer University by students and faculty alike. "When war was declared between the North and South, students and graduates of Mercer heroically responded to defend their constitutional rights and their sacred honor" (Dowell 1958, 110). Most members of the 1861 senior class enlisted with many students and graduates joining the 57th Georgia Infantry. Nine of the thirty-one classmates who joined the Confederate army died on the battlefield or succumbed to war-related injuries prior to the end of the war. One Mercer University student, Edwin T. Davis, left the academy to serve in Company A. Davis was captured at Vicksburg in 1863 (Gourley 2008). Alva Benjamin Spencer, a Mercer University alumnus, was thankful to have survived the July 1863 Battle of Gettysburg as well as other war-related hardships. In 1864, "Spencer passed the cold winter days by reminiscing of his 'schoolboy days' and 'living in anticipation of the happy time' in which he would see his future wife" (Gourley 2008, 153). Like many Southern college students turned army men, the "glory of combat" quickly lost its allure for Spencer.

Prior to Mercer University alumnus Spencer's wartime experiences, student support of the war and the desire to fight was strong. Indeed, the duty "to defend their constitutional rights and sacred honor," felt by most Mercer students and graduates was evident, as most of the 1861 and 1862 senior classes joined the Confederacy together (Mercer University 2009, 28). Even so, 29 Mercer University alumni died during the war. Per historian Spright Dowell, these "'Mercerians' bore themselves with conspicuous bravery and unwavering loyalty throughout the period of struggle in many hard fought and bloody engagement" (Dowell 1958, 110). This student enthusiasm, however, had a less than positive impact on the larger university community.

In his Report of Committee on Education for the annual Georgia Baptist Convention in 1862, Chairman S. G. Daniel described the campus atmosphere as it was steadily drained of its student body: "with much of painful solicitude we witnessed the circumscribing of its genial influence; the disappointments of its devoted instructors, and the increasing desertions of its honored halls; but as One who was wiser and mightier than we, has willed that it must be so" (1862, 11). The following year, Georgia Baptist Convention chairman H. A. Tupper noted that, "instead of studying history, they are making it; instead of disciplining the intellect by severe application, they are developing manhood, by the encounter of stern realities; instead of preparing for life, they are performing it. And many who have quitted the college for the camps, may be doing more towards shaping the destiny of their country, than they possibly could do in common times with all the resources conferred by the most elevated culture of their mental powers" (Georgia Baptist Convention 1862, 9). As students left to enlist, Mercer University's administration and faculty refocused their institutional efforts to recruit new students. The Baptist-affiliated institution's administrators hoped not only to keep the college's doors open, but also to make Mercer University an academically attractive and accessible option for those boys and young men not actively engaged in the Southern conflict (Georgia Baptist Convention 1862).

Despite the mass Civil War exodus of students from institutions of higher education across the American South, Mercer University remained open for the duration of the conflict (Georgia Baptist Convention 1864). This was not the case for most colleges and universities across the South, in the state of Georgia, and certainly not for other academies in the immediate area of Penfield. One neighboring institution, the Greensboro Female College, closed its doors at the beginning of the war. It was soon converted to serve "as a school for children until it was taken over by the Confederate government and used as a hospital for wounded soldiers" (Rice and Williams 1979, 216). By January of 1865, Greensboro was "filled with the wounded and dying soldiers" (Rice and Williams 1979, 216).

While no battles were fought at or near the Mercer University campus in Penfield, regional leaders in surrounding Greene County acted to assist military volunteers and mandated that $500 be appropriated for each volunteer company ordered to service. These monies were to be used to equip each volunteer for active military service. Thereafter, three Greene County military companies were formed. These military units consisted of Dawson Grays, the Greene County Rifles, and Stephens Light Guardians (Rice and Williams 1979). In addition to these companies, the university's administration sponsored the creation of the Mercer University Cadets, a volunteer student cadet corps. Professor Shelton Sanford took responsibility for the Mercer University Cadets. As with the governing body of surrounding Greene County, Mercer University's leaders spent a significant amount of money outfitting the college's cadets. On March 27, 1861, Professor Sanford ordered 80 "Minnie, Long Range" muskets for the cadets, at a cost of $1,600 (Sanford 1816–1896). Sanford made the purchase request to Georgia Governor Joseph E. Brown and identified himself as the acting captain of the Mercer University cadets. The money was sent in bond form with a request that, after the war, the muskets would be returned to Georgia's militia in good condition.

Though Sanford was keen to support military instruction, he was unsure of his students' roles in the Civil War. In October of 1861, Sanford queried Governor Brown on several related issues. The Mercer University professor explained to Brown that students had never been called to perform official military duties despite their involvement in military training. Now, Sanford explained, his cadets were being told that they would regularly drill with the Greene County Volunteer Corps (Sanford 1816–1896). While Sanford made no direct challenge to this edict, he did request guidance concerning the military dress of Mercer University cadets if they were to be required to participate in formal army-related activities. Sanford's uniform query followed a newspaper article published in the fall of 1861. The article's author questioned the value of military instruction offered at Mercer University. The article stated, "In our present condition our sons must have a Military education, and if they cannot get it at [Mercer University in] Penfield, we will be compelled to send them somewhere else" ("Military Training at Mercer" 1861, n.p.). The article's author proposed that a more formal system of military education should be imposed at the college, including uniforms that "be of Georgia goods—gray, brown, blue, or black; round jacket, with stripe down the pants and a military cap" (n.p.). This question of uniform color spurred Sanford to write to Brown. Sanford was keen to ensure that local community members viewed military instruction at Mercer University as on par with similar instructional activities occurring at colleges across the Confederate South—including uniform apparel.

Mercer University cadets continued to drill alongside the Greene County Volunteer Corps during the early years of the war. The college's military instruction had a profound influence on students' willingness to enlist in the Confederate army. In 1862, a report was presented to the Georgia Baptist Convention concerning student cadet support of the Southern cause. The report indicated that all graduates from the previous year, save one who was underage, enlisted. Two of the enlisted died not long after joining the Confederate forces (Georgia Baptist Convention 1863). Overall, the war greatly impacted campus life at Mercer University as student numbers declined precipitously. Thirty-five students enrolled in the spring of 1862, which was slightly better than the previous year but still a far cry from prewar enrollments. Faculty numbers were also influenced by the war. By 1863, only three professors remained at the campus—Shelton Sanford, J. E. Willet, and William Woodfin. Though these instructors avoided direct conflict in far-flung battlefields, they were each involved in the war effort both on campus and in their private lives. Willet, regionally acclaimed as a premier antebellum scientist, "placed his knowledge at the disposal of the Confederacy" (Dowell 1958, 110). He served as superintendent of the Confederate arsenal in Atlanta, then a laboratory for the manufacture of war materials. In his role as arsenal superintendent, Willet, like other military laboratory supervisors, would have been responsible for a number of Confederate army projects such as, "standardization of the production of ammunition as to caliber and quality; experimentation with projectiles, rockets and powders . . . the production of percussion caps, friction primers and other pieces of ordnance" (DuBose 2018, 13).

While many Mercer University students departed for the battlefield, others continued their studies. Likewise, several of the college's instructors maintained classes throughout the war. In an 1861 newspaper article, the university's faculty boasted about the institution's enrollment and declared that "hard times as yet have not affected our noble Institution" ("Mercer Triumphant" 1861, n.p.). Still, numbers soon declined while secessionist ideology permeated the institution's academics and daily operations. The Mercer University catalog for 1860–1861 included a short paragraph introducing a new feature to the college's course of study—the subject of slavery. In this new course section, students would be taught the importance of defending chattel servitude, a prominent feature of the American South championed by the Confederacy. This course, it was explained would provide pertinent fodder for related political and social debates that would, in addition to improving the student elocution, give all enrolled "a practical mastery of the argument on that question [of slavery], which of all others of earthly interest, is most important to the people of the Confederate States" (Mercer University Catalog 1860–1861, 32). This new course aligned with the broader Georgia Baptist Convention's views on the nature of slavery and the related mid-nineteenth-century conflict. Indeed, convention members declared that it was their "duty to avow that, both in feeling and in principle, we approve, endorse and support the Government of the Confederate States of America" (Georgia Baptist Convention 1861, 5).

Despite the inclusion of instructional material that defended slavery and championed the secessionist cause, enrollment at Mercer University continued to decline as students left for the battlefield. The remaining faculty and students maintained daily academic activities until Union general William Tecumseh Sherman's forces invaded nearby Greensboro, Georgia, on November 18, 1864. Sherman's men "burned all of the equipment of the railroad and hundreds of bales of cotton and buildings in the vicinity. Next to burn was the railroad bridge of the Ga. railroad over the Oconee. The Union forces camped for the night at Lee Jordan's plantation while the sky was aglow with the flames from the fires, taking what they could and burned 50,000 bushels of corn" (Rice and Williams 1979, 414). Despite the nearby decimation, Mercer University persisted. With the arrival of Sherman, "Greensboro was full of Yankees, and stealing and plundering . . . most of the [Greene County] mills were burned by Sherman's Raiders" (Rice and Williams 1979, 63).

Sherman's March through Georgia devastated the countryside near Mercer University. The destruction left in its wake an urgent need for simple necessities including food, clothing, and shelter. Survival was priority and "very few families had the means for sending their children to college or for helping to maintain an institution. To keep the college alive and in operation was no small problem" (Ragsdale 1932, 161). Despite the significant damage to surrounding Greene County, "there were very few and slight changes in college management and policies for the duration of the war" (Ragsdale 1932, 155). Other institutions, educational or otherwise, were not so fortunate. Due to the widespread burning and pillaging, the Georgia Baptist Convention's 1865 meeting, "which was to have met in Columbus that year, was called off, since the enemy had occupied, plundered, and partially burned the city" (Boykin 1881; Dowell 1958, 110).

FINANCIAL IMPLICATIONS OF WAR

Despite the abovementioned military and proslavery curricular revisions, war had permeated the state of Georgia, and Mercer University was not exempt. Even so, the university's Board of Trustees resolved not to suspend regardless of decreased enrollments and the loss of some professors (Campbell 1874). Indeed, hopes were high that, if the institution persisted through the war, regional students too young to enlist would enroll and those students who left to fight would eventually return to campus and reengage in their studies (Georgia Baptist Convention 1862). By the time of the Georgia Baptist Convention's annual meeting in 1862, however, the university's Board of Trustees had resolved to engage in cost saving measures such as the reduction of faculty salaries. At the same time, the board accepted the resignation of four additional professors so that they could enlist. These professors were not replaced, and the associated salary expenditures were retained by the board. With cost saving measures in place, members of the board once again reported that Mercer University had a strong financial footing despite the fact that tuition-based income had been greatly diminished. Members of the board worried that, given the region's political situation and increased involvement in the Civil War, continued reliance on tuition revenue was become increasingly unreliable (Georgia Baptist Convention 1862).

By the end of 1862, the number of faculty had decreased to three. This trio of college instructors experienced further diminished salaries. The president's salary was reduced to $1,600 while professor salaries were lowered to $1,200 each (Ragsdale 1932; Georgia Baptist Convention 1862). To offset decreased pay, faculty were permitted to recoup monetary losses via tuition revenue. While the war raged, faculty were compensated by student fees rather than stockpiling said monies for the long-term benefit of the college. In addition, faculty were given free housing. For example, Professor Wise occupied a wooden house on campus during the war. Even after his resignation, he was granted free housing (Georgia Baptist Convention 1862). Despite attempts to save money, tuition revenue further decreased as students continued to leave for the warfront. While Mercer University enrollment numbers peaked in 1861, they quickly dwindled following the siege on Fort Sumter in South Carolina. At the onset of the Civil War, members of the Georgia Baptist Convention published a statement imploring the state's young men that they could serve their country best by continuing their higher education until the time "when their services are required in the field." Unfortunately, this call fell on deaf ears (Georgia Baptist Convention 1861, 8). The university's Board of Trustees noted in their 1862 report to the Georgia Baptist Convention that many students left the college to enlist as members of various volunteer companies. As a result, the 1861–1862 academic year ended with only thirty-five students in attendance. By the end of 1862, enrollment had decreased to eighteen students, ten of whom were seniors (Georgia Baptist Convention 1862). In 1863, only twelve students enrolled. Of this number, nine left for the battlefield the following year. Eight bachelor of arts degrees were conferred in 1863, seven to students too young to fight (Dowell 1958; Ragsdale 1932).

The financial picture at Mercer University was further strained as the surrounding war resulted in increased costs for food and material resources. Due to regional inflation that accompanied the scarcity of goods and comestibles, faculty salaries were raised significantly in 1863. The college's governing board raised the president's salary to $2,400. They also raised faculty salaries to $1,800 per professor (Georgia Baptist Convention 1863). Further inflation resulted in yet another salary increase in 1864 (Ragsdale 1932), and although the college's overall endowment remained steady, members of the governing board reported that the cost to operate the university had, by this point, equaled the amount of income garnered via tuition and Baptist denomination support (Georgia Baptist Convention 1864). Despite further increasing the president's salary to $4,000 and professor salaries to $3,000, Mercer University's trustees were proud to have kept the college open. In fact, Civil War-era Mercer University is one of the only examples of increased faculty and administrative salaries during the war. Regardless of this success, war had taken its toll on the campus. As the late nineteenth-century historian Samuel Boykin explains, "During the continuance of the war, a skeleton, merely, of college organization was preserved, for the reason that the material for classes was almost entirely absorbed by the demands of the service; and, with the close of the war, came temporary confusion and demoralization" (1881, 251). Indeed, members of Mercer University's governing board held firm throughout the war and determined that the college should remain open despite significant Confederate losses in surrounding Georgia. In 1864, Sylvanus Landrum, the board of trustee's secretary, reported to the Georgia Baptist Convention in 1864:

> Two years ago, in one of the darkest periods of the war, at the Annual meeting of the Convention in LaGrange, the Board resolved to maintain the status of the University during the war; *provided* it could be done without incurring debt. The Convention approved the determination of the Board. The College has been kept open, and good results have followed. Indeed, now that so many Colleges have suspended, it seems to us all the more important that Mercer University should be kept open to the patronage of the denomination and the country. So far from falling into debt by continuing the exercises of the College, our funds, under the good providence of God, have considerably increased. (Georgia Baptist Convention 1864, 14)

This statement regarding the university's financial endowment, while made late in the Civil War, was perhaps made in haste. At the 1866 Georgia Baptist Convention, the Board of Trustees presented a much less favorable report regarding the pecuniary state of Mercer University. The 1866 report detailed that, while the college had remained open during the fighting, the academy's faculty and administration had "been impracticable to accomplish much" (Georgia Baptist Convention 1866, 15). Efforts to maintain and increase the college's endowment during the war proved futile. At the end of the war, Mercer University was left with little income. The wealth of area families had decreased, and enrollment remained low. As a result, tuition income was practically insubstantial to maintain the institution. Despite salary increases during the war, the university's financial condition had decreased so much that the faculty and administration went unpaid in 1865. Thereafter, Nathaniel Macon Crawford, the college's president, resigned and left Georgia to work at Georgetown College in Kentucky (Campbell 1874). After Crawford's resignation, Henry Holcombe Tucker was appointed to lead Mercer University as president. He remained in office until 1871. In 1874, Tucker assumed the presidency at the University of Georgia in Athens, Georgia (Dowell 1958; Dooley 2011).

The war's financial impact on Mercer University was outlined in the institution's 1868–1869 academic catalog. Though the endowment was totaled at $162,213 in the catalog, financial losses from the war were estimated at $27,899. Of that amount, $16,013 was lost to Confederate Securities, $10,000 in Bank of Georgia stock, and $1,886 in Confederate notes. This financial situation was further complicated by the university's policy regarding free tuition for disabled veterans. The university stated that "any soldier of the late

"Mercer University Faculty on Porch of President's Home," n.d. Pictured are Joseph Edgerton Willett, J. J. Brantly, Henry Holcombe (university president), Shelton Palmer Sanford, and William G. Woodfin. Image courtesy of Mercer University Archives, Macon, Georgia.

Confederate army, who is disabled from manual labor by reason of wounds, and who is unable to pay the expenses of education, is welcome to Mercer University as a student, and shall receive *tuition gratis.* This offer has been steadily made for the last six years and is still continued" (Mercer University Catalog 1868–1869, 27). Though this tuition waiver was granted to support Confederate veterans, the resultant loss in tuition revenue was significant.

Providing free tuition for disabled soldiers was not unique to Mercer University. In 1866, a state bill was passed to "educate the indigent maimed soldiers of Georgia and provide the necessary means for same" (Roberts 1965, 419). Disabled soldiers could take advantage of this benefit at a number of Georgia colleges and universities including the University of Georgia, Mercer University, Oglethorpe University, Emory College, or Bowdoin College. In addition, if veterans were under the age of 30, they received "free of charge . . . tuition, books, board and clothing, until the completion of their collegiate terms" (Roberts 1965, 419). The promise that "the state would pay up to $300 per year for their expenses and, in return, the indigent soldiers would teach in Georgia as many years as they had been in the university or college," remained in effect until March 1869, when "the General Assembly voted to end the program" (Roberts 1965, 419–20).

MOVING MERCER

Despite attempts to maintain Mercer University's financial solvency, the war-related monetary strain ultimately resulted in the institution's physical relocation. The subject of relocation proved contentious for years amongst Mercer University faculty and students, as well as members of the Georgia Baptist Convention (Ragsdale 1932). Debates regarding relocation had occurred as early as 1850. Similar discussions occurred periodically over the next decade (Bryant 2005). The lasting effects of the Civil War and subsequent Reconstruction, however, spurred renewed interest in campus relocation. In 1865, Sidney Root, an Atlanta, Georgia-based merchant, offered forty-five acres to relocate Mercer University to the capital city. This land "was located on the Macon & Western Railroad, just one and a half miles from the passenger station" (Bryant, 2005, 468). Root's offer was made four months after the war officially ended, and although the proposal was accepted by the Georgia Baptist Convention with some slight modifications, it was never acted on save a brief mention at the state Baptist convention meeting of 1866 (Bryant 2005). While Mercer University's Board of Trustees warmed to the idea of physical relocation, the Georgia Baptist Association ultimately opposed the move as "Penfield was the heart of the Georgia Baptist Association as well as the GBC" (Bryant 2005, 472). As such, the Baptist-affiliated Mercer University was to remain in Penfield.

During Southern Reconstruction, arguments over the university's relocation intensified between the college's faculty and members of the Georgia Baptist Association. Subsequently, enrollment at Mercer University significantly declined. Postwar enrollments increased until it peaked with 84 students in 1869. The next year, enrollment dropped to 44 (Dowell 1958, Bryant 2005). The relocation debate finally came to a head at the 1870 Georgia Baptist Convention. Heated arguments lasted for three days. During the debate, a Mercer University senior student pointed out that most students approved of relocation and warned that the student body was becoming agitated as regarded the delayed relocation (Ragsdale 1932). As historian James Bryant points out, students were frustrated with Mercer University's isolated location as well as the lack of social opportunities in Penfield. After the debate, a final vote approved the campus move to Macon—a hub for Georgia transportation and mercantilism. However, relocation was not finalized until 1871. Classes officially began at the new Macon site in October of 1871. Throughout the remainder of the nineteenth century, Mercer University's curricular structure was expanded. In 1873 a law school was added that contributed to the college's enrollment and financial growth (Bryant 2005, McMillen 1997).

While many students left Mercer University to fight for the Confederate army, many still completed their degrees following the end of the Civil War. In addition, Mercer University's faculty and administration awarded a Master of Arts degree to all students who served in the Southern armies. In 1866, Mercer University also award Gen. Robert E. Lee an honorary degree (Dowell 1958; Mercer University 2019). Following the war, Mercer University's faculty added, "a new feature of instruction, a systematic plan of public lectures given by members of the faculty which the students were required to attend" (Dowell 1958, 117). Further, "Mercer University was the first institution in Georgia to introduce this improved system [written exams] of examinations which has since been adopted by the state University, and perhaps by other colleges in the state" (Dowell 1958, 118). These curricular changes were welcomed by faculty, staff, and student families. Students engaged in the university's revised academic system were "noted for orderly conduct and great application to study; for they appeared to realize that the issue of the war had wrought a revolution in the fortunes, industries and employments of the Southern people, and that afterwards, the success of young men was to depend on personal effort, in which education entered as an important factor" (Boykin 1881, 252). As with many Southern colleges and universities, whether they remained open during the Civil War or reopened thereafter, application of study was important as livelihoods based on inherited wealth and slavery was a thing of the past. Now, in the New South, careers would have to be attained via study and vocational attainment. Certainly, the Civil War had reshaped Mercer University as it had so many other Southern institutions of higher education. Ninety-four years after the conclusion of the war, the Georgia Historical Commission, in 1959, erected a marker on the present Mercer University campus that acknowledges the institution's Civil War persistence. Per the marker, "Mercer was one of the few colleges in the South that remained open during the War Between the States and the only one for men in Georgia" (Seibert 2011). This official marker is one of a few that attests to a university's doggedness to remain open during a significant, socially and politically reforming event in US history.

REFERENCES

Boykin, Samuel. 1881 *History of the Baptist Denomination in Georgia.* Atlanta: Jas P. Harrison.

Bryant, James C. 2005. "From Penfield to Macon: Mercer University's Problematic Move." *Georgia Historical Quarterly* 89 (3): 462–84.

Burch, Jarrett. 2003. "Religious Pioneer of Nineteenth-Century Georgia." *The Georgia Historical Quarterly* 87 (1): 22–47.

Campbell, J. H. 1874. *Georgia Baptists: Historical and Biographical.* Macon, GA: J. W. Burke & Co.

Crawford, N. M. 1861. "Sketch of a Mercer Graduate." *The Christian Index* 40.

Dooley, Vince. 2011. *History and Reminiscences of the University of Georgia.* Chicago: Looking Glass Books, Inc.

Dowell, Spright. *A History of Mercer University 1833–1953.* Atlanta: Foote and Davies, 1958.

DuBose III, Beverly M. 2018. "The Manufacture of Confederate Ordnance in Georgia." *American Society of Arms Collectors Bulletin* 15: 10–15.

Geiger, Roger L. 2015. *The History of American Higher Education: Learning and Culture from the Founding to World War II.* Princeton, NJ: Princeton University Press.

Georgia Baptist Convention. *Georgia Baptist Convention Minutes.* 1822–1866. (Minutes of the Forty-Second Anniversary of the Georgia Baptist State Convention Held in Atlanta. April 22–25, 1864. Macon, GA: Burke, Boykin & Company.

Georgia Baptist Convention. *Minutes of the Fortieth Anniversary of the Baptist Convention of the State of Georgia, Held at the Baptist Church in LaGrange, the 25th, 26th & 28th of April, 1862.* Macon, GA: Jos. Jenkins & Co.

Georgia Baptist Convention. *Minutes of the Forty-first Anniversary of the Georgia Baptist State Convention, Held at Griffin, the 24th, 25th and 27th of April, 1863.* Macon, GA: Jos. Jenkins & Co.

Georgia Baptist Convention. *Minutes of the Thirty-Ninth Anniversary of the Baptist Convention of the State of Georgia, Held at the Baptist Church in Athens, the 26th, 27th and 29th of April, 1861.* Macon, GA: Telegraph Steam Printing House.

Gourley, Bruce. 2008. "Baptists in Middle Georgia During the Civil War," *Dissertation at Auburn University.*

McMillen, Neil R. 1997. *Remaking Dixie: The Impact of World War II on the American South.* Jackson: University Press of Mississippi.

Mercer Catalog. 1860. Catalog of the Officers and Students at Mercer University: 1859–1860. Penfield, GA.

Mercer Catalog. 1861. Catalog of the Officers and Students at Mercer University: 1859–1860. Penfield, GA.

Mercer Catalog. 1869. Catalog of the Officers and Students at Mercer University: 1859–1860. Penfield, GA.

"Mercer Triumphant." 1861. *Christian Index.* January 30, 1861.

Mercer University. 2009. "Charting Mercer's Future: Aspirations for the Decades Ahead." *The Mercerian*. Last modified January 29, 2009. https://issuu.com/mercerian/docs/mercerian_fall08_smpl/29

"Military Training at Mercer." 1861. *Christian Index*. August 28, 1861, n.p.

Mondy, Robert. 1956. "Jesse Mercer and the Baptist College Movement." *The Georgia Historical Quarterly* 40 (4):349–59.

Ragsdale, B. D. 1932. *Story of Georgia Baptists, Volume 1: Mercer University Penfield Period and Related Interests*. Atlanta: Foote and Davies.

Rice, T. Brockett and Williams C. White. 1979. *History of Greene County, Georgia, 1786–1886*. Spartanburg, SC: The Reprint Co.

Roberts, D. 1965. "The University of Georgia and Georgia's Civil War G. I. Bill," *The Georgia Historical Quarterly* 49 (4), 418–23.

Seibert, David. 2011. "Mercer University." The Historical Marker Database. https://www.hmdb.org/m.asp?m=44946.

Sheldon Sanford Papers 1816–1896. Special Collections (Baptist & University Archives), Mercer University, Macon, GA.

Sherwood, Adiel. 1860. *A Gazetteer of Georgia: Containing a Particular Description of the State, its Resources, Counties, Towns, Villages, and Whatever is Usual in Statistical Works*. 4th ed. Macon, GA: Brawner & Putnam.

"Some of Mercer's Benefactors." *Bulletin of the Mercer University, Macon, Georgia*. 7 (4): 42–44.

CHAPTER SEVEN

"So Firm a Hold"

Civil War Resiliency at Wesleyan Female College

Lauren Yarnell Bradshaw and Marcia Bennett

Located in Macon, Georgia, Wesleyan Female College has remained open since its inception in 1836 (Farnham 1994). Originally known as Georgia Female College, the institution's name was changed to Wesleyan Female College in 1843 in honor of John Wesley, after the Methodist Church took direct responsibility for the college (Huff 2006). To better examine the curriculum, people, and events that shaped history of Wesleyan Female College during the Civil War, this chapter is organized thematically rather than chronologically. Focusing on how exceptional leadership, the tenacity of its pupils, and a willingness to question gender norms enabled Wesleyan College to remain open through gross financial difficulties, violent battles in Georgia, and deadly plagues. Taking "so firm a hold" to ensure the college's survival, students and administrators alike fought to preserve the system of Southern education and values promoted at Wesleyan (Trustee Minutes 1865, 167).

GEORGIA FEMALE COLLEGE AND ANTEBELLUM WESLEYAN FEMALE COLLEGE

Wesleyan Female College is heralded as the oldest chartered degree-granting institution of higher education for women in the United States (Jones 1888). Macon residents initially became interested in establishing an institution of higher education for women in the mid-1820s, but support waned after a legislative bid to support the academy's founding failed. David Chandler, in his 1834 commencement address to the graduating class of the University of Georgia, passionately spoke of the need for women to receive higher education in the state of Georgia (Griffin 1996). The next year, several Macon businessmen met and devised a plan to found a college for women. Nine thousand dollars was secured for the college's construction (Huff 2006). College organizers appealed to the Georgia Conference of the Methodist Church, asking for the conference to supervise the new women's academy (Griffin 1996). Conference delegates agreed and a decision was made to create a governing board that would comprise "twenty trustees divided between the Conference and local citizens" (Griffin 1996, 59). On December 23, 1836, the state legislature granted a charter for Georgia Female College (Jones 1888).

On January 7, 1839, the doors of the Georgia Female College opened to ninety students. Courses were rooted in both the liberal arts and sciences. While enrolled in the college's four-year program, students were mandated to take courses in arithmetic, grammar, French, modern geography, ancient geography, composition, algebra, "geography of the heavens," "universal history," geometry, logic, chemistry, botany, trigonometry, natural philosophy, "mental and moral philosophy," astronomy, and "evidences of Christianity" (Catalog 1839–1840, 12). While curricula were set by members of the Board of Trustees, several students elected to take supplementary art courses for an additional fee. The college's administration waived residency requirements for students whose families resided in surrounding Macon so long as they could supply adequate documentation of their qualifications to enroll (Catalog 1839–1840).

In 1839, due to the limited opportunities available for women's higher education, the minimum age for admittance was reduced to twelve years of age. Before turning twelve, girls could attend the primary academy also housed at the college's campus. By 1839, fifty-three students were enrolled in the preparatory school, and the teaching staff consisted of five male professors who taught courses related to logic, astronomy, mathematics, natural science, music, modern and ancient languages, belles lettres, mental science, and "evidences of Christianity." In addition to one female music assistant, two female superintendents of drawing and painting and domestic economy also served on the faculty. By January of 1840, student enrollment had risen to 115 (Catalog 1839–1840). Further bolstering enrollment, the president of the Clinton Female Institute in Jones County, Georgia, accepted a teaching position at Georgia Female College and brought many of his students with him. By the end of the 1840 academic year, Catherine Elizabeth Brewer became the first of eleven women to graduate from the Macon-based institution (Blandin, 1909; Wesleyan College 2019).

At the end of the first academic year, the college's first president, George Foster Pierce, a native Georgian, delivered a rallying address, stating:

> Hail ye daughters of the South! I proclaim to-day the restoration of your birth-right; I commit to the flames the warrant of your exile. To your legitimate possession in the name of the State, and the Church, I give you your title and a welcome. Hail Georgia! Beacon star in the night of years, we greet thy beams with rapture and hail the sign of promise as did the Roman mother the lambent fire that played round young Tarquin's cradle. The first to rise on Woman's destine, shine on undimmed and bright, nor set till earth is childless and time's no more! (Pierce 1839, 19)

Pierce's fervor for women's higher education, as well as his support for the state of Georgia, were apparent in his speech. Yet, while Pierce maintained a strong commitment to the new women's academy, the college was facing a dire financial situation. In 1843, it was reported that the college had accrued over $10,000 in debt to the original building contractor. If this debt was not paid in a timely manner, the college would be forced to close. Local citizens, however, rallied together and paid the outstanding debt then "tendered the college building to the trustees for what it had cost them" (Jones 1888, 98). Thereafter, a new organization charter was granted in December of 1843 and the institution's title was changed to Wesleyan Female College (Jones 1888).

With secured finances and a new college name, academic pursuits increased at the rebranded academy. Likewise, social activity increased. In 1851, six students formed the Adelphean Society, a precursor to the Alpha Delta Pi sorority (Huff 2006). The Philomathean Society (later renamed Phi Mu) formed the following year. The two social organizations remained on campus until sororities were banned in 1914. The college's Board of Trustees banned the organizations due to a perception that they negatively influenced academics. In addition to early sororities, Wesleyan Female College graduates formed an alumnae association in the summer of 1859; the following year the first annual alumnae meeting was held during commencement week (Wesleyan College 2019).

STUDENT LIFE AT WESLEYAN, 1860-1866

Twenty-one years after the institution's opening, the campus of Wesleyan Female College had expanded and consisted of three buildings: the main college building, the chapel, and a dining saloon. The main college building provided accommodations for 112 pupils, the college's president, 3 professors, and a steward. Additionally, the facility housed music rooms, parlors, society rooms, and a library. The chapel was also multipurpose. In addition to serving as a religious locale, it contained a laboratory, recitation rooms, and study rooms for the college and preparatory departments (Catalog 1860–1861).

The 1860 academic year boasted a thriving campus, with students heralding from cities across the southeastern United States. Of the 215 students enrolled in 1860, 17 percent originated from Florida, Alabama, Mississippi, Louisiana, and South Carolina, while the remainder were from Georgia (Catalog 1860–1861). Enrolled students adhered to strict rules regarding social interactions, clothing, and spiritual practice. Pupils who lodged at the college stayed in "large and airy" rooms that housed four young women apiece. Students were restricted from bringing "heavy articles of furniture" but were expected to "furnish their own bed-clothing, towels, mirrors, pitchers, bowls, & etc." (Catalog 1860–1861, 31). The college's leadership took care to adhere to temporal standards of morality and modesty expected of young women during the nineteenth century. Such a lifestyle followed a "simple" and "clean" existence free from extravagance and materialistic distraction. Indeed, pupils were forbidden from opening "any accounts at stores." Additionally, visitors were restricted without the direct approval of parents or guardians as well as faculty supervisors. Students living off campus also complied with strict conduct regulations and were not "permitted to visit or receive visitors on the Sabbath" or within "the hours of study or recitation during the week" (Catalog 1860–1861, 34). All parents and guardians were requested to "withhold from their daughters and wards the means of expensive dress" and to refrain from sending "boxes of cake, meats, or confections" from home (Catalog 1860–1861, 31 and 35). Religious education was central to campus life. Students traveled to the nearby Macon, Georgia every Sunday to attend church. However, if the weather was not conducive to travel, religious services were held in the college chapel. All students attended weekly prayer meetings. Additional, optional meetings were held on Saturdays for supplemental religious counsel (Catalog 1860–1861). The faculty's insistence that students

"Old Wesleyan," c. 1870. Image courtesy of the Georgia Archives, Vanishing Georgia Collection, bib092, Morrow, Georgia.

adhered to moral and religious observations served as a defense against the opponents of higher education for women during peace as well as war times—chiefly, the period belief that secular education did more harm than good. Therefore, religion was seminal at several Southern women's colleges (Burnap 1848).

In addition to preparing women for the social mores of the regional Southern elite, Wesleyan Female College's faculty and administration cultivated a rigorous academic structure for all students. One aspect of this intense scholastic drive was the literary societies that formed early in the institution's history: the Adelphaean and Philomathean Societies. Each organization was assigned rooms within the main college building. Such communal proximity, it was believed, helped foster the social, economic, and political alliances needed for young women to enter society. These student organizations not only provided opportunities for networking between students and campus leaders, they afforded a space for students to express their support for the Confederate cause before and during the American Civil War. In July of 1861, students, eager to showcase their Confederate zeal, performed several compositions. One of which was titled "To Our Gallant Southern Soldiers." Not only did these organizations foster pro-Confederate orations, they served as a nexus for student-led fundraisers to support the Soldiers' Aid Society of Macon (Catalog 1860–1861, 59).

With war looming on the horizon, college and regional social life changed dramatically. After Georgia's formal secession from the United States in January of 1861, state leaders set about rewriting Georgia's constitution to better align with the Confederacy's edicts of state's rights and Southern slavery. Most college students in the state of Georgia were men who abandoned their studies to join the Confederate army. Businesses throughout the South supplied the new Confederate army with young men eager to fight in defense of the South. The city of Macon was demarcated and served as both armory and depository for Confederate gold. The war took its toll, however, and by the time Union general William Tecumseh Sherman began his destructive "March to the Sea" (November 1864), regional support for, and financial means to, send young female scholars to institutions of higher learning had decreased dramatically (Cohen 2012; Davis 2007).

When the Battle of Atlanta occurred in July of 1864, Macon denizens were watchful for potential Union invaders. Union Maj. Gen. George Stoneman hoped to liberate Union prisoners held in the Confederate prison camp at Andersonville but found his offense blocked by troops who had been notified of his advance. While no significant damage befell Macon, the city's residents felt the proximity of war more than ever before ("Stoneman's Raid" 1864). Traveling became far less common and families found the financial strain of sending their daughters to college too difficult to bear. By the start of the 1865–1866 academic year, much had changed for the students and faculty at Wesleyan Female College. As war neared the college and resources decreased, enrollment dropped to 111, with only 10 percent claiming residency external to Georgia.

Even the rules and expectations for Wesleyan Female College students changed to reflect the tone of a nation on the brink of failure. In 1865, students found many more rules in place than in previous years. In fact, while previous college catalogs provided vague guidelines regarding pupil behavior, the 1865–1866 academic catalog listed twenty-eight specific regulations to govern student behavior. New rules pertaining to student travel (both off campus and inside the main college building's residential quarters) now dominated the catalog. During the war, day scholars were prohibited from visiting the on-campus student residences. Additionally, day scholars could not travel into town during academic hours without the permission of the college president. All students were prohibited from taking lessons from instructors not employed by the college. Boarding students also found their movements restricted. Specific rules regulated when and where boarding students could wash laundry and what items could be removed from the dining room. Wasting food, academic supplies, or clothing was strictly forbidden. Infractions were met with demerits to discourage future rule-breaking (Catalog 1865–1866).

Federal occupation of Macon began in 1865 and continued throughout the 1865–1866 academic year. In light of Union military presence, the college's faculty and president needed to maintain a level of control over student behavior to protect both the students' virtue and the reputation of the institution. There was a particular interest in controlling when and where students could study, walk, and socialize. One particular rule was printed as follows: "No boarder was to come to the front door or enter either parlor until sent for by the president" (Catalog 1865–1866, 28).

Other regulations stressed frugality, as money was in very short supply by the conclusion of the war. With enrollment dwindling, faculty and students had to work together to ensure the college's survival. Commencement ceremonies for the 1865–1866 academic year reflected tougher times during Federal occupation. In 1860 students performed "Dixieland" and compositions pertaining to Socrates, Cleopatra, and Southern literature. Now, in 1866 any pro-Confederate performances had been replaced with "Farewell to Joy" and compositions such as "Posthumous Fame," "Retrospection," and "Power of Tears." After the war a melancholy but resilient student body continued its studies, unable to boast of the desired Confederate victory. Even with lowered enrollments and desperate to garner additional financial resources, Wesleyan Female College had endured (Catalog 1865–1866, 27–29).

COURSEWORK BEFORE AND DURING THE WAR

In 1860, the five-year course of study at Wesleyan Female College terminated in students receiving a "literary degree." Before students were admitted to the academy, applicants had to pass "strict examinations" that included English orthography, modern geography, and "The Five Fundamental Rules of Arithmetic and English Grammar" and to "be able to read without hesitation and write a legible hand" (Catalog 1860–1861, 26). If a student lacked proficiency in these areas, she was admitted into the college's preparatory department, where she studied "reading, spelling, writing, scripture questions, geography, grammar, arithmetic, composition exercises, and vocal music" until all admittance exams were passed. The college also hosted two classes of "irregular students," one composed of students who transferred from other female colleges and needed additional academic credits before they could enter the regular course of study. The second group of irregular students consisted of "grown young ladies who desire to spend a year or two in some good institution before quitting school" (Catalog 1860–1861, 28). The college's administration took "great care in reference to what [Southern] society expects of educated women at the present day," and institutional practices were "the result of years of experience and of the consultation with liberal minded men" (Catalog 1860–1861, 28). As historian Barbara White elucidates, the moral philosophy known as the "Cult of Domesticity" or "True Womanhood" prescribed that women should remain pure, submissive, domestic, and virtuous in their role as mothers, confined to a sphere of homemaking and childrearing (White 2003; Bernath 2010). Similarly, Wesleyan Female College instructors strove to provide young women with a socially justifiable liberal arts education that would reinforce the maintenance of both feminine and academic virtues.

Once admitted to the college, students followed an intense program of study that intensified each academic year. "First Class" (freshman) students began with courses in orthography, geography, arithmetic, English grammar, and biblical studies. The "Second Class" (sophomore) students took courses in algebra, rhetoric, Latin geometry, chemistry, and biblical history. Junior students undertook courses in trigonometry, botany, "natural and mental philosophies," further biblical studies, and French (as well as Latin). Finally, senior coursework included eight subject areas: astronomy, Latin, French, physiology, geology, logic, moral philosophy, and "evidences of Christianity." In addition, students in all grades were expected to engage in "reading penmanship, singing, and composition" throughout their academic career (Catalog 1860–1861, 26–27).

The curricula at Wesleyan Female College reflected coursework employed at similar Southern female institutions. In addition to traditional liberal arts instruction, pupils could participate in optional "ornamental arts" courses for additional fees. Ornamental arts included instrumental music, drawing, watercolor painting, oil painting, embroidery, and a language other than the required Latin or French. Participation in these elective courses was costly; the cost to partake in instrumental music instruction was equal to one year's tuition (Catalog 1860–1861). As the war progressed, interest in ornamental arts courses significantly decreased as students could barely cover the cost of regular tuition.

An examination of approved textbooks used at Wesleyan Female College allows historians an opportunity to explore the social, political, and moral ideals imposed upon students. As Joseph Moreau explains, textbooks reflect the identity of a school, college, or university (2011). The moral education promulgated at the Macon-based female academy was as much a reflection of Southern ideals regarding slavery as it was a means for social control (Hunter, 2000). Wesleyan's texts and curricula evolved during the war years to reflect the change in government—United States to Confederate states. In 1860, the college's leaders ensured that each student experienced a rich liberal arts higher education: math, sciences, logic, languages, and a Southern-friendly version of Christian morality. Senior students read Richard Henderson Rivers' *Elements of a Moral Philosophy* (first published in 1859), which depicted slavery as "established by Divine legislation." Rivers expands upon the biblical justification of chattel servitude, stating: "God commanded" that the "heathen" be "perpetual slaves" as the "descendants of Ham" (the biblical son of Noah from the Book of Genesis). Per Rivers, "these people were to be owned . . . they were chattels personal" and "to be inherited by the posterity of their masters." Rivers continues for fifty pages, proclaiming that the "highest commendation is bestowed upon slave holders" and the approval of "fugitive slaves being sent back to their owners" was outlined in scripture. Furthermore, the proslavery religious author stated that "slaves are exhorted to obedience—hearty, cheerful obedience to their masters" and "Masters are exhorted to be just to their slaves." This did not match "the philosophy of the modern abolitionists," who Rivers declared to be morally at fault, for if "slavery were a sin, God established it" (334–37 and 344).

While the promotion of proslavery morality continued at Wesleyan Female College, the ongoing war caused faculty to reduce course offerings and increase tuition. The requisite course in French became optional, and textbooks for other courses were replaced (Catalog 1865). The academy's faculty and administration found themselves in a period of financial and ideological transition throughout the war. As the college strained to remain operational, its instructional ethos altered from one of restrained sophistication to resilient doggedness. Rivers's *Elements of a Moral Philosophy*, with its rationalization of slavery through Christianity, did not suit the ideals of post-Civil War Reconstructionist government. As such, this text was replaced with untitled "Lectures" according to the college catalog for the academic year of 1865–1866. It is unknown whether these unpublished lectures included the similar proslavery attitudes.

Despite these curricular changes, the City of Macon and Wesleyan Female College fared better than most of Georgia during the Civil War. The college did close for two weeks in November of 1864, due to fears that Union forces would raid and burn Macon like other Georgian cities. Luckily, Sherman marched his troops through Milledgeville, thirty miles northeast of Macon, and the small metropolis was spared. After these two weeks of closure, the college reopened and students reenrolled. Thereafter, the college's leaders maintained continuous institutional operation (Akers 1976; Iobst 2009).

Less than three months after the conclusion of the war, in July of 1865, citizens of Union-occupied Macon rallied for the traditional, weeklong commencement exercises that culminated the pedagogical experiences of Wesleyan Female College students. Less traditional, however, was Mary Clare De Graffenreid's valedictorian address. De Graffenreid put aside her faculty-approved composition and delivered a passionate address that defended the Confederacy and condemned Union troops residing in Macon. Regional lore has it that Union general James H. Wilson heard De Graffenreid's speech. Angered, he threatened to close the college and sought to punish De Graffenreid. Eventually, the college's faculty and staff convinced Wilson that De Graffenreid was simply a spirited teenager and not a member of a larger network of Southern conspirators bent on upholding the failed Confederate States of America (De Graffenreid 2010). Motivated by Confederate pride, De Graffenreid acted in a manner directly at odds with the submissive image of antebellum womanhood. She used her platform as valedictorian to uphold the Confederacy and protest Union occupation. De Graffenreid, like her peer students, felt every change made to the college's regulations and curricular structure due to the war. Angered by the presence of so many Union solders, De Graffenreid refused to admit defeat and promoted a government that supported the South's antebellum economic and administrative structure.

WESLEYAN'S CIVIL WAR LEADERSHIP

In addition to the typical challenges of Civil War-era female higher education, students and faculty at Wesleyan Female College had to accommodate the challenges facing a proto-nation fighting for independence. Prior to the war, Southern secondary schools and institutions of higher education struggled to survive. Changes in leadership, regional politics, shifts in population, and low enrollments often resulted in antebellum institutional closures (Farnham 1994). Surviving prewar turmoils, the Macon-based college's faculty fought to ensure that wartime instruction would persist.

Wesleyan Female College, with its supportive female students, was a source of pride for regional supporters of the Confederacy. Reverend Osborne L. Smith, a former president of the academy and Civil War-era college trustee, offered a prayer in support of the Macon-based college at a meeting of the General Assembly in Milledgeville in November of 1861 ("General Assembly" 1861). Two years later, Confederate president Jefferson Davis visited the Georgia campus. LeRoy Gresham, whose sister Minnie attended Wesleyan Female College, wrote about his journey to see Davis at the college. Gresham suffered from a leg injury and tuberculosis, which rendered him unable to walk without assistance. Family-owned slaves pushed him in a wagon to hear Davis's war-related speech. Davis punctuated his speech by explaining that "the cause still demanded the utmost energies of the people" ("In Reception of the President" 1863). At the end of Davis's speech, Gresham recalled "All the college gals went down & shook hands with him [Davis]: Minnie among others" (Gresham 2018, 263–64). Supported by the administration and faculty, enthusiasm and sacrifice for the Confederate cause propelled Wesleyan Female College through the Civil War years.

REVEREND JOHN MITCHELL BONNELL

Reverend John Mitchell Bonnell, president of Wesleyan Female College from 1859 to 1879, was a fierce defender of the college; he fought for student and faculty well-being and maintained campus facilitates while battles raged in nearby communities. Bonnell not only administered the college and taught classes but also served as president on the academy's board of instructors (Catalog 1860). In this latter capacity, Bonnell served as an envoy between the faculty and the institution's governing board—a line of communication crucial at the best of times, and critical in times of war.

Born in Pennsylvania, Bonnell graduated from Jefferson College in Canonsburg, Pennsylvania, in 1838. Two years later, he accepted a position as a Methodist circuit preacher in north Georgia. He was later employed as a professor of Greek at Emory College in Oxford, Georgia, before serving at Wesleyan Female College. For a brief period, he served as the president of Tuscaloosa College in Alabama, but later returned to the Macon female academy as the college's president in 1859 (Ohles 1978). Bonnell, now thirty-nine, accepted this new position on the cusp of the Civil War. As a faculty member, Bonnell lived with his wife Mary, a native of Oxford, Georgia, and their three children in the main college building, along with the boarding pupils. While not a Southern native, Bonnell quickly adapted to the realities of Southern slavery. In 1848, he testified in support of an enslaved man by the name of "William." In the Wilkes County, Georgia court case Bonnell supported William's preaching "to people of his own color." Bonnell approved of William's "moral character and religious standing" and saw no reason he should not be ordained to preach God's love to other slaves. At the same time, the college president found no issue with William being considered property of Gabriel Toombs according to Georgia law ("Petition of Bonnell" 1848). Indeed, Bonnell himself owned at least one slave while teaching at Emory University, and frequently rented slaves owned by regional slaveholders during his tenure at Wesleyan Female College (US Census 1850; "To Hire" 1861).

Not long after Bonnell assumed the college's presidency, Georgia seceded from the Union. On the night of January 21, 1861, news of secession reached Macon on a wave of enthusiasm for the Confederate cause ("The City One Sea of Light" 1861). Bonnell, perhaps motivated to support his newly adopted state, suspended the rule that forbade students from keeping a candle lit after dark, so that his female wards could participate in the Confederacy's Illumination Night. This event marked the beginning of the war for Macon. One student, Lou Burge, recorded an incident in her diary illustrating why the rule was necessary: "the Adelphean candles burnt the windows and greatly injured their new carpet; whereas the P's [Philomatheans] were glad and the A's [Adelpheans] very angry" (Harwell 1952, 152). In addition to enforcing or relaxing institutional rules, it was Bonnell's job to bridge the gap between faculty and the college's trustees regarding both financial and scholastic matters, a position he used to advocate for the college throughout the war.

In June of 1863, Bonnell asked members of the Board of Trustees to reestablish history courses (one of the courses suspended to decrease costs). The college president hoped that, with the reinstatement of said classes, pupils would become more "historically" informed. He asserted, "our pupils rise to the grade of seniors with minds strong but empty. They can neither write nor converse as educated young ladies for the reason that they do not know what has been going on in the world" (Trustee Minutes 1863, 111). Wesleyan Female College catalogs reveal that the trustees must have agreed. Prior to the 1863–1864 academic year, history courses were not featured in the academy's curriculum, but reappeared in the curriculum by the conclusion of the war.

Emboldened by his success in revising the course of study, Bonnell asked for an even larger accommodation: a college endowment to mitigate the institution's growing financial troubles. Bonnell maintained that the college needed permanent funding to properly maintain the physical plant and insisted that the Board of Trustees find the needed funds despite Georgia's tumultuous political, wartime climate. Understanding that his request came at a difficult time, he concluded his request with "let my love of the institution be my apology" (Trustee Minutes 1863, 114). Bonnell proved once again persuasive, and the board found a donor willing to contribute $500 for an endowment. Unfortunately, the donation was made using Confederate money. After the war, these funds were rendered useless (Trustee Minutes 1863). Bonnell and the college's faculty not only plied the governing board for continued aid, they supported student efforts to promote the Southern cause.

With the permission of the faculty and administration, Wesleyan Female College students participated in Confederate fundraisers, social events, and morale boosting exercises "for the defense of the young [military] men" ("Headquarters" 1863). In June of 1863, a note appeared in the *Macon Daily Telegraph* playfully instructing all women between the ages of fourteen and twenty-five to engage in military drilling as an outward sign of Southern military support. The letter was signed by "Major General Cupid, Wesleyan Female College Commander" ("Headquarters" 1863). The students wasted no time in complying with the request. Two female military companies were formed on the college grounds: the "Bonnell Blues" (named in honor of college president John Bonnell) and the "Freeman Guards" (titled to acknowledge institutional support provided by the college's steward, Charles Freeman). Both units regularly participated in drilling activities and joined local Confederate troops in an "act of cooperation" (Banks 1969, 37). Though the female student drilling remained a visually supportive performance only, it stood in contrast to the stark realities faced by other students—men and women alike—throughout the South. Bonnell's son Willie, then thirteen years old, served as the captain of the Bonnell Blues and studied military drills for the young women to perform. Wearing uniforms of homespun dresses, blue or green sashes, paper hats, and armed with wooden rifles, both makeshift companies marched with ranks of officers and enlisted, and even included a young drummer boy (Banks 1969).

Sallie Love, a member of the Bonnell Blues, remembered one particular dress parade, when the female corps drilled before and after a local speech was given on the Siege of Vicksburg. Love stated, "I clutched my helpless wooden gun as I listened! While I somehow seem to have sensed at that time the ridiculous side of it all, still it was all so solemn an occasion that any smile was kept within" (Banks 1969, 39). The marching pupils were then treated to a feast of strawberries, and the event was remembered as "the Strawberry Festival" (39). While having young women dress as soldiers and march with mock weapons broke from traditional gender norms, the students of Wesleyan Female College were rather removed from severe war pangs. It is possible that Bonnell or another member of the faculty invented "Major General Cupid" to provide students with a means to show their support for the Confederate army. Alternatively, the activity could have served as a means to provide students with enjoyable exercise to prevent physical illness. Bonnell, a member of the publishing committee for the *Educational Repository and Family Monthly*, was quite progressive as concerned his views on women's physical education. Bonnell noted in an 1860 publication that "in connection with obedience to other laws of health . . . one generation" might "transform the inhabitants of this land from . . . low development" to "the highest form of humanity." In a postwar letter to the college's governing board, Bonnell pushed for increased physical education, stating that a "gymnasium should be fitted up, in which the young ladies shall be required, at proper times, to take exercise" (91).

FACULTY LEADERSHIP

Bonnell was not the only faculty member to assert leadership skills at the college during this time. Academic catalogs from 1860–1865 reveal that women held diverse positions at the institution, though the turnover rate was exceptionally high. While four male professors held their positions for the duration of the war, women usually taught or worked for only one or two years. Reasons for woman instructor turnover were not uncovered in archival sources, but it is possible that women faculty were easier to terminate than male professors at that time. Additionally, with male family members away at war, many women may have voluntarily left to help maintain homes and family businesses or even to marry Confederate soldiers before they departed for battle. However, one female professor challenged this pattern, becoming an administrator for the college. An 1858 graduate of Wesleyan Female College, Alice Culler ended her commencement speech by urging members of the Board of Trustees and Macon residents to support the college, charging audience members to "contribute . . . money and prayers" for the academy to "increase its facilities," "enlarge its influence," "and elevate its character" (Richey 2000, 285). Culler's passion for the academy did not wane during the war. She was both married and widowed in 1862 and soon after joined the literary faculty of Macon female college to help shape young women for "a brilliant career and a high destiny" (Richey 2000, 285). Culler accomplished a feat no other woman hired that year matched: she remained in her position for the duration of the war. Culler married Confederate Maj. John B. Cobb, a prominent Macon citizen, and had two children while maintaining her teaching duties at the college. After Cobb's death, she and her children moved into the main college building. In time, Culler eventually became dean of literature (McClary 1973).

While instructors and faculty lived on campus with students, salaries remained a vital component of their employment. In October of 1861, "in consideration of pressure of the times," professor Christian Schwartz voluntarily took a ten dollar cut in pay (Faculty Meeting Notes 1861, 9). Like most faculty, Schwartz lived and ate meals on campus. This makes it difficult to gauge the significance of this monetary sacrifice. However, according to the 1860 US Census, the value of Schwartz's estate was estimated at $300, while the estates of Professors Bass ($4,000), Forster ($1,200), and Smith ($4,500) were estimated at higher values (US Census 1860). While Schwartz was willing to reduce his own salary, it is evident that great economic disparities existed between members of the faculty.

In addition to faculty financial furloughs and administrative support of the Confederacy, some students sought opportunities to demonstrate their

Confederate zeal. Enthusiastic Southern patriots, they thrust themselves into a myriad of activities in support of the war effort. In May of 1861, a chapter of the Soldier's Relief Society was formed at Wesleyan Female College. The organization focused on raising additional funds for military needs. Newspaper reports indicate that members of the college-based relief society raised modest amounts throughout the war. In a similar show of Southern support, students performed the opera, *The Flower*, as part of the 1861 commencement ceremony and raised sixty dollars ("Ladies Relief Society" 1861). In addition, students raised money for the Wayside Home of Macon throughout the war ("Receipts of the Wayside Home from Dec 11th, '63, to Jan. 19th '64" 1864). Wayside homes were established in various Southern communities "for feeding and sometimes housing transient soldiers" (Betts 2016, 1).

Diminished funds, shifting access to faculty, and the ever-present threat of invading Union troops affected Civil War-era student life at Wesleyan Female College. Administrative and faculty leadership strove to maintain the college and inspired students to take an active role in the newly formed Confederate government. Campus facilities were maintained largely through the use of slave labor, attempts were made to adjust curricula and establish a lasting endowment, and students were promoted as an important part of the war effort—not pupils hidden away in a remote academy. These efforts created an ethos that would propel both students and faculty forward when attempts were made to close the institution towards the end of the war. The ardent desire to support Wesleyan Female College resulted in unified attempts to bolster the institution's survival. In time, the college's wards and instructors even pushed against the regional Confederate government to promote and protect their academy.

WESLEYAN SURVIVES THE WAR

Wesleyan Female College's Civil War persistence was not unique, considering other Southern colleges and universities that remained open, but it was a rarity in Georgia. The University of Georgia in Athens, the Medical College of Georgia in Augusta, Emory College in Oxford, and Oglethorpe College in Midway all closed during the war, while Mercer University in Penfield remained open and Wesleyan Female College not only remained open but also awarded degrees throughout the war (Mercer University 2018). Faculty and students strove to keep the college afloat, sometimes even challenging the Confederate government in the name of health, family, and education.

President Bonnell believed that a healthy student body was paramount to the success of a college, and the faculty of Wesleyan Female College promoted student health during the war by means of physical activity and protecting students from various diseases that ravaged the South. An estimated fifty thousand civilians died during the war—infections were reported as one of the leading causes (Faust 2008). The war caused food shortages and limited access to doctors and medicine, which only increased the number of deaths among Confederate soldiers and civilians alike. Wesleyan Female College acted as a refuge for many pupils throughout the war. While the college shielded the students some of the harsh realities of war, death still affected many within the academic community, including students Louisiana "Lou" Burge and Kittie Tooke. Tooke died in 1861, inspiring fellow Adelphean members to wear a badge of mourning for thirty days in her honor. Burge died two years later in 1863 after contracting both measles and whooping cough (Lunt and Robertson 1962; "Resolutions" 1861). Bonnell, responsible for the spiritual and emotional health of his wards, worked to ensure that students engaged in a grieving process consistent with mid-nineteenth-century social norms. Bonnell was no stranger to grief, having lost two daughters—Clara in 1861 and Loulie in 1863 ("Funeral Notice" 1861; Funeral Invitation" 1863). While no documentation exists to identify the cause of death, the loss of his daughters dealt Bonnell a devastating personal blow. The president continued to mourn even when his son decided to enlist in the Confederate army near the war's conclusion (Bonnell 1919).

Despite personal losses, Bonnell worked to ensure that his students remained safe from physical illness. In December of 1862, there was an outbreak of smallpox linked to regional rail transportation. As a result, the faculty decided to keep students at the college over Christmas break. The college's administration went so far as to warn parents that if they demanded their daughters to travel home via train, they would not be welcomed back to the campus for fear of a similar outbreak among the enrolled population ("Wesleyan Female College" 1862). While this decision was necessary for student health, the warning to parents was a gamble, as it had the potential to decrease enrollment. Even so, the college was deemed "flourishing" and healthy in 1861 (Catalog 1860–1861; "Georgia Annual Conference" 1861). Still, there were many concerns amongst the faculty and administration regarding building maintenance. Indeed, materials for general repairs as well as manual labor was difficult to acquire during the war. In 1861, Bonnell advertised in a local newspaper, hoping "to hire, two men and a negro girl" to assist with the day-to-day maintenance of the college, but even the use of slave labor was not enough to stem the flood of necessary repairs ("To Hire" 1861). This led to tragedy in 1863. That year, a young boy identified simply as "Mason" was killed when a portion of the large wall surrounding campus collapsed due to heavy rains ("Sad Accident" 1863). Due to the lack of Civil War-era funds, this incident illustrates the difficulty of campus upkeep and general safety during this tumultuous period of US history.

To enhance Wesleyan Female College's financial security, the institution's leaders permitted refugees displaced by the war to reside on campus (Akers 1976). Families displaced from their homes found safety behind the academy's walls, including the families of returning soldiers. When Confederate officers tried to take control of the college in the latter half of the war, these families supported Bonnell as he attempted to discourage military occupation (Bonnell 1864). In 1864, the medical director for the Confederate army at Macon, Dr. James Mercer Green, requested that the campus be converted into an army hospital (Bonnell 1864). Green cited the "breakup" of hospitals in Rome and Marietta, Georgia as well as the number of sick and wounded soldiers in Macon. The Confederate army had already laid claim to several Macon buildings for use as hospitals, including the city hall. In September of 1863, the Blind Academy relocated twelve students to convert the institution into a hospital at Green's request (Iobst 2009). Other colleges across the Confederate South had similarly become hospitals. Both Washington College in Virginia as well as South Carolina College were closed and became military hospitals. Other college campuses were commandeered by both Confederate and Union forces for a variety of purposes: military hospitals, barracks, stables, etc. Indeed, the University of Missouri was occupied by Union soldiers for significant portion of the war (Cohen 2012).

Wesleyan Female College's Board of Trustees was right to be concerned about military seizure. The institution nearly folded during a financial crisis a few years after its inception. Board members feared that closing the college's doors so that the facility could be repurposed as a hospital would most certainly create a situation from which the academy would never recover (Griffin 1966). If the college was converted for military use, faculty and staff would have to vacate their residences in the main college building, boarding students would be sent home, and campus refugees would be expelled. In a draft letter intended for the Confederate secretary of war James Alexander Seddon, Bonnell requested that military powers forgo commendation. While affirming his concern for sick and wounded Confederate soldiers, Bonnell argued that there were several reasons to spare the college. Between the boarding of war refugees, the instruction of students, and the employment of several Macon denizens, "we [Bonnell and the college faculty] think the benefits conferred by such an institution are too valuable to warrant its interruption" (Bonnell 1864, 2–3). Additionally, Bonnell and members of the Board of Trustees "believe[d] that the sick and wounded soldiers could be better provided for elsewhere, and there is no necessity for taking this [campus] unless such necessity has been created by the neglect of the medical director himself [James Mercer Green] to make adequate provision for the wounded and sick from Gen. Johnson's army" (1864, 4). Additionally, governing board members did not want any of the male faculty to be conscripted into military service

On June 11, 1864, an editorial was published in the *Macon Daily Telegraph* written by "a Trustee." The trustee stated that of the male faculty, only a few were physically able to endure the training regimens for military service ("Shall the Female College Be Taken for a Hospital?" 1864). Taking into consideration that most of the faculty were members of the clergy, the author pointed out that the Confederate army was most likely not in any dire need of more chaplains. The author defended the women's higher education, stating that "the stock of intelligent young people is diminishing at a fearful rate, and every instrumentality for conserving or replenishing the number should be cherished as a source of incalculable good ("Shall the Female College Be Taken for a Hospital?" 1864)." Days later, the *Macon Weekly Telegraph* printed another editorial. The editorial's author argued against converting the college into a Confederate hospital and stressed that civilian displacement "will puzzle the crowded tenants . . . to find a lodgment short of the wilderness, if forcibly dispossessed ("Wesleyan" 1864).

The following day, an article titled "A Voice from the School Girls" appeared in the *Macon Weekly Telegraph*, informing students of the potential campus commendation:

> With feelings of deep regret, I have heard it said that our college would be taken as a hospital. The smile has died from many a lip, and the rose faded from many a cheek, as some eager voice exclaimed, "O, girls, they intend to

> take our college for a hospital!" I have but little hope that my voice will be heard, but I know that it will at least do no harm to beg of the authorities that they will not deprive us of the means of obtaining our education. We are not unpatriotic. This we have proved, for we have parted cheerfully with our fathers, our brothers, and our friends, for the sake of our country. ("A Voice from the School Girls" 1864)

The author signed the article as "A Pupil." However, the diary of LeRoy Gresham reveals that his sister Minnie wrote the letter, which created a "sensation" at the college (Gresham 2018, 311). Minnie Gresham later shared valedictorian honors with her friend and student agitator, Mary Clare De Graffenreid.

Bonnell and the college's trustees took the fight to court and secured an injunction. Prior rulings in the 1864 *Home v. J. M. Green, Surgeon* case and supportive statements made by the obstructionist Judge O. A. Lochrane, created difficulties for the Southern military to seize occupied facilities. If the Confederate army needed another hospital in Macon, they would be responsible for building one (Neely 2015).

Following the war, Wesleyan Female College, like many of its Southern academic counterparts, experienced continued financial and enrollment difficulties throughout Reconstruction. However, the college maintained its focus on women's higher education in the latter half of the nineteenth century. In 1917, the institution's name shortened to Wesleyan College and survives to this day as the oldest chartered degree-granting college for women in the United States (Akers 1976). The Civil War decimated cities, industries, railroads, schools, and colleges throughout the South. Yet with disease and death approaching from all sides, the faculty and staff of Wesleyan Female College fought to prevent students from becoming casualties in a war that touched more civilians than any other in US history. The resiliency students, faculty and administrators, their spirit to overcome, to fight, and ultimately rebel, allowed the college to remain open and contribute to the higher education of Southern women for years to come.

REFERENCES

"A Voice from the School Girls." 1864. *Macon Daily Telegraph*. June 16, 1864.

Akers, Samuel Luttrell. *The first hundred years of Wesleyan College, 1836–1936*. Macon: Wesleyan College, 1976.

Banks, Sallie Love. 1969. *Memories*. Pasadena, CA: Sallie Love Marston.

Bernath, Michael T. 2010. *Confederate Minds: The Struggle for Intellectual Independence in the Civil War South*. Charlottesville: University of North Carolina Press.

Betts, Vicki. 2016. "Southern Wayside Homes, Soldiers' Homes, and Soldiers' Rest." *Special Topics*. Paper 24. Last modified February 10, 2020. https://pdfs.semanticscholar.org/3a8d/3dc9602453d90218a8953bcf8defb1fcea53.pdf.

Blandin, Isabella Margaret. Elizabeth. 1909. *History of Higher Education of Women in the South Prior to 1860*. New York: Neale Pub. Co.

Bonnell, John M. "Impressment Draft Letter." John Mitchell Bonnell Papers, 1848–1864, Stuart A. Rose Manuscript Archives and Rare Book Library, Emory University.

Bonnell, Alice J. 1919. "Confederate Pension Applications, Georgia Confederate Pension Office." RG 58-1-1. 1919. Georgia Archives.

Burnap, George. 1848. *The Spheres and Duties of a Woman a Course of Lectures*. Baltimore, MD: John Murphy Publishing.

Catalogs. Wesleyan Female College, 1860–1865. Special Collections, Wesleyan College.

"The City - One Sea of Light." 1861. *Macon Daily Telegraph*. January 22, 1861.

Cohen, Michael David. 2012. *Reconstructing the Campus: Higher Education and the American Civil War*. Charlottesville: University of Virginia Press.

Daily Constitutionalist. 2012. "Georgia Annual Conference," November 30, 1861.

Davis, Robert Scott. 2007. "A Cotton Kingdom Retooled for War: The Macon Arsenal and the Confederate Ordnance Establishment." *The Georgia Historical Quarterly* 91 (3): 266–91.

De Graffenreid, Thomas Pritchett. 2010. *History of the De Graffenreid Family: From 1191 A. D. to 1925*. Markham, VA: Apple Manor Press.

"Died." *Macon Daily Telegraph*. February 7, 1861.

Faculty Meeting Notes. Wesleyan Female College, 1980–1871. Special Collections, Wesleyan College.

Farnham, Christie Ann. 1994. *The Education of the Southern Belle: Higher Education and Student Socialization in the Antebellum South*. New York: New York University Press.

Faust, Drew Gilpin. 2008. *This Republic of Suffering: Death and the American Civil War*. Waterville, ME: Thorndike Press.

"Funeral Invitation." 1863. *Macon Daily Telegraph*. March 26, 1863.

"Funeral Notice." 1861. *Macon Daily Telegraph*. September 18, 1861.

"Fire." 1863. *Macon Daily Telegraph*. September 16, 1863.

"General Assembly." 1861. *Macon Daily Telegraph*. November 17, 1861.

Gresham, LeRoy Wiley, and Janet Elizabeth Croon. 2018. *The War Outside My Window: The Civil War Diary of LeRoy Wiley Gresham, 1860–1865*. El Dorado Hills, CA: Savas Beatie, LLC.

Griffin, Richard W. 1996. "Wesleyan College: Its Genesis, 1835–1840." *Georgia Historical Quarterly* 50 (1): 54–73.

Harwell, Richard B. 1952. "Louisiana Burge: The Diary of a Confederate College Girl." *The Georgia Historical Quarterly* 36 (2): 144–63.

"Headquarters, Macon, Georgia. Special Order, No. 1." *Macon Daily Telegraph*. June 2, 1863.

Mercer University. "The History of Mercer." 2018. https://about.mercer.edu/history/.

Wesleyan College. "The History of Wesleyan College." Last modified July 31, 2020. https://www.wesleyancollege.edu/about/wesleyan-college-history.cfm.

Hunter, James. 2000. *The Death of Character; Moral Education in an Age Without Good or Evil*. New York: Basic Books.

Huff, Christopher Allen. 2006. "Wesleyan College." *New Georgia Encyclopedia*. Last modified October 31, 2020. https://www.georgiaencyclopedia.org/articles/education/wesleyan-college.

"Impressments." 1864. *Macon Daily Telegraph*. June 13, 1864.

Jaschick, Scott. 2017. "A College and Klan Traditions." *Inside Higher Ed*. Last modified November 13, 2020. https://www.insidehighered.com/news/2017/06/23/wesleyan-college-georgia-apologizes-decades-which-institution-embraced-ku-klux-klan.

Iobst, Richard W. 2009. *Civil War Macon: The History of a Confederate City*. Macon, Georgia: Mercer University Press.

Jones, Charles Edward. 1888. *Circular of Information of the Bureau of Education, for Education in Georgia*. Bureau of Education.

"Ladies Relief Society." 1861. *Macon Daily Telegraph*. July 7, 1861.

Lipscomb, A. A. "The Relations of the Anglo-Saxon Race to Christian Womanhood," *1859–1860 Catalog Wesleyan Female College*, 1860. Special Collections, Wesleyan College.

Lunt, Dolly Sumner, and Robertson, James I. 1962. *The Diary of Dolly Lunt Burge*. Athens: University of Georgia Press.

McClary, Ben Harris. 1973. "The First Professorship of English Literature in America." The Georgia Historical Quarterly 57 (2): 274–76.

Moreau, Joseph. 2004. *Schoolbook Nation*. Ann Arbor: University of Michigan Press.

Neely, Mark E. 2015. *Lincoln and the Triumph of the Nation: Constitutional Conflict in the American Civil War*. Chapel Hill: University of North Carolina Press.

"Office S. C. Hospitals." 1864. *Macon Daily Telegraph*. July 26, 1864.

Ohles, John F. 1978. *Biographical Dictionary of American Educators*. Westport, CT: Greenwood Press.

Pierce, George F. 1839. *An Address on Female Education: Delivered in the Chapel of the Georgia Female College*. Macon, GA: Office of Southern Post.

"Receipts of the Wayside Home from Dec 11th, '63, to Jan. 19th '64." 1864. *Macon Daily Telegraph*. January 20, 1864.

"Resolutions." 1861. *Macon Daily Telegraph*. February 14, 1861.

Richey, Russell E., Kenneth E. Rowe, and Jean Miller Schmidt. 2000. *Methodist Experience in America, Volume 2: Sourcebook*. Nashville: Abingdon Press.

Rivers, R. H. 1859. *The Elements of Moral Philosophy*. Nashville, TN: Southern Methodist Publishing House.

"Sad Accident." 1863. *Macon Daily Telegraph*. May 30, 1863.

"Shall the Female College Be Taken for a Hospital?" 1864. *Macon Daily Telegraph*. June 11, 1864.

"Soldiers Relief Society." 1861. *Macon Daily Telegraph*. May 7, 1861.

"Stoneman's Raid." 1864. *New York Times*, August 15, 1864.

"To Hire." 1861. *Macon Daily Telegraph*. August 17, 1861.

"Tribute to the Memory of Kitty Tooke." 1861. *Macon Daily Telegraph*. February 14, 1861.

Trustee Minutes. Wesleyan Female College, 1836–1874. Special Collections, Wesleyan College.

US Census. 1860. Population Schedule. Macon, Georgia. NARA Microfilm. M6553. Washington, DC: National Archives and Records Administration.

US Census. 1850. Slave Schedule. Newton, Georgia. NARA Microfilm. M6553. Washington, DC: National Archives and Records Administration.

"Wesleyan Female College." 1862. *Georgia Weekly Telegraph*. December 12, 1862.

"Wesleyan." 1864. *Macon Daily Telegraph*. June 15, 1864.

White, Barbara. 2003. *The Beecher Sisters*. London: Yale University Press.

CHAPTER EIGHT

Witness to Civil War Student Life and Military Strife

The University of Virginia as College and Army Hospital

Holly A. Foster and R. Eric Platt

The University of Virginia was founded in 1819 near Charlottesville and remains a historic testament to the educational ideology of Thomas Jefferson, third president of the United States (1801–1809). Jefferson not only helped found the institution, he influenced its early development, curricular design, and physical environment. Jefferson deemed that a flexible course schedule was preferable to the rigid academic structure of other early American and European colleges. It was his intention that University of Virginia students choose their courses according to personal interests and engage in a learning environment meant to mold minds via academic discourse fueled by science, literature, and philosophy. The institution of slavery also influenced the university from its beginnings. Buildings were constructed using slave labor, slaves attended students as personal servants, and the whole of the academy, per Jefferson, was meant to safeguard Southern sons from Northern abolitionist ideologies (Wilder 2013). Indeed, the university's early student population was comprised of members of slave-holding planter and mercantile families.

In addition to the presence of slave labor, student accommodations at the university reflected the wealth of their Southern families. One student described his personal college room as carpeted, with a "cheery wood fire crackling away." Student rooms not only had carpets and fireplaces, they also contained comfortable armchairs where one could relax after taking a bath (Gratz 1862, n.p.). Besides academic excellence, comfort and slavery were chief components of the early Virginia academy.

Owing to the University of Virginia's history as a leader in Southern academic instruction, its connections with various notable political figures, and attempts to provide modern curricula, the institution has held a significant place in the history of American higher education (Thelin 2019). Not only has the university educated and graduated various US leaders, thinkers, and artists such as famed horror author and poet Edgar Allan Poe, influential modernist artist Georgia Totto O'Keeffe, Mississippi novelist and Nobel Prize laureate William Cuthbert Faulkner, and twenty-eighth US president, Thomas Woodrow Wilson ("Notable Alumni" 2019), it was also one of the few Southern institutions of higher education to remain open for the entirety of the Civil War. Prior to its Civil War existence, the University of Virginia was often described as a picturesque athenaeum that offered its pupils rigid instruction and diverse curricula—all in an effort to promote Southern intelligentsia. During the war, however, the regionally celebrated academy was converted into a military hospital while student instruction was relegated to the periphery. Owing to the war, student and faculty enlistment, and scarce material resources, the institution remained open with a meager staff and student body. With the end of the Civil War in 1865, the University of Virginia, like many other Southern institutions of higher education, had to readjust to the realities of a post-slavery society, political reconstruction, and changing educational landscape.

MR. JEFFERSON'S UNIVERSITY

The original University of Virginia campus, sometimes referred to as the "academical village" or "grounds," "consisted of eight independent schools [medicine, law, mathematics, chemistry, modern languages, ancient languages, moral philosophy, and modern philosophy] and offered a radical departure from the rigid curriculum, strict discipline, and theological dogmatism that characterized many American colleges" (Moyen, Thelin, and Edwards 2003, para. 3). The university, its alumni, former faculty, and administrators possessed both a history of Southern honor and academic respect but also a history of slavery, peer dishonor, and raucous student behavior (Wagoner 1986;

Nelson and Zehmer 2019). Throughout the college's early years, students were known to terrorize the campus and local community. Scenes of student public drunkenness, fights with faculty, slave abuse, and campus riots were not unusual and did much to tarnish the young institution's regional reputation. These sons of wealthy planters were more akin to leisurely, unchaperoned life than they were to strict study and academic scrutiny. However, prior to the Civil War, college discipline had been tightened and student life had calmed. As such, the university became more widely regarded for its curricular prowess and architectural significance (Bowman and Santos 2013, McInnis 2019).

From its founding onward, the university was well known for its rich Palladian, Greek-revival architecture, red brick and white columned buildings, and its symmetrical campus layout punctuated by a large, domed rotunda. Built to resemble the Roman Pantheon, the structure was fashioned from bricks manufactured by slave hands (Nelson and Zehmer 2019). The campus was often described as a visually charming environment that enhanced the mental abilities of all who attended. In 1861 a Richmond, Virginia-based newspaper described the ornate antebellum campus with its large amphitheater and well-adorned buildings as including a row of one-story student dormitories with decorated faculty houses. In addition to these structures there were lecture halls and a chapel. The reporter, an anonymous correspondent, described the entire scene as "a rather pleasing picture" ("Notes on the War" 1861, n.p.). The elegance of the campus was meant to attract refined intelligentsia and the sons of wealthy American gentility. Indeed, with its Doric colonnades, pedimented buildings, and sprawling lawns, the pre-Civil War campus resembled ancient Rome ("Notes on the War" 1861).

STUDENT ACTIVITY AND THE START OF WAR

Prior to the Civil War, enrollment hovered around six hundred. Students were predominantly the sons of wealthy planters, businessmen, or lawyers. In the years before the war, the University of Virginia's student population was rather homogeneous. Indeed, historian Jennings L. Wagoner described the university as "the most expensive as well as the most prominent college in the South and its students were drawn from the upper class of the region" (1986, 154). Wagoner also addressed reasons students attended the University of Virginia; for many of them, it was not to learn but to solidify their social status, as "merely attending the University of Virginia in the company of other Southern gentlemen improved one's standing as a member of the elite of Southern society" (Wagoner 1986, 170). In addition to social networking, the college, its early curricular structure, and reliance on slave labor went far to replicate the social mores of the antebellum South. While students forged social alliances with their peers and attended classes meant to sharpen their minds for futures of plantation ownership and political prowess, slaves tended the library and laboratories, cleaned classrooms, and rang the campus bell to signal the beginning and end of courses.

Though students enrolled more for social networking than academic achievement, many engaged in campus debate. Debating societies were a significant part of the university curriculum and student culture. As James Moore Goode explains in his unpublished master's thesis: "The debating societies maintained the greatest patronage of the student bodies" (1966, 25). While students debated over topics such as history, politics, and current events, there was little debate over the tensions that were beginning to split the nation in two—slavery, abolitionism, and states' rights (Goode 1966). Once, in 1832, one student argued in favor of emancipation. "A disapproving faculty," as historian Brendan Wolfe explains, banned students "from orating on any point of state or national controversy" (2016, para. 41). However, in 1850, a University of Virginia student group, referred to as the Southern Rights Association, championed states' rights and the rights of white citizens to engage in slave purchasing, ownership, and sale. As tensions surrounding state's rights and potential secession mounted in the late 1850s, harsher rules were put in place regarding political speech. In 1858, one of the college's two primary debate clubs, titled the Washington Society, "adopted a resolution that no debates would be tolerated on political issues then dividing the Union" (Goode 1966, 53). However, in early 1860, as Southern patriotism increased, both debating societies lifted bans on secessionist discussion. As political and secessionist banter increased, more students favored disunion. By the time Virginia seceded from the Union on April 17, 1861, "the entire student body supported secession" (Goode 1966, 57). Indeed, as the possibility of war increased, anti-Union discussions dominated at the university (Garnett 1912).

When war broke out in 1861, there was great excitement among the University of Virginia's students, as many left to join the Confederate army. Other students from Deep South states such as Mississippi and Georgia left to rejoin their families (Goode 1966). According to one student, his peers left "by every train." It is estimated that 515 students left the university to enlist during the semesters preceding the end of the 1860–1861 academic year (Bruce 1920). The imagined honor one could earn in battle was too great a temptation for many young men to ignore. Enlistment and the possibility of future military escapades excited students. One student stated, "it [enlistment] makes my blood tingle with patriotism" (Dixon 1861, n.p.). Similarly, another student wrote to his family, "we're all anxious to leave here and have a fight" (Preston 1861–1862, n.p.). Remaining at the university instead of leaving to fight was, according to many students, dishonorable. While some left to support their families or join burgeoning regiments, others simply took advantage of the excuse to shrug off studies and other academic labors (Lenoir 1861).

Thereafter, enrollment decreased rapidly (Goode 1966). In October 1861, the University of Virginia administrators sent enrollment advertisements to newspapers across the South. In New Orleans, the following solicitation was printed in the *Daily Picayune*: "The University of Virginia will be ready for the reception of students, at the beginning of its regular session, the 1st of October" ("The Richmond Papers Announce" 1861, 2). In October, the university enrolled less than fifty students. Institutional administrators and faculty alike hoped that the student population would increase to one hundred or more, but such numbers were never achieved ("The News in Brief" 1861). The loss of active students and bustling college activity resulted in a campus that was described by remaining students as "dull" or on the verge of "breaking up" (Gratz 1864, n.p.). Diminished faculty numbers due to military conscription exacerbated internal problems, and external perceptions of the university's ability to persist were grim. Five of the University of Virginia's original fourteen instructors resigned to serve in the Confederate army. Another three served intermittently throughout the war (Goode 1966).

After the initial excitement of war had died down, the remaining University of Virginia students tried to return to their studies, though often unsuccessfully due to regular war-related distractions (Goode 1966). Students reacted differently to reports of battle as the war progressed. While some maintained a strong sense of Confederate patriotism, others questioned the necessity of secessionist violence. Conflicting student views led to heated disputes with unrestrained foul language (Preston 1861). Despite a growing melancholia amongst students as concerned the war, there were still some campus incidents that excited the remaining University of Virginia population. At the start of the war, students watched as two drunken men wandered onto campus and engaged in a heated argument. The debacle resulted in one man shooting the other in the knee. At other times physical brawls broke out during classroom lectures that ended with blood soiled floors. On another occasion, a student was suspended for firing a pistol on the college lawn. Despite this infraction, he was later reinstated. Yet another pupil, "in a fit of insanity . . . burnt up his bed and did other damage to his room" (Journals of the Chairman 1863, n.p.). While these events were recorded in detail, the overwhelming student perception of daily, wartime college life was far from enthralling. Indeed, one student described life at the university as dragging out day-by-day with little entertainment. Campus, with its occasional furloughed student "veterans and striplings" was depicted as mundane and melancholic (Abernethy 1953, 24).

While some students wrote about the boredom of campus life or their longing to see family members and enlisted friends, others extoled their continued support of the Confederate cause and explained that they would join the fight should it become necessary. Of those students enlisted, several hoped for furloughs to rejoin the university's enrollees—war, students eventually realized, was far less desirable than many originally imagined (Chairman's Journal 1863–1864). As the war progressed, attitudes shifted. While some students maintained their patriotic zeal for the Confederacy, others felt less excited about the possibility of fighting and worried about conscription. One student wrote: "I shall go on studying with equal a mind as possible . . . hoping something will prevent my [military] departure" (Gratz 1864, n.p.). As news of bloody battles, Southern defeats, and death reached the campus, the desire to enlist decreased. Some who left the university did so with great regret. University of Virginia student John Henderson sent a letter to his mother on February 14, 1863, that described the shrinking sophomore class as well as the many students who had already been conscripted. Henderson was concerned to see his friends leave and worried that he might never see them again. Though Henderson informed his mother that his fellow pupils left to join the war in good spirits, the letter was void of the same wartime excitement that filled so many student letters two years prior (Henderson, 1863). Like Henderson's letter, there are multiple student accounts that reflect emotions far from the usual excitement described in existing wartime literature. Most contain little enthusiasm for the war in general. As enrollments continued to drop and battles neared the campus, positive spirits were difficult to maintain.

Students aside, most of the University of Virginia's professors opposed secession prior to the war (Lenoir 1861). However, once the war was underway, professors shifted their views in support of the South, and many entered the Confederate army. As the war progressed, finances at the university became strained due to the lack of student tuition and dwindling state support. As a result, faculty salaries were reduced to offset the institution's diminished budget ("The Virginia Legislature" 1864). In 1863, University of Virginia's Board of Visitors reduced faculty salaries by approximately 40 percent (Goode 1966). Regardless of their decreased wages, faculty maintained regular course schedules and made curricular alterations to better provide for the remaining students who, during the war, pressed for formal military training. The faculty acquiesced to student requests, and military instruction was incorporated into the curriculum. In May of 1861, the Board of Visitors authorized the establishment of an academic department of military science and civil engineering to prepare students as officers for the Confederate army. Marching and parade drill took place on the university's main lawn in front of the rotunda, while military strategy was taught in the classroom (Goode 1966). Despite these pedagogical changes, lectures and course schedules were often interrupted for a variety of reasons including, but not limited to, "students discharging military duty," professors who volunteered for full-time or part-time regimental duties, caring for wounded soldiers, and "Confederate Days of Fasting and Prayer" (Goode 1966).

With military curricula on the rise, the university, with its remaining students and wounded veterans, was described as "little more than a military school" (Preston 1861–1862, n.p.). Still, the Richmond, Virginia, branch of the Whig Party praised the university's governing board for implementing military curricula and establishing a military department (Whig 1861). The board viewed the military department's creation as "useful" for every white man interested in better serving the Southern war effort. Still, some faculty did not approve of increased military instruction and expressed that regimental cadet training was "seriously interfering with the ordinary pursuits of college life" (Goode 1966, 71).

Despite the remaining faculty's best efforts to retain students, the loss of so many pupils and instructors quickly led to a general impression that operations at the university had been suspended. Regardless of the loss of so many students and faculty and the common belief that the university would suspend operations, members of the faculty declared that all courses would continue as usual, with no possibility of course suspension ("There Seems to Be" 1861). Consequently, operations continued for the duration of the war. Though classes with a handful of students persisted, the university remained open and functional largely due to the need for medical accommodations. Medical studies existed at the institution since the late 1820s (Cunningham 1986). Adept students aided army surgeons who practiced in campus buildings. As the number of wounded soldiers poured in, unused student living quarters were converted into hospital wards ("During the War" 1865). The remaining faculty were instrumental in caring and providing for soldiers suffering from musket-ball wounds, cannonball shrapnel, bayonet lacerations, etc. when the university became what was described as a "vast hospital for the sick and wounded" (Gemmill 1962, 98).

WOUNDED, DYING, AND THE UNIVERSITY AS ARMY HOSPITAL

Those instructors who remained not only taught classes and managed rowdy students but also nursed suffering soldiers who were wounded in nearby skirmishes and provided physical space for army medical officers to perform procedures such as amputations and the like (Goode 1966; Albemarle County Historical Society 1962). The students and faculty felt their great contribution early in the war was their ability to serve wounded soldiers. Several students gave up their beds for ailing military men, and the university's enslaved servants helped professors tend to the wounded (Gemmill 1962). "Battles such as First and Second Bull Run, Cross Keys, Port Republic, and Cedar Mountain added to the carnage" (Maurer 2008, para. 14) and battered, bloodied military men were transported to the university to be cared for. In his 1920 book *The History of the University of Virginia*, Philip Alexander Bruce recounts the story of George L. Christian, a Confederate soldier who was wounded, brought to the campus for medical treatment, and "lost one entire foot and the heel of the other." After recuperating, Christian enrolled in classes along with other wounded soldiers who had been cared for at the university. While Christian required the use of crutches to walk and had no clothes other than his military fatigues, he was given the same academic treatment as other University of Virginia students and was assigned an unfurnished dormitory room. Not long after he enrolled, Christian was assigned a roommate, W. C. Holmes. Holmes, like Christian, had been wounded in battle. His right arm

"Confederate Monument, University of Virginia Cemetery," n.d. U.Va. Prints and Photographs File. Accession #RG-30/1/10.011. Image courtesy of University of Virginia History Collection, Small Special Collections Library, University of Virginia, Charlottesville, Virginia.

was severely damaged, and he was left unable to write with his dominant hand. Still he was set on garnering his higher education and, with his roommate Christian sharing class notes, he was able to participate in courses. The two soldiers were often seen helping one another—Christian helping Holmes with writing and Holmes assisting Christian with walking. The two even shared blankets to keep warm in their unfurnished room (Bruce 1920).

Eventually the number of wounded increased so dramatically that the university's main buildings, lecture rooms, and remaining dormitories were filled with young men wearing Confederate uniforms stained with blood (Davis 1861–1862). As student enrollment had significantly decreased, the university's instructors were able to offer the empty residential buildings to the Confederate wounded. The campus filled with the wounded and dying, while other nearby town buildings and private homes served as additional medical facilities (Goode 1966). Still, the University of Virginia served as the region's main hospital. By 1862, it was estimated that over 1,400 patients were treated at the university (Journals of the Chairman 1862). By the end of the war it was estimated that the institution had housed approximately 1,500 patients ("Notes of the War" 1861). Socrates Maupin, the faculty chairman, described the conversion of so many campus buildings into a grand army hospital as a great advantage to future medical students, for the two university instructors gleaned extensive experience attending and aiding military surgeons (Maupin 1861). Though university faculty and students attended the wounded and provided rooms for rehabilitation, approximately 1,097 Confederate soldiers died on or near campus and were buried in the University Cemetery adjacent to the campus. The cemetery was conceived of in 1828 after the death of professor Henry William Tucker, MD. Though founded for the interment of faculty and students, the stone-walled cemetery was expanded in 1862 for the Confederate dead (Ford 2019). In 1893, the local Ladies Confederate Memorial Association erected a large stone memorial with the interred soldiers' names inscribed on bronze plaques (Maurer 2008). A bronze Confederate soldier with rifle in hand surmounts the granite pillar. The base of the memorial is engraved with the following epithet: "Fate denied them victory but crowned them with glorious immortality" (Clukey 2019, para. 3).

The university-turned-hospital operated so well that a local journalist commented on its efficiency. The reporter opined that the university hospital was in a far better state of affairs than other existing medical care facilities and stated that "the sick [were] better attended [at the university] than any [hospital] previously seen" (Long 1862, n.p.). Even before the war, the University of Virginia's medical department (founded 1825) had been well regarded as one of a handful of successful medical institutions in the antebellum South (Greer, Platt, and Woods 2018). Now, medical students and faculty served the wounded and practiced their trade while the war raged on. Harkening back to descriptions of the university's impressive architecture and serene locale, another journalist described the academy and its wartime status as a medical care facility as "seated at the center of a lovely valley, girdled by the billowy ranges of the Blue Ridge [Mountains], with an abundant supply of pure water, and a complement corps of medical practitioners immediately at hand" ("Notes of the War" 1861, n.p.). Despite his admiration for the Charlottesville campus, the same reporter commented on the painful shock of such beauty set against the "sad reality of the impressive suffering on which it [the university] looks down. Amputated limbs, taken off at the hip and thigh and shoulder, ghastly flesh wounds, half healed stumps, and bandaged heads, meet your eye on every side [of the campus]" ("Notes of the War" 1861, n.p.).

Although the faculty and students of the University of Virginia supported the Confederacy and helped care for the wounded and dying, the instructors soon realized that their campus facilities were filled with ailing military men. As such, difficulties arose regarding the admittance and housing of new students (Bruce 1920). The faculty ruminated on the university's longevity if new students were not admitted due to the overwhelming number of soldiers (Gemmill 1962). Given the faculty's desire to keep the university open and in the business of providing higher education, the board of directors were faced with a daunting decision—allow the institution to maintain its medical role and close the campus to new students or remove the wounded and return the campus to its singular, pedagogical purpose. In the summer of 1862, the board of directors demanded the removal of all sick and wounded as well as compensation for damages caused to the university buildings due to its hospital conversion and overpopulation of army patients. Thereafter, soldiers were transferred to other Virginia-based care facilities (Jordan 2016).

The university's conversion into an army hospital had significantly altered daily student and instructional life. Before the war, a typical day for University of Virginia students began at dawn. Students studied before breakfast, ate, and then attended three to four classes before lunch. Study and additional courses continued after lunch until dinner. After the evening meal, students spent approximately one hour in the gymnasium studying or engaging in recreational activities until bedtime at 10:00 p.m. (Goode 1966). However, the presence of the sick and wounded changed campus life. Prior to the departure of soldiers and military personnel, students were subject to regular class cancelations and course schedule changes due to faculty tending for military men wounded in battle. Regardless, the students and faculty persevered, and the college continued to function (Lenoir 1860–1861; Massie 1862). Even so, many students remained worried about conscription. In time, fears of conscription turned to concerns over family wealth due to the collapse of Confederate finances and Southern currency (Goode 1966).

Conditions at the university improved as student numbers increased (and revenue as well), but normalcy did not last long. News of further Confederate losses changed the tenor of life in Charlottesville. When students and faculty were notified of the death of Virginia-born Confederate general Thomas Jonathan "Stonewall" Jackson in 1863, it was stated that "a universal gloom covered everything" (Gratz 1863). Despite this, lectures continued. For some students, the lectures greatly resembled those they experienced before the war. Other students, however, described the challenges both professors and students faced as they struggled with "wandering thoughts" due to war-related melancholy (Minor 1962, 48). One student described the minds of both the students and faculty as distracted and "completely unhinged." While some instructors faltered at their jobs and allowed academic rigor in their classrooms to slip, others maintained high expectations. Some students described diligently studying late into the night during the latter war years. Another student managed to "study himself down" until he was sick from self-neglect (Lenoir 1860–1861). Along with lectures, examination schedules were maintained (Goode 1966). Examinations were thorough, and despite morose student and faculty attitudes, pupils were expected to prepare accordingly and answer all questions germane to each academic course (Goode 1966; Gratz 1863–1864).

Students, however, faced more than curricular inconsistency and academic challenges. Approximately seventy-two miles from Charlottesville was Richmond, the capital of the Confederate government. Charlottesville, as a major Southern train depot, was a "key point for the movement of Confederate troops" (Goode 1966, 64). Indeed, Charlottesville's service as a railroad hub made it an important locale for Southern soldiers as they moved from the Confederate capital to battlefronts across the South and eastern seaboard (Goode 1966). Throughout the war, thousands of troops, traveling from the Confederate capital city to Richmond, often stopped near the university for rest and provisions. Therefore, the University of Virginia's residential facilities not only housed students in addition to sick and infirm soldiers but also sometimes functioned as temporary barracks for Confederate troops. Indeed, Confederate soldiers disrupted campus life with their comings, goings, and military drills (Chairman's Journals 1862–1863).

The presence of troops continued throughout the war. Several students wrote about the military activity on campus, some finding particular interest in members of the Confederate Second Cavalry camped just outside of Charlottesville (Dabney 1863–1869; Graves 1861–1862). While Confederate troops elicited local excitement, Federal troops also passed through the region. Their presence caused both excitement and fear. Following the 1863 emancipation proclamation, increased Southern losses, and invading Union soldiers, the university's faculty maintained classes and even published essays on the detriment of miscegenation and the biblical justification of slavery (Howard and Brophy 2019). Regardless of these academic attempts to justify a dying way of life, Union soldiers continued to pour into the area surrounding Charlottesville and the university. In 1864, the number of Federal troops had increased to the point that some speculated that a battle might occur nearby. While some students worried, others brimmed with anticipation at the thought of a battle (Graves 1864).

FEDERAL OCCUPATION AND CONFEDERATE DEMISE

Student excitement waned as 1865 dawned, and the prospect of Union occupation consumed Richmond. Similarly, Charlottesville residents prepared for the worst as Federal troops marched towards town (Leake 1962). When Union troops came within twenty miles of Charlottesville, locals set fire to depot stores (Graves 1865). Soon after, ten thousand men under the command of Union general Phillip Henry Sheridan arrived in Richmond and camped near the university. One student wrote that at least two thousand soldiers passed through the University of Virginia's main lawn (Graves 1865). In April of 1865, students were so unsettled by occupying Federal forces that lectures were suspended for the remainder of the spring semester (Dabney 1865). Regardless of class cancelations, students still found moments to be merry. While Union soldiers camped nearby, some University of Virginia students attended soirees hosted by their fellow students and balls given by the ladies of Charlottesville (Goode 1966). Despite Federal occupation, one student, after attending a ball in Charlottesville, described the Virginia depot city as "quite gay now" (Graves 1865). This social entertainment was especially important for bolstering student morale, as all other campus social activities had ceased (Bruce 1920).

While students found ways to enjoy themselves, they still faced serious issues such as the expense of tuition and the lack of food and clothing supplies. Despite early preparations to stock food supplies, consumables had considerably decreased. In addition, the cost of food and other supplies had increased in the face of the decreased value of Confederate currency. Boarding costs rose to $300 per month, and one student, suffering from a loss of personal capital and undernourished, withdrew from the university. Costs for other goods and services had likewise risen. The price of a haircut had increased more than four-fold, tuition at the university nearly doubled during the war, and by 1863, living costs exceeded most students' ability to pay (Bruce 1920). As prices skyrocketed, students found it impossible to purchase textbooks. That same year, most students stopped purchasing ink for their writing pens. Instead, they manufactured their own writing ink from elderberry juice. To defray the cost of paper, some students used wallpaper as stationery (Goode 1966).

While costs increased and supplies decreased, colleges across the South, including the University of Virginia, experienced dire straits. College closures and decreased instructional and student resources had become so pervasive that, in 1865, a reporter from the *Richmond Times* newspaper observed that while the war raged "the educational resources of the South were terribly reduced and neglected" ("During the War" 1865, 4). As the war came to a close, the University of Virginia, like its few peer institutions that had remained open during the conflict, was financially strapped. To aid their college, two University of Virginia professors borrowed from a local bank to help defray the cost of restoring the campus. Though not destroyed by Federal troops, the university had sustained significant damage from years of physical plant neglect, army hospital conversion, and a dormitory fire that was the result of student carelessness (Bruce 1920).

On March 3, 1865, Union troops arrived at the campus and were met by students and professors holding a flag of truce. The university instructors requested that the Federal officers protect the town and the university from violence as they, the faculty, and city residents had surrendered both the academy and city (Minor 1962). On March 14, the *New York Daily Herald* included a report from Gen. Sheridan to Edwin McMasters Stanton, Union secretary of war, which stated, "this division . . . entered Charlottesville at two P.M. the next day. The Mayor of the city and the principal inhabitants came out and delivered up the keys of the public buildings" ("Sheridan" 1865, n.p.). While the officers agreed not to harm the town or campus and were even welcomed into residents' homes, acts of violence were still committed in the area. Though troops did not burn the university, they cut telegraph wires, destroyed eight miles of railroad and iron rail bridges, and demolished "every bridge on the road, and in many places miles of road" ("Sheridan" 1865, n.p.). Charlottesville and the University of Virginia had been successfully cut off from the Confederacy. While former war-related events such as the Federal destruction of an artillery camp three miles outside of Charlottesville caused campus excitement that one student described as "gay as a carnival," the 1865 military occupation intensified student depression ("The Situation" 1865).

Even though the university remained open, the student body had significantly changed. By the war's end, there were only fifty-five students enrolled—many of whom were not eligible to enlist. Those who remained were described as either too young to register for military service (younger than eighteen years of age) or wounded veterans (Abernethy 1953; Cashin 2002). The student population was described as a "pitiful array of boys too young to enlist, disabled veterans walking amidst almost empty lecture halls and deserted arcades" (Bruce 1920, 323). Despite the fact that student numbers had been reduced to a handful, faculty tried to stymie the consistent exodus of students determined to take up arms. In 1864, the chairman of the faculty, Socrates Maupin, wrote to the secretary of war, James Seddon, asking that University of Virginia students be excused from military duties (Chairman's Journals 1863–1864). His request was denied, and student enrollment continued to decrease until the Confederacy's surrender at Appomattox, Virginia—less than sixty-three miles from the college campus. The retention of younger students and military veterans was due largely to the former's conscription exclusion. The latter was retained due to the university faculty's decision to waive tuition for wounded veterans (UVA Alumni 1912; Goode 1966). One student in 1864 described a law class where two-thirds of the attendees were either missing an arm or a leg (Goode 1966). Sadly, the remaining students who were too young to fight viewed veteran pupils with disdain and considered their veteran peers "as fools and of an inferior class of whom none are above mediocrity" (Gratz 1863–1864).

With the fall of the Confederacy and the end of the war, there was considerable uncertainty about the future of the University of Virginia. The college's buildings were in disrepair, grounds were severely damaged, teaching materials had been destroyed, university slaves had been set free, and the college's treasury was practically empty. On May 8, 1865, members of the University of Virginia faculty convened at the home of faculty chairman Socrates Maupin to consider the institution's future and assure one another that, above all, the university would remain open.

Though both faculty and students struggled with Reconstruction conditions, the university was still intact. Despite difficult conditions, classes were reinstated, the dormitories continued to operate, and lectures were continued. Even though the Confederacy had fallen, the University of Virginia's faculty turned their attention towards preparing for the 1865–1866 academic session (Bruce 1920). In 1865, the *Daily National Intelligencer Advertisements* announced that the University of Virginia's next session of fall classes would begin on time and emphasized the fact that the university remained open throughout the war ("Multiple Classified Advertisements" 1865). The fall of 1865 saw increased enrollment, with a student population of 230, comprised mostly of former members of the Confederate army ("Miscellaneous" 1865).

While the university prospered prior to the war, students, faculty, and soldier patients suffered numerous hardships during the war. Prewar enrollments had exceeded six hundred, and student life had flourished. While war-era student enrollment drastically decreased, those faculty and students who remained experienced significant challenges. Still, the University of Virginia rebounded after the war, and on August 24, 1865, Charlottesville was identified as a literary center of the South ("Charlottesville Is Fairly Entitled" 1865). Today, the University of Virginia remains a well-enrolled, financially endowed Southern institution. Visitors to the campus can walk the grounds, visit the dormitory room once occupied by Edger Allen Poe, explore the nearby Confederate cemetery, and, in more recent years, engage in walking tours that illustrate the university's ties to slavery, the Confederacy, and the Civil War (University of Virginia 2013).

Like many colleges and universities in the American South, the University of Virginia has struggled with its antebellum legacy of chattel servitude and involvement in the Confederacy. To increase transparency and communicate the institution's multifaceted racial history to the larger public, the "President's Commission on Slavery and the University" was founded at the University of Virginia in 2013. The commission was charged to explore the university's ties to the antebellum slave trade and post-Civil War racial segregation (University of Virginia 2013). Like other Southern academies, the Virginia-based institution remains a living piece of history that further illustrates higher education's connection to the American Civil War.

REFERENCES

Abernethy, Thomas Perkins. 1953. *The University of Virginia: Historical Sketch*. Charlottesville: University of Virginia Press.

Albemarle County Historical Society. *The Magazine of Albemarle County History*. 1963–1964. University of Virginia, Albert H. Small Special Collections Library.

Boles, John B. 2017. *Jefferson: Architect of American Liberty*. New York: Basic Books.

Bowman, Rex and Carlos Santos. 2013. *Rot, Riot, and Rebellion: Mr. Jefferson's Struggle to Save the University that Changed American*. Charlottesville: University of Virginia Press.

Bruce, Philip Alexander. 1920. *History of the University of Virginia, 1819–1919*. 5 vols. New York: Macmillan Company.

Burke, Colin B. 1982. *American Collegiate Populations: A Test of the Traditional View*. New York: New York University Press.

Cashin, Joan E, ed. 2002. "Deserters, Civilians, and Draft Resistance in the North." In *The War Was You and Me: Civilians in the American Civil War*, 262–85. Princeton, NJ: Princeton University Press.

"Charlottesville Is Fairly Entitled to be Called the Literary Center of the South." 1865. *Boston Daily Advertiser*. August 24, 1865.

Clukey, Abby. 2019. "Another Statue: UVA Faces its Own Challenge in Who to Memorialize, and How." *C-Ville*. Last modified June 29, 2019. https://www.c-ville.com/another-statue-uva-faces-its-own-challenge-in-who-to-memorialize-and-how/.

Cornelius Dabney Diary. 1863–1869. University of Virginia, Albert and Shirley Small Special Collections Library.

Coulter, Ellis Merton, Wendell Holmes Stephenson, and George Brown Tindall. 1967. *A History of the South*. Baton Rouge: Louisiana State University Press.

Cunninghman, H. H. 1986. *Doctors in Gray: The Confederate Medical Service*. Baton Rouge: Louisiana State University.

Cunningham, James. Letter. 1864. University of Virginia, Albert and Shirley Small Special Collections Library.

"Domestic Intelligence." *Harper's Weekly: A Journal of Civilization*. March 25, 1865.

"During the War the Educational Resources of the South were Terribly Reduced and Neglected." 1865. *Richmond Times*, July 13, 1865, 4.

Earl C. Leake Papers. 1890. University of Virginia, Albert and Shirley Small Special Collections Library.

Earl C. Leake Papers.1900. University of Virginia, Albert and Shirley Small Special Collections Library.

Earl C. Leake Papers.1962. University of Virginia, Albert and Shirley Small Special Collections Library.

"The First News from Sigel: Destruction of the Railroad between Lynchburg and Charlottesville." *The Christian Recorder*, May 21, 1864: n.p.

Fisk, Wilbur. Wilbur Fisk Davis Papers. 1861–1864. University of Virginia, Albert H. and Shirley Small Special Collections Library.

Ford, Benjamin. 2019. "The African American Burial Ground." In *Educated in Tyranny: Slavery at Thomas Jefferson's University*, edited by Maurie D. McInnis and Louis P. Nelson, 225–45. Charlottesville: University of Virginia Press.

Frost, Dan R. 2010. *Thinking Confederates: Academia and the Idea of Progress in the New South*. Knoxville: University of Tennessee Press.

Garnett, James M. 1912. "Personal Recollections of the University of Virginia at the Outbreak of the War of 1861–65." In *Alumni Bulletin of the University of Virginia*. Third Series, vol. 5, no. 3. University of Virginia. Albert and Shirley Small Special Collections Library.

Gemmill, Chalmers L. 1962. "The Charlottesville General Hospital 1861–1865." In *The Magazine of Albemarle County History*, 1963–1964. University of Virginia, Albert H. Small Special Collections Library.

"General Scott and His Enemies." 1861. *Fayetteville Observer*. March 7, 1861.

Goode, James Moore. 1966. *The Confederate University: The Forgotten Institution of the American Civil War.* Master's thesis. University of Virginia.

Greer, Tiffany, R. Eric Platt, and Shamekia Woods. 2018. "Towards a History of Medical Higher Education in the American South: Southern Nationalism, Racial Ethos, and the Flexner Report of 1910." *Curriculum History* 20: 70–85.

Harry St. John Dixon Papers. 1860–1861. University of Virginia, Albert and Shirley Small Special Collections Library.

Henderson, John F. February 14, 1863. Letter to his Mother. *Documenting the American South.* University of North Carolina: Chapel Hill. Last modified July 11, 2019. http://docsouth.unc.edu/unc/unc09-12/unc09-12.html.

Howard, Thomas and Alfred Brophy. 2019. "Proslavery Thought." In *Educated in Tyranny: Slavery at Thomas Jefferson's University*, edited by Maurie D. Mcinnis and Louis P. Nelson, 141–70. Charlottesville: University of Virginia Press.

Jordan, Ervin L., Jr. 2016. "The University of Virginia during the Civil War." In *Virginia Encyclopedia*. Last modified May 10, 2020. http://www.encyclopediavirginia.org/university_of_virginia_during_the_civil_war_the#.

Journals of the Chairman. 1827–1864. University of Virginia, Albert H. Small Special Collections Library.

Kendi, Ibram X. 2016. *Stamped from the Beginning: The Definitive History of Racist Ideas in America*. New York: Bold Type Books.

Lenoir Family Papers. 1860–1861. University of Virginia, Albert and Shirley Small Special Collections Library, University of Virginia.

Long, Grals. 1862. "For the Observer." *Fayetteville Observer*. November 10, 1862: n.p.

Massie Family Papers. 1850–1862. University of Virginia, Albert H. Small Special Collections Library.

Maupin, Socrates. 1861. "University of Virginia." *Weekly Raleigh Register* 38 (September 25, 1861).

Maurer, David. 2008. "Set in Stone: The Serenity of UVA's Cemeteries Belies a Colorful Past." *Virginia*. Last modified August 4, 2020. https://uvamagazine.org/articles/set_in_stone/

McInnis, D. Maurie. 2019. "Violence." In *Educated in Tyranny: Slavery at Thomas Jefferson's University*, edited by Maurie D. Mcinnis and Louis P. Nelson, 97–112. Charlottesville: University of Virginia Press.

Minor, John B. "John B. Minor's Civil War Diary." 1962. In *The Magazine of Albemarle County History, Albemarle County Historical Society, 1963–1964*, edited by Anne Freudenberg and John Casteen, 45–46. Albert H. Small Special Collections Library, University of Virginia.

Miriam Gratz Moses Papers (Gratz Cohen Series), 1864. University of Virginia, Albert and Shirley Small Special Collections Library.

"Miscellaneous." 1865. *New Daily Palladium*. November 28, 1865: n.p.

Moyen, E. A., John Thelin, & Jason Edwards. 2003. "University of Virginia—Early Years, The Twentieth Century and Future Directions." In *Encyclopedia of* Education, 2nd Ed, edited by James W. Guthrie. Last modified April 24, 2016. http://education.stateuniversity.com/pages/2521/University-Virginia.html#ixzz4ZfKKQ1ec.

"Multiple Classified Advertisements." 1865. *Daily National Intelligencer*. September 14, 1865: n.p.

Nelson, Louis P. and Jams Zehmer. 2019. "Slavery and Construction." In *Educated in Tyranny: Slavery at Thomas Jefferson's University*, edited by Maurie D. Mcinnis and Louis P. Nelson, 27–41. Charlottesville: University of Virginia Press.

"Notes of the War." 1861. *Charleston Mercury*. August 28, 1861: n.p.

Preston, Walter. Walter Preston Letters, 1861–1862. University of Virginia, Albert and Shirley Small Special Collections Library.

"The Richmond Papers Announce." 1861. *Daily Picayune*. September 1, 1861: 2.

Sarah Ann Graves Strickler Fife Diary, 1861–1902. University of Virginia, Albert H. Small Special Collections Library.

"There Seems to Be, We Learn, a General Impression Throughout the Country, that the Operations of the University of Virginia have Been Suspended." 1861. *Natchez Weekly Courier* 47 (November 13, 1861): n.p.

"Sheridan." 1865. *New York Daily Herald*. March 14, 1865: n.p.

Shields, W. S. 1859. "General Lafayette's Visit to Monticello and the University." *The Virginia University Magazine* 4 (3): 113–25.

"The Situation." 1865. *New York Dailey Herald*. March 6, 1865: n.p.

Thelin, John R. 2019. *A History of American Higher Education*. 3rd ed. Baltimore: Johns Hopkins University Press.

"University of Virginia." 1861. *Weekly Raleigh Register*. October 23, 1861: n.p.

University of Virginia. 2013. "President's Commission on Slavery and the University." Last modified November 1, 2020. http://slavery.virginia.edu/enslaved-african-americans-at-the-university-of-virginia-walking-tour-map/.

University of Virginia. 2019. "Notable Alumni." Last modified November 18, 2020. https://as.virginia.edu/notable-alumni.

UVA Alumni. 1912. *Alumni Bulletin of the University of Virginia*. Third Series, vol. 5, no 1.
University of Virginia, Albert and Shirley Small Special Collections Library.

"The Virginia Legislature." 1864. *Daily Richmond Examiner*. January 11, 1864: n.p.

Wagoner, Jennings L. 1986. "Honor and Dishonor at Mr. Jefferson's University: The Antebellum Years." *History of Education Quarterly* 26 (2): 155–79.

Whig, Richmond. 1861. "Military Department at the University." *Fayetteville Observer*. June 13, 1861: n.p.

Wilder, Craig Steven. 2013. *Ebony and Ivy: Race, Slavery, and the Troubled History of America's Universities*. New York: Bloomsbury Press.

Wolfe, Brendan. 2016. "Slavery at the University of Virginia." *Encyclopedia Virginia*. Last modified November 12, 2020. https://www.encyclopediavirginia.org/Slavery_at_the_University_of_Virginia#start_entry.

CHAPTER NINE

Confederate Compatriot

The Virginia Military Institute and the Vicissitudes of War

Michael M. Wallace

In the fall of 1860, a Virginia Military Institute (VMI) cadet named Thomas Andrew Stevenson wrote to his sister about the rumors of Civil War: "All I have said, Dear sister, amounts to a mere probability, believe me. There will be no such issue as these extravagant fanatics' prophesy. We consider it as trifling talk but have preparedness in case of an emergency. We have commenced the skirmish drill and cartridges have been distributed to the amount of twenty-five hundred. But believe me in the whole, it will amount to nothing" (Stevenson 1860). Despite Stevenson's reassurances, he and his fellow VMI peers would play a central role in the Confederate war effort. At the beginning of the war, the state of Virginia and VMI's administration agreed that the institution would remain open during the conflict. During the war years, hundreds of students flocked to VMI to receive a formal higher education punctuated by military instruction. Additionally, the VMI Corps of Cadets was very active outside of the classroom serving as reserve troops, public execution guards, attending burial parties, apprehending military deserters, and eventually fighting as combat troops.

PRE-CIVIL WAR VMI

The Virginia Military Institute was founded in Lexington, Virginia, in 1839, to provide state students with formal higher education and military instruction in exchange for said students guarding one of Virginia's arsenals, which contained weapons from the War of 1812. Over its first twenty years of existence, VMI earned a reputation in Virginia and throughout the American South for both traditional academics and military arts. This was due to the efforts of VMI's first superintendent Francis H. Smith. Smith was a West Point alumnus who strove to combine the military and engineering strengths of the United States Military Academy at West Point with the practical curricular needs of the Commonwealth of Virginia. Academically, VMI offered courses that concentrated on mathematics, engineering, and mechanics. It was one of the few colleges in the antebellum South to predominantly offer such courses. Additionally, from 1842 to 1859, VMI produced 160 teachers (Couper 1939). Many VMI-trained teachers either established or taught at military academies in various Southern states. When hired to teach at nonmilitary institutions, the alumni often established military programs that resembled their VMI experiences (Allardice 1997). VMI's prodigious reputation for military instruction was due, in large part, to two of its professors: the prewar commandant of cadets and instructor of infantry tactics, Maj. William Gilham, and instructor of artillery tactics, Maj. Thomas J. Jackson—both were West Point graduates and had served in the Mexican-American War (1846–1848).

The beginning of VMI's Corps of Cadets service to the state of Virginia actually occurred before the start of the Civil War (McMurry 1999). After John Brown's abortive raid on Harper's Ferry in October 1859, he was put on trial and was found guilty of murder, treason to the Commonwealth of Virginia, and conspiring with enslaved individuals to commit treason. Brown's raid was an abolitionist attempt to inspire a slave revolt by forcibly commandeering a US arsenal (DeCaro 2015). Due to his insurrectionist actions, Brown was sentenced to public execution via hanging on December 2, 1859. Virginia's governor, Henry Wise, ordered VMI's cadets to report to Charlestown to provide security for Brown's execution (Couper 1939). After the execution, state leaders took steps to include VMI faculty and cadets in Virginia's military forces. An act passed in March 1860 stated, "the Corps of Cadets, in the course of their regular military education, may readily be employed to prepare munitions of war, as may be demanded by the wants of the State" (Wise 1915, 116). In accordance with a separate militia bill passed in April of 1860, officers of the Virginia Military Institute were officially recognized as part of the state's military. The state's governor was authorized to issue commissions to VMI instructors in accordance with the regulations of the institute, but these commissions conferred no rank in the active militia (Couper 1939). As a result, VMI's Board of Visitors changed the status of cadets in the spring of 1860 to include state military status. When the institution's governing board informed new cadets of their academic appointment, the board also provided notice that they had joined the military service of Virginia upon entering military academy (Board of Visitors Minutes 1860).

VMI AND THE EARLY YEARS OF WAR

Virginia's state leaders voted to secede from the Union on April 17, 1861, five days after the bombardment of Fort Sumter. Thereafter, VMI quickly shifted from an academic institution with a heavy military component, to a completely military academy. On April 17, Commandant of Cadets John T. L. Preston began to prepare the institution and its students for war. VMI cadet Andrew Gatewood wrote on April 18, "We have drilled 3 times today. We have suspended all Academic duty except Tactics. All of us are studying Tactics. We don't do anything at all but study Tactics and drill" (Gatewood 1861). Likewise, preparations for war were being made throughout the Virginia Commonwealth. On April 20, Governor Letcher published a call for volunteers to defend against the Federal foe. The state's Central Fair Grounds, located a mile and a half north of Richmond, was designated as the camp of instruction for new army recruits. That same day, couriers from Richmond arrived at VMI and informed Maj. Gilham that he had been placed in charge of the camp, the instruction of new army recruits, and was to "immediately send Corps of Cadets to Richmond" as drill instructors (Couper 1939). This order from Richmond may have come as little surprise as VMI's cadets were considered the best-drilled and most proficient military organization in the state at that time.

VMI cadets were quartered in the fairground's exhibition buildings. The grounds, renamed Camp Lee, were originally intended to train only Virginia recruits. However, recruits from various Confederate states soon reported to the converted fairgrounds for training. Despite the overwhelming attendance of so many Southern recruits, VMI cadets took their new duties seriously. However, their eagerness did not endear them to the recruits in training. A Virginian recruit, George Bagby, wrote about his life as a recruit, the shock of stem military training compared to his rather lackadaisical antebellum existence, and the demanding VMI cadets, "I was three and thirty years old, a born invalid whose habit had been to rise late, bathe leisurely and eat breakfast after everybody was done . . . [T]o be drilled by a fat little cadet, young enough to be my son . . . that indeed was misery. How I hated that little cadet! He was always so wide-awake, so clean, so interested in the drill; his coat tails were so short and sharp and his hands looked so big in white gloves. He made me sick" (Couper 1939).

Additional cadets were dispatched to train troops throughout the state of Virginia. Regarding the cadets and their acumen for military instruction, Confederate general Robert E. Lee wrote to Superintendent Smith, "they are wanted everywhere" (Couper 1939). After training new recruits, VMI cadets joined the companies and regiments they had instructed. So many cadets enlisted this way that, by early July, the number of VMI cadets serving at Camp Lee had decreased to thirty (Conrad 1997). When new recruit training ended, Confederate officials granted officers commissions to those VMI cadets over twenty-one years of age (Couper 1939). This action enhanced the perception that individuals having a formal military education would receive an officer's commission.

Back at the VMI campus, militia companies assumed guardianship of the institute's arsenal until they were ordered to serve in Northern Virginia, which lead to a shortage of soldiers to guard the arsenal. Additional VMI cadets were urgently needed for said guard duty, but few could be spared from duty in Richmond and across Virginia. To increase enrollment, the acting superintendent ran newspaper advertisements in Richmond and other cities, stating that the course of instruction at VMI was devoted exclusively to military tactics and that no tuition would be charged except for material fees for the foreseeable future (Couper 1939). Local boys and young men, viewing this enrollment offer as a means to receive quality military training that would result in an officer commission, flocked to VMI. By May 1, 1861, one hundred students from across Virginia enrolled as new "cadets."

From April to July 1861, VMI cadets and faculty trained both recruits and future officers for duty in the Virginia and Confederate armies with tremendous success. However, the VMI cadets and faculty had also been swept up by the war effort and an ardent desire to serve the Confederate South. Accordingly, VMI students, faculty, and administrators had accepted positions in the armies of the Confederacy (McMurry 1999). As a result, enrollment drastically decreased. As there were so few cadets to instruct, the

VMI Board of Visitors voted to cease academic operations on July 2, 1861. The Virginia adjutant general and VMI Board of Visitors member William Richardson believed that closing VMI was a mistake and would hurt the Confederate war effort. He asserted that VMI should maintain its academic and military programs to produce officers for the Confederate army while the war raged (McMurry 1999). VMI would, in effect, become the "West Point for the Confederacy." Richardson also pointed out that the board had no legal right to close the institute. He soon convinced his fellow board members and a tentative date to reopen VMI was set for October 1, 1861. However, if VMI was to reopen and remain in existence throughout the war years, the academy's superintendent had to be made exempt from service in the Confederate army.

The superintendent of VMI, Col. Francis H. Smith, was not in favor of reopening the academy. He had received a Confederate colonel commission and was content with his orders to defend his hometown of Norfolk, Virginia. He also harbored doubts about VMI's ability to remain open during the war; specifically, due to the restlessness of cadets, and the impossibility of securing supplies and provisions during the conflict. Adjutant General Richardson, aware that Smith did not want to return to VMI, plied Virginia's Governor Letcher and Confederate president Jefferson Davis to support the institution's reopening under his, Smith's, leadership. Both Davis and Letcher agreed that VMI's continued operation was more important than Smith's field service. As a result, Davis released Smith from active duty in November to oversee the military college's reopening and operation (Conrad 1997, 45). The Confederate government also granted permission for VMI professors to leave active service and return to the classroom. With a few exceptions, notably Confederate general Thomas Jonathan "Stonewall" Jackson (the Virginia military academy's former professor of natural philosophy and artillery tactics), most of the prewar professors returned to campus (Couper 1939).

Following VMI's brief closure, applications increased. Enrollment grew in part because many of Virginia's colleges had closed due to lack of students, leaving VMI as one of the few extant wartime institutions of higher education in the state (Gibson 2005). However, the primary reason for the considerable number of applicants was the fact that the academy offered a formal education in military tactics. Parents believed that VMI would provide training and experience that would prove useful if their sons enlisted or were conscripted (McMurry 1999). With a new rank in the Virginia Militia, yet excluded from conscription, Maj. Gen. Smith reopened VMI on January 1, 1862. The academy's short, three-month closure did little to dissuade new enrollees. Upon reopening, 153 freshmen were admitted (Gibson 2005). Further, students from other area colleges transferred to VMI specifically to gain military knowledge and prepare themselves for army service. Other cadets were former soldiers, both officers and enlisted, who enrolled at VMI to start or, in some cases, finish their higher education while recuperating from wounds received on the battlefield. In all, ninety-five VMI cadets had experienced some form of active military service before attending the Virginia military academy (McMurry 1999).

Though VMI had little trouble attracting new cadets during the war, the institution's administration struggled to retain them. Historian Richard McMurry's study on the Corps of Cadets during and immediately following the Civil War concluded that for the classes of 1863 through 1868, there were 969 matriculants with only 94 graduates, a significant disparity. For many cadets, receiving a military college degree could not compete with the concept of winning honor on the battlefield and commendations for military service. Most cadets waited until they were of enlistment age to enlist. With or without their parents' permission, VMI cadets would resign from the academy or simply desert to enlist and fight for the Confederacy. A cadet in 1862 wrote, "the cadets are resigning very fast . . . all think they ought to be in the army" (Snodgrass 1862). Some students attempted to garner expulsion for disciplinary or academic infractions. Superintendent Smith appealed to the cadets and urged them to remain at VMI. One cadet wrote that, "As General Smith says, be soldiers in the next army, after the present one has been killed off" (Snodgrass 1862). However, as the war continued, Smith could not stem the tide of war-hungry students who left the campus to join the fray. The number of cadets fluctuated day to day, with old cadets leaving VMI and new cadets arriving. From January to July 1862, only 143 out of 268 cadets remained (Conrad 1997).

CADET LIFE AND CONFEDERATE SERVICE

The VMI cadets were called into Confederate service during April and May of 1862 to support Stonewall Jackson's Shenandoah Valley Campaign. When the 1862–1863 academic year commenced on September 1, 1862, the war was far enough removed from Lexington that VMI was able to hold classes without having to engage in military service; it was the only term during the war that cadets, faculty, and administrators were able to do so (McMurry 1999). During this time, the cadets were kept busy with military requirements, yet they still practiced regular drilling in addition to academic coursework. Cadets received only thirty minutes for leisure activities after each meal during the week (Wise 1915). As Cadet Reid wrote to his parents in the fall of 1862, "In place of studying this week they try to drill us to death. We get up at Rev at 5, to squad drill at 5 ½, & drill till 6 ½, go to breakfast parade at 7, go on guard mounting at 8, squad drill from 11 to 12, Dinner parade at 1, squad drill again at 5 to 6, dress parade from 6 ¼ to 7 ¼, evening parade at 7, & tattoo at 9 ½ Besides we are on guard twice in every week, stand one hour in the night each time" (1862).

New cadets, referred to as "Rats," also had to deal with mistreatment and hazing from senior cadets. First-year cadets were required to stand when an upperclassman entered their rooms or spoke to them (Wise 1915). The more common form of hazing for VMI Rats was known as "bucking," which consisted of tying a cadet's hands together, placing the bound wrists over the cadet's knees. A stick was then placed between the new cadet's legs and hands. Once this was accomplished, the cadet was turned over and his backside was exposed. Older cadets would then use a bayonet scabbard to write, via cutting, the Rat's name, county, state, "VMI," and class year on his posterior. Cadet Gatewood who experienced this painful initiation ritual wrote to his parents and stated, "I do tell it hurts awful bad" (Gatewood 1860). Until the academic year was completed on July 4, a new cadet could be "bucked" by a senior cadet for "expressing an opinion upon any subject" (Wise 1915, 20). Hazing incidents grew so numerous during the Civil War that board member William Richardson wrote to Superintendent Smith that the atrocious abuses of new cadets, "ought to be put out [underlined in original], and until it is put down effectually and under the regulations, I hope the Legislature will not appropriate another dollar to the Institute" (1863).

Like other Southern colleges and universities that remained open during the war, VMI faced severe food and clothing shortages. Likewise, there was a significant lack of textbooks and academic supplies. As textbooks were in short supply cadets were encouraged to return books to the quartermaster so they could be reissued. A cadet whose brother sent him some textbooks wrote to his parents that he wished his brother, "had sent a dozen coppies

“VMI Cadet Andrew Gatewood and Unidentified Cadet” c. 1861. VMI Archives Photograph Collection. Image courtesy of the Virginia Military Institute Archives, Lexington, Virginia.

[sic] of French Grammar as . . . I could sell every coppy [sic] for two $ apiece” (Langhorne 1862). Similarly, fuel for gaslight was scarce. When the VMI barracks were built from 1850–1851, they were among the first facilities in the Commonwealth of Virginia to install gas lighting (Couper 1939). However, the war caused oil shortages and as Cadet Hanna wrote on April 27, 1864, “We used candlelight, gas having given out” (Hanna, 1864).

Fabric for cadet uniforms, bought in Northern states prior to the war, was now difficult to locate and purchase. Cloth obtained from Richmond during the early part of the war was of such poor quality that its use was discontinued. Eventually, every cadet was required to provide his own cloth for uniforms (Couper 1939). Soon cadet uniforms were anything but uniform, differing in color, length, and texture. Cloth and clothing items sent to cadets from all over Virginia and the Confederate South resulted in uniforms that varied from "Melton gray to Georgia butternut" (Wise 1915, 14). One VMI graduate wrote that during the war the general cadet uniform consisted of "a simple forage cap, blue or gray . . . coarse sheep's gray jacket and pants, seven buttons and a black tape stripe . . . plain leather waist belt and cartridge box, with harness buckle . . . and muzzle-loading Belgian rifles, as clumsy as pickaxes" (Wise 1915, 13–14). Shoes, in particular, were in short supply, and the cadets' constant marching during military service further aggravated the situation. Cadet Langhorne wrote to his parents, "General Smith says he cannot and will not furnish us shoes, and I am nearly barefooted" (Langhorne 1862).

The quality and quantity of food was a constant source of cadet complaints. At the beginning of the war the Board of Visitors granted Superintendent Smith sweeping powers to deal with all questions of discipline and to obtain necessary supplies (Smith 1912). Smith purchased three hundred head of cattle, ten hogshead barrels of sugar, and fifty barrels of molasses. He managed to convince a Confederate quartermaster to transport barrels of molasses from Vicksburg, Mississippi, to Lexington for cadet consumption (Conrad 1997). After the war, Smith stated, "with these large supplies, judiciously used, we were able to give great comfort to the cadets" (Smith 1912, 183). VMI cadets perceived the quality of food quite differently from the academy's administration, especially as the war progressed. Cadet Edmund Berkeley wrote, "We have very poor fare here. Today for breakfast we had only two pieces of bread and about half a gill of milk with what we call growly—which is made of mutton, beef, beef feet or anything else they can make. For dinner we have beef or cabbage or turnips one day and beef-steak and soup the next. We have nothing that I would have eaten at home, but I am so hungry when I go to means that I think even turnips delicious" (Couper 1939). Cadet John Shields described breakfast: "The boys have a rule at our table, one side stay away one morning, and the other side the next, in order that what we have, may go around at breakfast" (Shields n.d.).

Cadet complaints became so numerous that VMI Board of Visitors member Richardson investigated their claims on behalf of the institution's governing council. In a letter to Superintendent Smith, an aggravated Richardson noted: "the Corps of Cadets is far better subsisted than any private family I know. General Lee himself lives almost entirely upon vegetables, leaving what meat there is for the soldiers—and to descend from the sublime to the ridiculous, I am very near the point of having no meat on my own tables" (Richardson 1863). VMI's administrators eventually instituted a payment-in-kind system where parents could send meat and crops to Smith in lieu of tuition. Smith also employed agents in Europe to buy and ship supplies to Virginia through blockade-runners. The most important of these agents was VMI alumnus Col. Benjamin F. Ficklin (Smith 1912). Smith, selling some of the cattle he had purchased to support VMI, gave Ficklin $10,000 to buy supplies in Europe. The supplies were successfully transported from Nassau in the Bahamas through the Confederate blockade on Ficklin's boat, the *Giraffe*. However, getting supplies through the blockade was far from guaranteed. In November 1863, a shipment of supplies for VMI left Europe on the steamer *Dare* (Conrad 1997). Among the cargo was cloth, as well as "a large supply of buttons, and 1,000 pairs of shoes" (Richardson 1863). Sadly, the *Dare* was beached near Georgetown, South Carolina, in late January and was plundered by members of both the Union and Confederate armies (Richardson 1864). Richardson noted that both sides left the textbooks.

In addition to trying to obtain supplies, the cadets were called upon to help defend the Shenandoah Valley. Beginning in August 1863 and continuing well into 1864, Union Brig. Gen. William Woods Averell's cavalry conducted raids into the valley. The three raids conducted by Averell in late summer, fall, and winter of 1863 resulted in the service of VMI's Corps of Cadets to help defend the Shenandoah Valley. As a result, each raid disrupted academic duties and related activities. Not a shot was fired by the cadets, nor were the students under fire during the raids, but as VMI historian William Couper pointed out, the raids indirectly benefited VMI. The raids, wrote Couper, "compelled the adoption of a policy of defense for the State property at Lexington; it secured better arms for the cadets and by far the most important, it served to accustom the cadets to service in the field and harden them for more arduous campaigns in the session" (1939, 2:207).

In his early December 1863 raid, Averell again pushed into Virginia, aiming for the East Tennessee and Virginia Railroad at Salem, southwest of

Lexington. Confederate Cdr. Gen. Imboden, in an attempt to capture Averell, requested the VMI Corps of Cadets occupy passes at local Panther Gap and Goshen (Conrad 1997). Commandant of Cadets Scott Ship set out with 180 cadets, but two days of incessant rain caused them to halt at Bratton's Run. There the cadets waded in freezing, waist-deep water to build a bridge for artillery to cross. The cadets reached Cold Sulphur Springs on December 17, "through mud & water a foot deep near ten miles" (Stanard 1961, 24). A house near the cadets' campsite contained a still and "every boy got enough to drink to make him sleep and to keep him from taking cold. In fact, most of the boys were quite merry" (Stanard 1961, 24). The next day the cadets were ordered to march back to Lexington, again in freezing rain. The march back was torture as many of the cadets were hungover and barefoot. All cadets struggled with the relentless cold on the return trip. Cadet Stanard wrote to his mother: "Well dear Mother we reached our journeys end Monday evening and nar'e yankee did we kill or see after marching us all over this plagued mountainous country, and ruining our feet, we being badly shod [underlined in original] at the time. . . . Although we were so near drowned, yet there was no grumbling" (1961, 24).

During the three Shenandoah Valley raids cadets were absent from VMI a total of thirteen days, but with rehabilitation needed after each march and the disruption of their studies, the fall semester was an academic loss. Constant marching had taken a physical toll on the cadets as well as on their clothing and equipment (McMurry 1999). On December 18, VMI board member Richardson wrote to Superintendent Smith that the Confederate government was furnishing the academy with 250 pairs of shoes to be deducted from the supply of Gen. James Longstreet's corps (Richardson 1863). On December 21, Richardson wrote again to say that the Confederate Secretary of War had decided, "whenever the cadets are out upon the call of the Confederate Gov't—they shall be supplied by the Confed Gov't" (Richardson 1863). Richardson was also concerned with the effect that constant military service was having on the cadets' academic studies. On December 19, he wrote, "it is time now, I think, to define distinctly what military service is legitimately due from them, for if they care to be called out upon all occasions the school must be abandoned" (Richardson 1863). Richardson wrote again about the cadets' studies on Christmas Eve: "it appears to me that if these calls continue to occur as frequently as heretofore, the whole course of education at the Institute will be broken up, and that it is full time that the question should be made and determined, what is the extent of service that they may be called on to perform" (Richardson 1863).

LATE WARTIME SERVICE

The spring of 1864 ushered in a new military campaign season for Virginia, but this season would prove to be unlike any Gen. Lee or the Confederacy had yet faced. On March 9, 1864, President Abraham Lincoln appointed Ulysses S. Grant as general of the Union armies. Grant immediately instituted a new strategy to end the war using his armies to coordinate strikes that would overwhelm Confederate forces. As part of these strikes, numerous smaller Union regiments were active throughout the South. Among these were Union Maj. Gen. Franz Sigel and his men in the Shenandoah Valley. Sigel's forces advanced through the valley to deny the Confederate soldiers crops from the recent spring harvest (Couper 1939).

Confederate forces were sparse in Shenandoah at this time. As a result, Superintendent Smith, via VMI Board of Visitors member Richardson, sent a letter to Gen. Lee offering the use of the VMI Corps of Cadets for military operations in late April 1864. A few days later Sigel's troops advanced into the valley. This caused Confederate general John Breckenridge to call the VMI cadets into service on May 10 (Annual Report 1864). On the morning of May 11, 1864, 247 cadets under the command of the new commandant of cadets, Scott Ship, left Lexington towards Staunton, Virginia. The cadets arrived the following day and departing for New Market, Virginia, on May 13. The cadets marched eighty-one miles in four days to reach Breckinridge's troops at New Market (Couper 1939). The damp, cool morning of May 15 found the cadets sheltered behind the main Confederate line. Breckinridge planned to use the cadets as a reserve and called them forward to a position close to the main military line (Davis 1975). The cadets advanced in parade formation and took a few casualties from Union artillery. They continued, filling gaps in their lines as they marched until they were sheltered, out of sight of the artillery. At midday, Sigel arrived with the main body of his troops and established a defensive line on Bushong's Hill, above a farm of the same name (Turner 1912). Breckinridge decided to assault the Union line and ordered his forces to advance. Union artillery, firing into the center of Breckinridge's line with double-loaded grapeshot, inflicted substantial casualties. The advance stalled and a gap opened in the center of the Confederate line. Breckenridge realized that he would have to commit the VMI cadet reserves to fighting but agonized over sending the young men into battle. His assistant ordnance officer, Maj. Charles Semple, told Breckenridge that the cadets would fight like veterans and that if the gap in the military line was not closed the battle would be lost (Conrad 1997). In response, Breckinridge told Semple to "put the boys in, and may God forgive me for the order" (Davis 1975, 119).

The cadets advanced in parade formation and attracted the attention of Union artillery soldiers. Thereafter, the cadets began to receive fire, which forced them to take cover behind a wood fence in a nearby orchard. At this time, Sigel ordered Union troops to advance. All the while, it had begun to rain over the battlefield. Union troops sustained significant casualties, and the attack was beaten back by Confederate forces. As the storm broke, the Confederates again charged the Union lines. The VMI cadets advanced with the Confederate line, losing their shoes in the muddy battlefield and once more taking casualties from Union artillery. Reaching the Union lines, they rushed through the Federal infantry to an artillery battery, where they captured a cannon and its crew (Davis 1975). The Confederate troops succeeded in breaking Union lines, and the remaining Union forces retreated down the Shenandoah Valley with the Confederate troops and VMI cadets in pursuit, ending the Battle of New Market. Breckenridge rode up to the cadet battery after the battle, telling them: "boys, the work you did today will make you famous" (Conrad 1997, 99). Regardless of Breckinridge's encouraging words, ten VMI cadets died that day as a result of wounds received on the battlefield: Cadets Samuel F. Atwill, Thomas G. Jefferson, William H. Cabell, Henry J. Jones, Charles G. Crockett, William H. McDowell, Alva C. Hartsfield, J. Beverly Stanard, Luther C. Haynes, and Joseph C. Wheelwright. (Bierle 2019; Virginia Military Institute 2019)

The Battle of New Market was relatively inconsequential compared to other battles in the Shenandoah Valley, but it did temporarily secure the agricultural region for the Confederate army (Davis 1975, 184). With Sigel no longer a threat, Breckinridge transferred his brigades from the Shenandoah Valley to supply Gen. Lee with additional troops for the Battle of Cold Harbor near Mechanicsville, Virginia (Gindlesperger 1997). The cadets had been vital in the Battle of New Market. Still their contribution to the Confederate victory dealt a significant blow to VMI as several of the cadets who engaged in the battle died (Davis 1975).

Traveling to Richmond after the battle, the cadets returned to Lexington on June 9, 1864. The next day, Sigel's replacement, Union general David Hunter, pushed up the valley and was just north of Lexington, skirmishing with Confederate Brig. Gen. John McCausland's Confederate forces. McCausland, an 1857 graduate of VMI, fought to keep Hunter out of Lexington, but his forces were too weak to make an extended stand (Conrad 1997). Superintendent Smith realized that the defense of Lexington was futile against Hunter's forces and evacuated as much property and supplies from VMI as could be carried. He ordered canal boats to be loaded with all VMI artillery, large amounts of ammunition, as well as institutions more vital records. Most of the scientific equipment and the library were left due to lack of time. Brig. Gen. McCausland ordered the evacuation of Lexington that evening (Smith 1941).

On June 11, 1864, McCausland's rear guard fell back across the North (now Maury) River Bridge. Once his forces were across, VMI cadet sappers burned the bridge while cadet howitzers fired on the bridge's pilings to destroy them before falling back to the campus. Soon thereafter, an artillery duel occurred between Union guns across the river and McCausland's artillery at the institute. When Union shells struck VMI's main college building, Superintendent Smith moved the cadets first under the parapet in front of the barracks and then to the nearby campus of Washington College (today Washington and Lee University) for protection. Near the college president's home on the Washington College campus, the cadets tore up the VMI flag carried during the Battle of New Market and distributed the pieces among themselves, so it would not fall into Union hands (Couper 1939). The cadets then marched to Lynchburg, Virginia. After ransacking VMI and "liberating" the statue of George Washington, Gen. Hunter burned VMI on the morning of June 12, despite the protests of his officers (Gibson and Whiting 1995). Hunter, disregarding a Federal army order prohibiting the damage of educational institutions, saw VMI as part of the military establishment of the South and set the college ablaze.

The cadets were ordered back to Lexington and arrived on June 24, 1864. With the VMI edifice destroyed, they took quarters at Washington College. The destruction of the main VMI building demoralized the cadets, but in a letter to Richardson, Smith took another view: "(T)he Virginia Military Institute still proudly and defiantly stands. The brick and mortar which gave temporary shelter . . . constituted not the Military school of Virginia. Thank

God, that still lives" (1864). The first reports of the burning of VMI reached Richmond on June 17. VMI Board of Visitors member Richardson called a meeting of the academy's governing board. The immediate topic of discussion was where to relocate it. Washington College, Lynchburg College, Randolph-Macon College, and the University of Virginia were mentioned as possibilities. On June 27, members of the class of 1864 graduated in Lexington, and the rest of the Corps of Cadets was furloughed until September 1 (Conrad 1997).

The Board of Visitors met in Lexington from July 15 until July 21, 1864, and decided to rebuild the Lexington campus if possible. Preparations to reopen VMI at its original site fell behind schedule, and the date for the fall semester was first moved to October 1. It was then pushed to October 20 and finally, November 1. However, with Confederate general Jubal Early's defeat at the Battle of Fisher's Hill in September, the Shenandoah Valley was again open to Union forces. Richardson directed Superintendent Smith not to organize the Corps of Cadets until the fate of the Shenandoah Valley was decided (1864). With the cadets on furlough, the Confederate government decided that the young soldiers would be better employed in defenses around Richmond, rather than waiting at home for classes at VMI to reconvene. On September 29, Union forces took Fort Harrison, one of the most important positions in the outer defenses of Richmond. Calls went out throughout Virginia for all available men to gather in Richmond to bolster defenses. Approximately thirty cadets reported for duty under the command of Cadet Capt. Pizzini, a veteran of the New Market campaign (Couper 1939).

By November 11, 262 cadets were employed in the defense of Richmond. Superintendent Smith, who was still in Lexington, realized that if the cadets were not under VMI leadership, the Confederate government could absorb them into military ranks surrounding the city. Smith ordered VMI commandant of cadets Scott Ship to organize and take control of the cadets in Richmond. The cadets were soon dispatched to bolster Confederate defenses near Williamsburg, then under attack by Union Maj. Gen. Benjamin Butler's Army of the James. Ship requested that the cadets be taken into active Confederate service. The request was granted, and the cadets were transferred from the reserve forces to Confederate general Ewell's Department of Richmond (Conrad 1997). With the Shenandoah Valley continuing to be a target for Union military forces, the City of Richmond offered the Alms House (also known as the Richmond Nursing Home) as a site to reopen VMI. The Alms House was a relatively new structure built just before the war started. It was soon converted to a military hospital. Its use as a hospital had taken a physical toll, and the facility was not a cheerful place. On December 12, 1864, the cadets were released from field duty and mustered at the Alms House. The cadets were then furloughed until December 23, but some had difficulty returning to Richmond due to Union advances. As a result, several did not reach Richmond until January (McMurry 1999).

Continuous Union activity around Richmond, in addition to the poor condition of the Alms House, spurred restlessness the cadets. As a result, several students informed VMI's administration that they wanted to leave the academy to enlist. In response, the Board of Visitors passed a resolution urging the Confederate secretary of war, Judah Philip Benjamin, to allow cadets in good academic standing to enlist (Couper 1939). Most cadets joined cavalry or artillery units rather than enlist in the infantry due to a general fear that they would be immediately called into battle (Richardson 1865). Cadet James Witt wrote in February 1865, "It is evident that if we remain as a body or Corps we will be in service this coming spring, and all are desirous to choose their command and not go in service as a 'corps of Cadets'" (Witt 1865).

VMI cadets and other reserve military men were ordered to repel Union general Philip Sheridan's cavalry on March 12, 1865. The cadets constructed hasty entrenchments near Westham Plank Road and waited, but an attack never materialized, and they returned to the Alms House on March 13. The cadets were called out for the last time on April 1, 1865. In previous months, Union advancement alarms had been a constant occurrence. This particular alarm, however, proved significantly different (Couper 1939). Cadet F. H. Smith Jr., in his memoirs (January 3, 1914), noted that, "it was apparent to us that something out of the ordinary was taking place. Rockets and other signals were seen, and a general air of excitement seems to prevail. At taps many of us kept our clothes on and watched from the windows, expecting orders of some sort calling out the corps. We did not have to wait long, for in a short time a horseman rode rapidly to the front of barracks and . . . asked for the Superintendent."

The cadets marched through Richmond to take over rifle pits so that Longstreet's corps could aid Gen. Lee in Petersburg, Virginia. According to Cadet Smith (1914), the corps "were placed in the rifle-pits early Sunday morning, April 2. We were separated from the enemy by a heavy body of pines. Our pickets and those of the enemy were in speaking distance." The cadets were facing the enemy with no other friendly troops in support and were terrified that an attack could come at any time. "We remained there," continued Cadet Smith, "constantly expecting attack, and when the tremendous cheering of the enemy was heard, from time to time, we were sure our time had come. If anything, more uncomfortable than this waiting could have been found, we didn't care to experience it" (1914). The cadets were relieved by dismounted cavalry in late afternoon and walked back into the city (McMurry 1999). Along the way, some of the cadets' fathers from Richmond informed them that Petersburg had fallen, and Richmond would soon follow. Before returning to the Alms House, the cadets continued to the city's Capital Square, where the scene was one of panic and confusion. There, the cadets were "disbanded and directed to escape the best way we could, as in a body we could not reach any organized Confederate field force" (Couper 1939, 3:92). The academy's battle flag was taken by the cadet color sergeant, wrapped around his body, and carried through Union lines to his home in Lynchburg, Virginia. He returned the flag to Superintendent Smith a year later. Cadet Joel M. Hannah, sick with fever from serving in the Richmond trenches, was left in Richmond and died on April 17. He was the final VMI cadet to die in the war. Of the approximately 1,930 VMI alumni alive at the beginning of the Civil War, 1,827 served in the Confederate army. Of those who served, 240 died, and 171 were killed or mortally wounded in action (Conrad 1997). Leaving Richmond, small groups of cadets attached themselves to other Virginia units, while others headed to North Carolina. By late April, all cadets had been captured, surrendered, or had reached their homes (McMurry 1999). For the cadets of the Virginia Military Institute, their military service to the Confederacy and state of Virginia had ended. Both the Federal and Reconstructionist Virginia state governments were hesitant to support a college that had produced large numbers of officers in the Confederate army but allowed VMI's classes to reconvene shortly after the end of the war on October 16, 1865. With the buildings still in ruins, cadets were billeted in private homes and forbidden by the Provincial Government of Virginia from wearing uniforms or drilling with arms (Flood 1981).

VMI survived the postwar years on private donations and faculty salary reductions. The faculty had been hit especially hard by the war. Eighteen of the prewar faculty were killed, and others had to leave their teaching positions at VMI due to the loss of family fortunes. Through the efforts of Superintendent Smith, Adj. Gen. Richardson, and VMI alumni, the institute soon expanded and grew academically, attracting a new cadre of faculty. George Washington Custis Lee (Gen. Robert E. Lee's son), John Mercer Brooke (sailor and engineer ultimately responsible for the Trans-Atlantic Cable), and Matthew Fontaine Maury (early oceanographer and author of the 1855 book, *The Physical Geography of the Sea*) all joined VMI's faculty in the five years following the war (Brooke 1981; Williams 1963). Reconstruction, however, forced VMI to reemphasize its academic mission over its military one, due both to the policies of the new state government and the fact that VMI was one of the few colleges still open in Virginia. Even so, the Virginia Military Institute progressed through Reconstruction and into the twentieth century.

Today, vestiges of VMI's involvement in the Civil War remain on campus. The graves of the ten cadets that died at the Battle of New Market front the Nichols Engineering Building. Their headstones are fronted by a bronze statue titled *Virginia Mourning Her Dead*. It was crafted by VMI alumni Moses Jacob Ezekiel and dedicated in 1903. Ezekiel fought alongside the cadets who perished on the battlefield and went on to become a famed US artist renowned for his various sculptures. Perhaps the most regarded pieces of Ezekiel's professional portfolio are his statues that honor the Southern Lost Cause such as *Tyler Confederate Memorial Gateway*, Hickman, Kentucky, and *Confederate Memorial*, Arlington, Virginia. Other Virginia Military Institute Civil War memorials and traditions include a large mural depicting the VMI cadets at the Battle of New Market (painted by Benjamin W. Clinedinst, 1880 VMI graduate) in the campus chapel and an annual military ceremony where a roll call of the deceased Civil War cadets is read. Rejoining each name, a cadet replies "Died on the Field of Honor." These ceremonies and memorials reinforce the memory of VMI's involvement in and persistence though the American Civil War.

REFERENCES

Allardice, Bruce. 1997. "West Points of the Confederacy: Southern Military Schools and the Confederate Army." *Civil War History* (December 1997): 313–30.

Annual Report of the Superintendent, 15 July 1864. Virginia Military Institute, VMI Archives, Lexington, Virginia.

Board of Visitors Minutes, 1853–1864. Virginia Military Institute, VMI Archives, Lexington, Virginia.

Bierle, Sarah Kay. 2019. *Call Out the Cadets: The Battle of New Market, May 15, 1864*. El Dorado Hills, CA: Savas Beatie, LLC.

Brooke, George M. 1981. *John M. Brooke, Naval Scientist and Educator*. Richmond: University of Virginia Press.

Conrad, James Lee. 1997. *The Young Lions Confederate Cadets at War*. Harrisburg, PA: Stackpole Books.

Couper, William. 1939. *One Hundred Years at VMI*. 4 vols. Richmond, VA: Garrett and Massie.

Couper, William. *Papers*. Virginia Military Institute, VMI Archives, Lexington, Virginia.

Davis, William C. 1975. *The Battle of New Market*. New York: Doubleday.

DeCaro, Louis, Jr. 2015. *Freedom's Dawn: The Last Days of John Brown in Virginia.* Lanham, MD: Rowman & Littlefield.

Flood, Charles Bracelen. 1981. *Lee: The Last Years*. Boston: Houghton Mifflin.

Gatewood, Andrew C. L. Letter to Parents. August 4, 1860. Andrew C. L. Gatewood Papers, VMI Archives, Lexington, Virginia.

Gatewood, Andrew C. L. Letter to Sister. 18 April 1861.

Gibson, Keith E. 2010. *Virginia Military Institute.* Charleston, SC: Arcadia Publishing.

Gibson, Keith E. Director, VMI Museum, Lexington, Virginia. 2005. Interviewed by Michael Wallace, Fort Leavenworth, Kansas. 8 October 2005.

Gindlesperger, James. 1997. *Seed Corn of the Confederacy*. Shippensburg, VA: Burd Street Press.

Hanna, John F. 1864, Diary. John F. Hanna Papers. Virginia Military Institute, VMI Archives, Lexington, Virginia.

Langhorne, J. Kent. Letter to Aunt. September 28, 1862. J. Kent Langhorne Papers. Virginia Military Institute, VMI Archives, Lexington, Virginia.

McMurry, Richard M. 1999. *Virginia Military Institute Alumni in the Civil War*. Lynchburg, VA: H. E. Howard, Inc.

Reid, J. Henry. Letter to Father. August 26, 1862. J. Henry Reid Papers. Virginia Military Institute, VMI Archives, Lexington, Virginia.

Richardson, W. H. Letter to Francis H. Smith. August 5, 1863. W. H. Richardson Papers. Transcribed by William Couper. Virginia Military Institute, VMI Archives, Lexington, Virginia.

Richardson, W. H. Letter to Francis H. Smith. November 11, 1863.

Richardson, W. H. Letter to Francis H. Smith. November 18, 1863.

Richardson, W. H. Letter to Francis H. Smith. December 18, 1863.

Richardson, W. H. Letter to Francis H. Smith. December 19, 1863.

Richardson, W. H. Letter to Francis H. Smith. December 21, 1863.

Richardson, W. H. Letter to Francis H. Smith. December 24, 1863.

Richardson, W. H. Letter to Francis H. Smith. January 18, 1864.

Richardson, W. H. Letter to Francis H. Smith. May 3, 1864.

Richardson, W. H. Letter to Francis H. Smith. September 24, 1864.

Richardson, W. H. Letter to Francis H. Smith. February 21, 1865.

Shields, John. Partial Letter. N.d. John Shields Papers. Virginia Military Institute, VMI Archives, Lexington, Virginia.

Shipp, Scott. Letter to Francis H. Smith. November 2, 1864. Scott Shipp Papers. Virginia Military Institute, VMI Archives, Lexington, Virginia.

Smith, Francis H. 1912. *The Virginia Military Institute: Its Building and Rebuilding*. Lynchburg, VA: J. P. Bell Co.

Smith, Francis H. Letter to William Richardson. July 27, 1864. Superintendents Outgoing Correspondence. VMI Archives, Lexington, Virginia.

Smith, Francis H., Jr. 1914. "Military Service of the Corps of Cadets." *The Cadet*, January 3, 1914.

Smith, Francis H., III. 1941. "Old Spex of the VMI." Unpublished manuscript.

Snodgrass, John B. Letter to Sister. March 29, 1862. John B. Snodgrass Papers. Virginia Military Institute, VMI Archives, Lexington, Virginia.

Special Orders Book. 1861. VMI Archives, Lexington, Virginia.

Special Orders Book. 1864. Virginia Military Institute, VMI Archives, Lexington, Virginia.

Stanard, Beverly. 1961. *Letters of a New Market Cadet*. Chapel Hill: University of North Carolina Press.

Stevenson, Thomas A. Letter to Sister. November 20, 1860. Thomas A. Stevenson Collection. VMI Archives, Lexington, Virginia.

Superintendent's Records: Outgoing Correspondence. 1853–1864. Virginia Military Institute, VMI Archives, Lexington, Virginia.

Turner, Edward R. 1912. *The New Market Campaign*. Richmond: Whittet & Shepperson. Virginia Military Institute, VMI Archives. Last modified November 17, 2020. https://vmi.edu/archives/civil-war-and-new-market/vmi-in-civil-war-faq/.

Virginia Military Institute. "Died on the Field of Honor." 2019. Virginia Military Institute Museum and Archives. Accessed December 12, 2019. vmi.edu/archives/civil-war-and-new-market/battle-of-new-marker/died-on-the-field-of-honor/.

VMI Order Book. 1861. Virginia Military Institute, VMI Archives, Lexington, Virginia.

VMI Order Book. 1862. Virginia Military Institute, VMI Archives, Lexington, Virginia.

VMI Order Book. 1863. Virginia Military Institute, VMI Archives, Lexington, Virginia.

Williams, Frances Leigh. 1963. *Matthew Fontaine Maury: Scientist of the Sea*. New Brunswick, NJ: Rutgers University Press.

Wise, Jennings C. 1915. *The Military History of the Virginia Military Institute from 1839 to 1865*. Lynchburg, VA: J. P. Bell Co.

Wise, John S. 1889. "The West Point of the Confederacy." *Century Magazine*, 463. N.p.

Witt, James. Letter to Miss Fannie. February 8, 1865. James Witt Papers. Virginia Military Institute, VMI Archives, Lexington, Virginia.

CHAPTER TEN

A "Charitable Institution"

The University of North Carolina in the Era of the Civil War

Don Holmes

It was a cold, rainy day on January 15, 1795, when the University of North Carolina (UNC) opened its doors. There were no students present, and the few people in attendance simply inspected the newly erected buildings and went home (Linderman 2018). A month after the opening ceremony the university's first student, Hinton James, made the long, 137-mile trek from his home in Wilmington, North Carolina, to the village of Chapel Hill. Owing much to his early education at UNC, James would become a successful civil engineer after his graduation in 1798 (Snider 1992). From its inception, UNC was to be physically located where any of North Carolina's white sons could gain a respectable higher education no matter their social or political class. In the official 1789 "Act Establishing the University of North Carolina," the North Carolina General Assembly recorded its duty to educate young men. The opening of the act reads in part: "WHEREAS in all well-regulated governments it is the indispensable duty of every Legislature to consult the happiness of a rising generation, and endeavor to fit them for an honorable discharge of the social duties of life, by paying the strictest attention to their education" (North Carolina Act 1789).

In its early years, UNC flourished as a public institution that welcomed a "long line of seekers after knowledge" (Snider 1992, 4). However, the institution faced its greatest nineteenth-century challenges during the American Civil War, when student enrollment declined, and public funding drastically decreased (Powell 1992). Still, UNC remained open throughout the fray. Only during the postwar, Reconstruction era did the institution waver owing to the wartime aftermath of an economy rife with political and financial uncertainty. The story of UNC's ability to remain open during the war centers on its longest serving president, David Lowery Swain. The former state executive led the university through the Civil War and, after Swain's fall from political grace, UNC fell with him.

PRESIDENT SWAIN

Before Swain became president of the University of North Carolina, he was a popular state governor. In 1831, the North Carolina General Assembly elected Swain to the university's Board of Trustees—an influential body that maintained a powerful grip over university affairs. The following year, Swain was elected governor for a one-year term. Historian Carolyn A. Wallace (1996) notes that Swain's rise to governor was a surprise to many North Carolina politicians. His appointment was an attempt to garner the support of North Carolinians in the western counties, National Republican Party members, and advocates of state's rights—all of whom were in opposition to eastern North Carolinian Democrats. By the end of his yearlong gubernatorial administration, Swain had become quite popular, which led to two additional terms as governor. During his state administration, Swain advocated for the expansion of North Carolina's railroad system and presided over two internal improvement conventions, which included a revision of assessment laws such as a deceased poll tax, a public income tax, and increased revenue to support public construction projects (Wallace 1996). A pivotal focus of Swain's campaigns was railroad construction, which, it was argued, would better connect the politically divisive Western and Eastern counties of North Carolina. However, as Wallace (1996) suggests, little was completed in the way of enhancing the state's railway systems, public education facilities, and constitutional reform during Swain's first term as governor.

When Joseph Caldwell, the longtime, first appointed president of UNC died (1835), the post remained vacant for a year. Thereafter, the university's Board of Trustees concluded that the institution was in dire need of stable leadership and appointed Swain as president due to his reputation for effective state management. He began his appointment as president in January

1836. Swain, however, was not the scholar Caldwell had been. Given the board of trustee's desire that the university increase its enrollment and finances, board members felt that a skilled executive would be necessary to increase the institution's standing rather than a traditional academic leader. Swain, it was believed, could do just that and was appointed UNC president in hopes that he would increase the college's regional popularity (Wallace 1996). Swain led UNC through the antebellum era, oversaw the college's Civil War survival, and remained president through the early months after the war ended, a total of thirty-three years. During Swain's tenure, UNC saw an increase in student enrollment and, for the first time, an expansion of campus facilities, which made the university more attractive to prospective students and prosperous in terms of finances (Inscoe 2008). Still, Civil War loomed on the horizon and the University of North Carolina, like many Southern academies, would have to contend with associated hardships.

THE UNIVERSITY'S MARCH TO SECTIONALISM

Civil and political sectionalism cast a shadow over the university beginning in 1856 when Benjamin S. Hedrick, who historian William Snider (1992) referred to as a "mild-mannered professor of chemistry," revealed his choice for the national presidential election. Hedrick favored John C. Fremont, a "Free Soiler." After the Mexican-American War in 1848, the United States acquired much of what is now the West Coast, including California. Vigorous debates in the US Congress ensued as to whether to expand slavery to the newly acquired territory. A major political opponent to the expansion of slavery was the Free Soil party. The Free Soilers were a short-lived faction that, as a core issue, fought the western expansion of slavery (Foner 1995). Even though this debate was waged on a national level, the issue inspired dissention within the halls of UNC.

For many in Chapel Hill, Hedrick's support of Fremont threatened the practice of chattel servitude in North Carolina. Slavery was a major economic factor for a state that relied on plantation-grown tobacco (Crow 2006). In response to Hedrick's overt support of Fremont, William Woods Holden, editor of the *Raleigh Standard* and future governor of North Carolina (1865 and 1868–1871), authored an editorial in defense of North Carolina's Democratic faction. Holden wrote that "the expression of Black Republicanism in our minds in incompatible with our honor and safety as a people. Let our schools and seminaries of learning be scrutinized and if Black Republicanism be found in them, let them be driven out" (Snider 1992, 65). Holden's critique of Carolina's faculty, chiefly professor Hedrick, was the first in a long line of editorials that admonished university officials for political beliefs that did not reflect state's interest—slavery in particular.

After Holden's rejoinder on September 13, 1856, questions about what should be taught and practiced at the state-run university became an increasingly contentious topic for many North Carolinians. Such discussions positioned the university as a battleground of policies that did not reflect the political ambitions of administrators like Swain. For many, Holden's editorial was a rallying cry. For instance, Joseph A. Engelhard, a North Carolina Democrat and an alumnus of the UNC law school, wrote of "poisonous influences" at the university in a letter to the *Standard*: "If our information be entirely correct in regard to the political tendencies and Fremont bias of this professor, ought he not to be 'required to leave,' at least dismissed from a situation where his poisonous influence is so powerful, and his teachings so antagonistical [*sic*] to the 'honor and safety' of the University and the State? Where is the creative power? To them we appeal. Have they no restrictive clause in the selection of instructors or limiting code in regard to their actions" (Hamilton 1910, 10)? Such public response was indicative of many North Carolinians' belief that they had a say in the university's ideological direction—academic, political, and otherwise. Moreover, Engelhard and Holden's publications affirmed that any threat to the university's "honor and safety" would be a threat to the state itself. Symptomatic of Hedrick's Free Soiler sympathies was a nascent secessionist ideology that took root at UNC. Though there was no gunfire, such political ideals eventually led to mob-style violence against Hedrick while he attended a state educational convention in Salisbury, North Carolina (Snider 1992).

In November of 1856, the *Weekly Standard* newspaper reported on the success of the state educational convention. The convention upheld many resolutions, including the establishment of the North Carolina Educational Association. Such organizations did not distinguish between common schools and the state's colleges or universities. With a purview to regulate all education in North Carolina, higher education or otherwise, language in related resolutions admonished outspoken teachers and professors, like Hedrick, who supported political groups opposed to the Democratic majority: "*Resolved*, That the members of this Convention fully impressed with the importance of the Common School System of North Carolina, will use their active assertions as professors in Colleges, and as teachers, as officers of the system, and as citizens of the State, to promote its further usefulness and efficiency" ("State Educational Convention" 1856, 2). According to Sharon K. Knapp, North Carolina newspapers found in Hedrick the antithesis of the state's aims to uphold the institution of slavery. It was of little surprise that the chemistry professor was vilified at the education convention (Knapp 1996). Indeed, convention rabble-rousers mocked Hedrick and paraded an effigy of his likeness (Snider 1992).

Hedrick, as a result, could do little to prevent his eventual dismissal from the University of North Carolina. Following Engelhard's publication, Hedrick sought to explain his Free Soiler ideas and cordon slavery to the American South. In October of 1856, *The Standard* published the professor's sentiments: "I have very little doubt that if the slaves which are now scattered thinly over Tennessee, Kentucky, and Missouri, were back in Virginia and North Carolina, it would be better for all concerned. These old States could then go on and develop the immense wealth, which must remain locked for many years to come. Whilst the new States, free from a system which degrades white labor, would become a land of Common schools, thrift and industry, equal if not superior to any in the Union" (Hamilton 1910, 15). Hedrick believed that keeping slaves in the South would further benefit the Southern economy and reinforce the already powerful planter class. However, within his letter was a strong condemnation of the continuation of slavery itself. Hedrick could not, in his words, "believe that slavery is preferable to freedom, or that slavery extension is one of the constitutional rights of the South" (Hamilton 1910, 13).

Though his rationalization fell on deaf ears, Snider has argued that the Southern economy was better insulated without the expansion of slavery (1992). Nevertheless, Hedrick's "self-defense" proved to be his downfall, as the nation was already perilously divided regarding the institution of slavery. After Hedrick's letter was published, public condemnation increased. Hedrick was labeled a "Black Republican," which, according to Engelhard, was a term associated with men who fostered antislavery and believed in the Northern Republican agenda to emancipate enslaved persons (Hamilton 1910). Soon after, an effigy of Hedrick was once again created, and this time was set ablaze on the UNC campus. Calling all students and community members to the conflagration, the university's bell tower rang throughout the night (Hamilton 1910).

President Swain, in favor of anti-sectional Whig polices, meant to keep the university out of the political fray. As such, Swain withdrew from the furor Hedrick had created in the public eye (Snider 1992). In a letter dated October 4, 1856, Charles Manly, a former state governor and the current UNC secretary and treasurer, pressed Swain to encourage Hedrick's resignation. Manly wrote, "the opinions and advice of other Trustees here, not members of the Committee, were heard, the resolution was withdrawn, and it was finally agreed unanimously that [Swain] shall be requested to use your influence in persuading [Hedrick] to resign" (Hamilton 1910, 16). Swain wrote back to Manly explaining that "proceedings of the Faculty in relation to the publication of Prof. Hedrick" were already underway (Hamilton 1910, 18). Swain commissioned a faculty committee to study the divisive case. Unsurprisingly, the faculty sought to silence Hedrick. Public support was necessary to keep the university's doors open and Hedrick's actions had done little to help. Members of the faculty met and penned the following to the *Standard* in October of 1856: "It was natural that the conduct of Mr. Hedrick should excite anxiety in the minds of the President and Faculty; and in promptly repudiating both his conduct and his dangerous and unconstitutional political opinions, they have not only guarded themselves in advance against the remotest suspicion of sympathizing with him in his views, but they have shown themselves faithful to the people of the State, whose University is their immediate charge, and have met, we doubt not, the expectations, as their proceedings will receive the unanimous approval of the Board of Trustees" (Hamilton 1910, 19). Despite Swain's efforts to stay away from such politics, his implicitness in silencing Hedrick showed, if anything, that he leaned more towards the sectionalists.

Snider noted, "airing partisan political opinions was contrary to the usages of the university" (1992, 65). Penning a response to the above stated, Hedrick made enemies of the very men who once supported his UNC tenure. Rather than tarnish the name of the university by continued association with the chemistry professor, the committee felt it appropriate to silence Hedrick. After the board forced Hedrick out of UNC, he relocated to the nation's capital, where he eventually rose to political influence in President Andrew Johnson's administration. There he was known for determining which Old Confederates should be pardoned after the Civil War ended. He also promoted black suffrage in North Carolina. More than anything, Hedrick's case represents the first time President Swain and the Board of Trustees were directly involved in sectionalist appeasement (Snider 1992). Their role in campus sectionalism did much to undergird the university's political position concerning the approaching war and set the tone for UNC students and faculty during the entirety of the conflict.

It was not the belief that Hedrick could materially damage North Carolina, which caused panic among Southern Democrats. Rather, his detractors feared the influence he had over UNC's students (Hamilton 1910). In response, North Carolina Democrats ensured that they would maintain some authority over the university, even if Swain sought to align himself as a neutral Whig Party member prior to Hedrick's expulsion. Anything in opposition to the Democratic agenda, the support of state's rights, and the proslavery argument was seen as endorsing Free Soiler and Northern Republican ideologies. Though the Free Soiler party lasted only a few years, most Southern Democrats believed that the Republican Party absorbed Free Soiler ideologies, especially those members championed by John C. Frémont, the first Republican presidential candidate in 1856 (Foner 1995). Despite Swain's desire to remain above the political fray that divided the nation in the 1850s, his administrative decision to force Hedrick's resignation may have saved the university from a complete Democratic takeover, which, in time, could have led to a more pronounced call to send students to join Confederate military ranks. Without students UNC could not operate. Student enrollment issues during the war remained a heightened issue as Swain and other university officials struggled to keep the academy afloat. By preserving political silence within the faculty ranks, university officials laid the groundwork for maintaining the college's continued existence, even when blood began to soak the soil in nearby battlefields.

UNC DURING THE CIVIL WAR

Talk of secession and war had been common in Chapel Hill long before the skirmish at Fort Sumter in 1861. When Confederate soldiers fired on a Union garrison in neighboring South Carolina, Chapel Hill residents responded with support and intense enthusiasm to take up arms. Though members of the Whig Party had ruling authority over North Carolina politics when

Swain's tenure as UNC president began, Democrats, by the start of the Civil War, had complete control over both the state's general assembly and the university's Board of Trustees (Snider 1992). Unlike the Democratic machine, Whig politicians did not openly support the sectionalist movement. This lack of sectionalist support did little to turn the tide of war but was instrumental in keeping UNC's doors open during the war. Though the slave-owning, planter class-controlled state politics, President Swain and other Whig-affiliated faculty insisted that the university would remain open for all qualified students. Still, UNC, like its peer regional institutions struggled to keep students enrolled in the face of enlistment solicitations.

In a letter to his family, UNC student Edward H. Armstrong wrote about his intention to join the Confederate war effort. He also wrote about Swain's desire to keep the university out of North Carolina's political disputes. On April 20, 1861, eight days after the Civil War began, Armstrong wrote, "The Orange Guards left Hillsboro this morning, and I am told that there were few dry eyes in the crowd congregated to see them depart. . . . Gov. Swain in alluding to the war said that the south was invincible by any force that our enemies can send against us. He thought that further bloodshed could be avoided by every man in the South shouldering his musket. Lincoln would then see our strength. . . . I beg you to let me be one to proceed to Federal Point" (Armstrong 1861, 2–3). Even though Swain favored the Confederate's efforts, his outwardly expressed political neutrality in the years preceding the Civil War aided his ability to keep students at UNC. While Swain's Confederate leanings perhaps inspired students like Armstrong—who died from battle wounds sustained in 1862—an overt sense of student and faculty conscription into the Confederate army was not supported by Swain.

In a curious case, UNC student John Halliburton may have been the only professed Union supporter enrolled. He aired his pro-Union sympathies at a secessionist gathering held on campus. On April 22, 1861, Halliburton was asked to give a speech in front of his fellow students, the UNC faculty, and President Swain. During his speech, Halliburton expressed his love for the American Union through two lines of a poem: "For the Union of hearts the Union of hands, and the flag of our Union forever" (Halliburton 1861, 4). Still, Halliburton insisted, "Everybody here is talking about war. Many have gone to hunt it up" (Halliburton 1861, 3). Surely the "everybody" Halliburton wrote about to his future wife, Juliet, were his fellow students. In his letter to Juliet, Halliburton described the excitement war brought to the campus:

young men and boys eager to test their manhood on the battlefield while old men, like Swain, concerned themselves with the preservation of academic life and the maintenance of the university.

The Civil War escalated quickly, affecting not only Confederate soldiers but also those who were left behind at homes, on farms, and enrolled in colleges and schools. Despite attempts to maintain regular daily life, the ever-present reality of war stripped all sense of normalcy for most Southerners (Manning 2008). Chandra Manning (2008) suggests that the war generated a tension between the needs of the Confederacy and the needs of Southern families, who were long without men for labor, and, in the case of UNC and other Southern colleges and universities, pupils to teach. Rumors spread that the university would suspend operations in July of 1861. President Swain refuted such concerns in a letter dated July 31, 1861: "The troubled state of the country, caused by the existing war, and the paralysis which affects every kind of business, have very much diminished our numbers. We trust, however, that we shall not suffer a permanent loss from this source; and shall certainly endeavor to deserve success, whatever may be the result" (Swain 1861, 1). On the eve of the war, UNC boasted 456 students. James L. Leloudis (2004) notes this number as the highest enrollment of any antebellum Southern college save the University of Virginia. But by September of 1861, only ninety-one students remained.

Enrollment dropped drastically for several reasons. Some students willingly joined Confederate ranks, while others were involuntarily conscripted under the Conscription Laws of 1862. To prevent the total depletion of students, Swain entreated President Jefferson Davis to exempt UNC students from conscription. Davis approved, but Swain's victory was short lived. In 1864, the Confederate Secretary of War, James Seddon, reinforced conscription for UNC students except those in their senior year of study (Leloudis 2004). University of North Carolina student John Henderson wrote to his mother on February 14, 1863, and described fellow pupils carted away from campus and forced into Confederate ranks: "The enrolling officer has been here; he carried several of the students to the conscript camp at Raleigh, where they were immediately sworn in as soldiers in the armies of the Confederate States" (Henderson 1863, 1).

In the fall of 1863, UNC's Board of Trustees wrote directly to Secretary Seddon, entreating him to consider the institution's low enrollment numbers resulting from military conscription. The board described the university as a traditional and historical site, more so than an educational institution that needed students if it were to survive the war. The petition, in part, read:

> It will be seen by reference to the numbers of the Sophomore & Freshman Classes, & their ages, but five, very few soldiers can be added to the army of the Confederacy. Whilst the removal of that small number may so reduce the Class, as to render it necessary to discontinue the exercises of the Institution—one of the oldest and largest in the Confederacy; and disband the able & venerable corpus of Instructors, some of whom have devoted their services to the Institution for more than a quarter of a century, and others for nearly a half century. (Manly 1863, 2)

In a November 6, 1863, letter, Peter Mallett, commandant of conscription for North Carolina, informed President Swain that the Board of Trustees' further request to exempt UNC's two senior classes from conscription was approved (Mallet 1863).

The effort to keep some students on campus was a success, but it came at a cost. With the shrinking number of students to pay tuition, university finances took a major hit. Before the war, particularly in the 1850s, there were hundreds of men studying at the university. In 1862, the graduating class had just twenty-four students (Snider 1992). To help ease the university's financial burden, members of the faculty elected to receive reduced pay to keep UNC afloat (Battle 1912). Despite low enrollment and dwindling funds, Swain kept UNC's doors open, much to the chagrin of Confederates, who desired every able-bodied Southerner to join the fight despite their claim that Swain and the faculty had "no heart for the cause" (Snider 1992, 67). Even so, the fear of closure remained ever present.

In a letter dated December 12, 1864, Professor William J. Martin wrote to Charles Phillips about his concerns should the university close during the war:

> I think it best to take it as a fundamental notion that the college must be kept up [underlined in original]. Come what may, its organization should not be destroyed. The idea that it is a "sinking ship" is not to be tolerated for a moment [underlined in original]. It must be kept afloat somehow during the war, and then with proper management a prosperous voyage & glorious results are certain [underlined in original]. I feel very earnest on this point, for I believe that if the college is disbanded now it will begin its new life after the war a sickly affair, as will be the fate of the numerous colleges in the South. (Martin 1864, 1)

Closing the doors, no matter how short the duration, made Swain and other university officials fearful they would never be able to revive the university. For instance, when the leadership of South Carolina College (now the University of South Carolina) met in 1861 to officially close the university because of war, they did so not only because of low enrollment but also because the Confederacy had transformed the small state college into an army hospital (Cohen 2012). The University of North Carolina escaped such a fate and, without a significant number of students, remained in operation as an institution of higher education, even during America's deadliest war.

On April 11, 1865, two days after Confederate general Robert E. Lee surrendered to Union forces at the Appomattox Courthouse in Virginia, Zebulon B. Vance, the governor of North Carolina, wrote of the state's charitable institutions to Union general William Tecumseh Sherman. Vance sought to protect the university from pillaging and physical destruction by raiding Union troops. Even though Vance did not directly mention UNC in his letter to Sherman, he sought the general protection of entities that would otherwise be defenseless, and the University of North Carolina was among the governor's list of institutions that included academies and hospitals. Though the mayor of Raleigh, William H. Harrison surrendered the city to Federal officers, Vance requested "the extension of [Sherman's] favor to its defenseless inhabitants generally; and especially to ask [Sherman's] protection for the charitable institutions of the State located here" (Vance 1865, 1). President Swain and fellow UNC faculty negotiated with Gen. Sherman in person on behalf of Governor Vance (Vance 1865).

Though UNC was spared both destruction at the hands of the Union army and closure resulting from the war itself, the institution suffered greatly during Reconstruction. Due to the war's lasting effects on human and monetary capital, the university was forced to close for the first and only time in its history. Kemp Battle, President of the University of North Carolina from 1876 to 1891, wrote about the university's troubled, postwar economic situation in his 1912 book, *History of the University of North Carolina*: "The University kept its doors open in all the hardships of the war, but it was left in desperate circumstances. The endowment was gone. Professors for the payment of their salaries depended on tuition receipts and, owing to the general paralysis of business, students were few in number, and some of them on the beneficiary list" (2). In the years preceding the American Civil War, UNC had been a well-known higher educational entity. As a result, enrollment doubled between 1850 and 1860 and the number of faculty grew to twelve (Linderman 2018). Though the ensuing war resulted in the steady decline of students, the war itself did not have the power to force closure. The lingering influence of regional rebuilding and political Reconstruction, however, stymied the institution's "long line of knowledge seekers"—so much so that UNC closed in the early years of Reconstruction.

RECONSTRUCTION AND THE FALL OF UNC

Despite Swain's efforts to keep the university open after the war, the institution faced further uphill battles exacerbated by poorly crafted policies and precarious acquaintances. To make matters worse, the university simply did not have the financial leverage it possessed during the antebellum era. Without the constant flow of students and other economic allotments such as valuable land grants and state bonds, the university had nearly depleted its endowment by the end of the 1860s (Powell 1992).

Though the Civil War officially ended in 1865, the after-effects of sectionalism remained palpable at UNC. After the war, Swain entertained Union Brig Gen. Smith B. Atkins, who would eventually marry President Swain's daughter, Eleanor Hope Swain. William D. Snider (1992) noted that the courtship between Eleanor and Atkins began when the general sent his regimental band to play in Swains' yard. The Northern general also gifted Eleanor a prize horse, which came to be seen as the university's own "Trojan Horse." Cornelia Spencer, an early supporter and unofficial record keeper of the university, claimed it was a great mistake for Swain to entertain Northern men who could sully the Southern institution's reputation (Inscoe 2008). For many in Chapel Hill and throughout North Carolina, Atkins was a reminder of the South's military defeat and a disruption to their plantation-based economy. As such, Swain's friendship with the Northern general did little to encourage local citizens to support UNC, which hastened the university down a path that ended in closure (Inscoe 2008).

In addition to fostering a marital alliance between his daughter and a Northern general, Swain further damaged his standing as university president by soliciting massive financial loans for the declining university (Snider 1992). Swain's outspoken cry to procure loans to financially enhance the university spawned potent rumors that UNC was in dire circumstances, which only decreased Swain's credibility as president. In September of 1865,

Cornelia Spencer wrote to Ellen Caldwell Summerell that "the future is both dark and uncertain" at the university (1865, 9). Spencer went on to write, "Chapel Hill people are very poor. We are all so dependent on the prosperity of the university, that its decline carries the whole village down" (1865, 9). The university's debts totaled more than $100,000, with $7,000 owed in faculty salaries (Snider 1992). Facing considerable debt, worthless Confederate securities, and nearly two thousand shares in insubstantial bank stock, potential students, many of whom were descendants of UNC alumni, chose to attend other Southern institutions, such as the University of Virginia or Gen. Robert E. Lee's Washington and Lee College in Lexington, Virginia, instead of the ailing University of North Carolina (Leloudis 2004).

In 1867, Swain and the Board of Trustees were successful in petitioning North Carolina's General Assembly to allot $7,000 to repay faculty salaries (Snider 1992), but the money did little to ease the university's large-scale financial burden. In addition, public confidence in Swain's ability to lead the university continued to decrease. A letter dated August 12, 1867, from Charles Phillips to Kemp S. Battle, warned of the university's misdirection: "I take it for granted that the life of this institution has been misdirected for some years. Some may say in one direction, others in another. Some say by one mistake, other suggests another. But when the best scholars among the graduates for thirty consecutive years concur, as they do in our case, in saying that something is wrong in the education of our University, for one, I am willing to listen to their complaints and to heed their suggestions" (Phillips 1867, 2). To change the university's curricular and administrative structure and provide academic programming that would entice Southerners interested in higher education that warranted lucrative careers, UNC's Board of Trustees appointed a committee to determine how best to reorganize the institution. Resulting from the board's actions, Swain and several university faculty members offered their resignations, which were accepted in the fall of 1867. Swain's post as university president was one of the last significant positions he held during his life. One year after resigning from UNC, Swain died from injuries he sustained from falling off of Atkins's prize horse. At the time of his death, he was no longer regarded as the strong leader he once was prior to the war.

President Andrew Johnson appointed Republican William W. Holden as governor of North Carolina in 1865. Holden, like many other North Carolina officials, no longer supported Swain as university president and sought to push out the "old rookery." In doing so, he briefly closed the university in 1868. Holden appointed Reverend Solomon Pool to lead the institution's reorganization in 1869. While reviewing the actions of his presidential predecessor, Pool wrote of his distaste for UNC's old administration and its affiliation with regional, upper-class families: "The aristocratic family influence that has controlled the University ought to be crushed and the institution should be popularized" (Pool 1869, 1). Cornelia Spencer did not believe in Pool's ability to lead the institution. Spencer used her anti-Republican voice in the *North Carolina Presbyterian* (and other, similar publications) to write weekly columns in which she attacked the Holden-Pool camp. Spencer's polemic language characterized post-Civil War UNC leaders as ineffective and incapable of restoring the university to prosperity (Inscoe 2008). Even though Chapel Hill residents opined that Spencer did more harm than good, she continued her war of words. Though Holden and Pool did not sit quietly as Spencer levied her attacks, their voices were all but muted as she assumed different author aliases and even wrote retorts to her own arguments, all to keep the university leadership issue in the newspapers. Influenced by Spencer's attacks, many prospective students chose not to attend the state college. When the university reopened on January 3, 1869, only one student sought admittance.

In a commencement speech Holden remarked, "it will be one university, the University of North Carolina," open to all North Carolina residents, so long as they were white and male (Snider 1992, 81). Holden hoped to attract a larger student body by petitioning the state assembly to appropriate funds for free tuition for 170 students. Unfortunately, his request was declined. By 1870, Holden and the Republican-led General Assembly were contending with state railroad bond issues (Snider 1992). Even more pressing, Holden battled the Ku Klux Klan by sending in black troops to rebuff the white supremacist group. In response to murders and lynchings, "black members of the Republican-sponsored Union League struck back by burning mills, barns, and homes of their former masters" (Snider 1992, 83). In the face of regional racial and economic turmoil, Holden could not allocate sufficient time to aid the university. Despite President Pool's efforts to keep the doors open with only fifteen students in 1870, the university closed on February 1, 1871, with no plans of revitalization. Still, four years later, UNC did reopen and was slowly expanded to become a leading publicly funded research university in the American South.

"David Lowry Swain," n.d. Image courtesy of the Dialectic and Philanthropic Foundation, Louis Round Wilson Special Collection, University of North Carolina, Chapel Hill, North Carolina.

It is true that the Civil War negatively impacted the University of North Carolina. Despite the war's significant influence, UNC remained an active institution largely due to Swain's ability to ward off overt political divisiveness on campus, maintain a modicum of student enrollment, and dispel wartime rumors that the university would close. Had it not been for Swain's insistence that both faculty and students refrain from intense and direct political discourse, it is possible that the university would have been caught up in the state's political discord and, as a result, have suffered even more so. Despite the university's prominence and a strong reputation during the antebellum years, UNC faced its greatest battles not during the war, but after. The editorials penned by Cornelia Spencer, the poor administrative leadership of Reverend Solomon Pool, and the failed political support of Governor William Holden resulted in diminished university popularity with North

Carolina's gentry. Such negativity impacted the institution's standing as a premiere public institution.

Throughout the remainder of the nineteenth century and well into the twentieth century, the University of North Carolina continued to grow, but often grappled with the racist and sexist practices that stained its history and hindered its progress. Women were first permitted to enroll in 1896. African Americans could not call UNC home until 1951. Recently, the university struggled with division over Confederate campus iconography (i.e., the UNC "Silent Sam" Confederate monument) and a rash of hateful and racist rhetoric sprawled across the campus and local community (Svriuga 2019). Though the Silent Sam statue was removed in 2019, vestiges of the Confederacy remain a point of contention at the University of North Carolina. The institution's students, faculty, administrators, alumni, and stakeholders will hopefully work together to promote an environment that welcomes all and any in the "long line of seekers after knowledge."

REFERENCES

Act Establishing the University of North Carolina. 1789. *Documenting the American South.* University of North Carolina: Chapel Hill. Last modified November 12, 2020. https://docsouth.unc.edu/unc/unc01-08/unc01-08.html.

Armstrong, Edward H. April 20, 1861. Letter to Thomas G. Armstrong. *Documenting the American South.* University of North Carolina: Chapel Hill. Last modified July 11, 2019. https://docsouth.unc.edu/true/mss06-07/mss06-07.html.

Battle, Kemp P. 1912. *History of the University of North Carolina.* E-book. Edward and Broughton Printing Company.

Crow, Jeffrey J. 2006. "Slavery." *Encyclopedia of North Carolina,* edited by William S. Powell. Chapel Hill: University of North Carolina Press.

Halliburton, John. April 22, 1861. Letter to Juliet Halliburton. *Documenting the American South.* University of North Carolina: Chapel Hill. Last modified July 11, 2019. https://docsouth.unc.edu/unc/unc09-04/unc09-04.html.

Foner, Eric. 1995. *Free Soil, Free Labor, Free Man: The Ideology of the Republican Party before the Civil War.* London: Oxford University Press.

Hamilton, Joseph G. 1910. "Benjamin Sherwood Hedrick: Electronic Edition." *Documenting the American South.* University of North Carolina: Chapel Hill. Last modified July 24, 2008. https://docsouth.unc.edu/true/hamilton/hamilton.html.

Henderson, John. February 14, 1863. Letter to his Mother. *Documenting the American South.* University North of Carolina: Chapel Hill. Last modified July 11, 2019. https://docsouth.unc.edu/unc/unc09-12/unc09-12.html.

Inscoe, John C. 2008. "To Do Justice to North Carolina." In *Carolinians in the Era of the Civil War and Reconstruction,* edited by Paul D. Escott, 129-154. Chapel Hill: University of North Carolina Press.

Knapp, Sharon E. 1996. "Benjamin Sherwood Hedrick, 13 Feb. 1827–2 Sept. 1886." In *Dictionary of North Carolina Biography*, edited by William S. Powell, 95. Chapel Hill: University of North Carolina Press.

Leloudis, James L. 2004. "Civil War and Reconstruction." *Documenting the American South*. University of North Carolina: Chapel Hill. Last modified July 11, 2019. http://docsouth.unc.edu/unc/essay/unc_ess08.html.

Lindemann, Erika. "Aftermath of the Civil War." *Documenting the American South*. University of North Carolina: Chapel Hill. Last modified November 14, 2020. https://docsouth.unc.edu/true/chapter/chp06-02/chp06-02.html.

Lindemann, Erika. "The Establishment of the University." *Documenting the American South*. University of North Carolina: Chapel Hill. Last modified September 6, 2019. https://docsouth.unc.edu/true/chapter/chp01-01/chp01-01.html.

Lindemann, Erika. "Civil War." *Documenting the American South*. University of North Carolina: Chapel Hill. Last modified November 12, 2020. https://docsouth.unc.edu/true/chapter/chp06-01/chp06-01.html.

Mallet, Peter. November 6, 1863. Letter to David L. Swain. *Documenting the American South*. University of North Carolina: Chapel Hill. Last modified July 11, 2019. https://docsouth.unc.edu/unc/unc09-59/unc09-59.html.

Manning, Chandra. 2008. "The Order of Nature Would be Reversed: Soldiers, Slavery, and the North Carolina Gubernatorial Election of 1864." In *Carolinians in the Era of the Civil War and Reconstruction*, edited by Paul D. Escott, 101–28. Chapel Hill: University of North Carolina Press.

Phillips, Charles. August 12, 1867. Letter to Kemp P. Battle. *Documenting the American South*. University of North Carolina: Chapel Hill. Last modified July 11, 2019. https://docsouth.unc.edu/unc/unc09-02/unc09-02.html.

Pool, Solomon. January 23, 1868. "Letter to Charles Pool." *Documenting the American South*. University of North Carolina: Chapel Hill. Last modified July 11, 2019. https://docsouth.unc.edu/unc/unc09-76/unc09-76.html.

Powell, William S. 1992. *The First State University: A Pictorial History of the University of North Carolina*. 3rd ed. Chapel Hill: University of North Carolina Press.

Snider, William D. 1992. *Light on the Hill: A History of the University of North Carolina at Chapel Hill*. Chapel Hill: University of North Carolina Press.

Spencer, Cornelia Phillips. September 30, 1866. Letter to Ellen Caldwell Summerell. *Documenting the American South*. University of North Carolina: Chapel Hill. Last modified July 11, 2019. https://docsouth.unc.edu/unc/unc09-32/unc09-32.html.

"State Educational Convention." *The North Carolina Standard*. November 5, 1856. N.p.

Swain, David L. July 31, 1861. Letter to UNC Faculty. *Documenting the American South*. University of North Carolina: Chapel Hill. July 11, 2019. https://docsouth.unc.edu/unc/unc09-84/unc09-84.html.

Svrigua, Susan. 2019. "UNC Memorial to Enslaved People Vandalized with 'Racist and Other Deplorable Language.'" *Washington Post*, April 3, 2019.

The First Century of the First State University. (n.d.). "The University During the Civil War and Reconstruction." *Documenting the American South*. University of North Carolina: Chapel Hill. Last modified March 26, 2020. https://docsouth.unc.edu/unc/browse/civilwar_recons.html#closing.

UNC Board of Trustees. October 15, 1863. Letter to James A. Seddon. *Documenting the American South*. University of North Carolina: Chapel Hill. Last modified July 11, 2019. https://docsouth.unc.edu/unc/unc09-58/unc09-58.html.

Vance, Zebulon B. April 11, 1865. Letter to William T. Sherman. *Documenting the American South*. University of North Carolina: Chapel Hill. Last modified July 11, 2019. https://docsouth.unc.edu/unc/unc09-29/unc09-29.html.

Wallace, Carolyn A. 1996. "David Lowry Swain, 4 Jan. 1801–29 Aug. 1868." In *Dictionary of North Carolina Biography, Vol* 5, edited by William S. Powell, 486. Chapel Hill: University of North Carolina Press.

William, Martin J. December 12, 1864. Letter to Charles Phillips. *Documenting the American South*. University of North Carolina: Chapel Hill. Last modified July 11, 2019. https://docsouth.unc.edu/unc/unc09-62/unc09-62.html.

CHAPTER ELEVEN

Trinity College

Duke University's Persistence in Civil War Years

Lauren Lassabe

Duke University was founded in 1838 as a private elementary academy titled Brown's Schoolhouse in a small, central North Carolina community in Randolph County. In 1841, the growing institution was renamed Union Institute Academy, and by 1851, its name was changed again to "Normal College"—a fully-fledged institution of higher education. Eight years later, the academy was affiliated with the Methodist denomination, renamed Trinity College, and placed under the leadership of president Braxton Craven. Due to local affinity for the renamed academy, the surrounding community was renamed "Trinity" (Durden 1993). Like most Southern colleges during the Civil War, Trinity College was ultimately forced to close its doors in the final months of conflict when its grounds came under the occupation of Confederate refugees. Even so, the institution did not remain shuttered for long. The resolve of Trinity College's administration to persevere through circumstances of army conscription, Confederate monetary inflation, and military occupation render it an example of Southern higher education's Civil War endurance. During four years of war, students, faculty, and the president himself served the Confederacy as soldiers, company leaders, and prison overseers. The administrative decisions of Trinity College's wartime presidents, Braxton Craven and William T. Gannaway, provide insight into the circumstances that the institution faced during and after the war. Similarly, the papers of student-soldier John Franklin Heitman provide telling details of wartime college life from a student's perspective.

TRINITY COLLEGE BEFORE THE CIVIL WAR

The immediate years before the Civil War were a time of unprecedented growth and prosperity for Trinity College. Sprawling across seventeen acres, the campus comprised two, three-story brick buildings. These structures not only hosted classes, they contained four libraries with over ten thousand volumes, a museum, society halls, and a chapel. Just before the war commenced, the college's president had awarded a $14,000 contract to a local construction firm to build a third campus facility. (Unfortunately, the war interrupted construction.) Between 1859 and 1862 the average Trinity College enrollment was 204 (Dowd 1939). The academic year of 1860–1861 alone saw 215 young men enrolled, the second highest matriculation in the college's history. According to historian Michael David Cohen, only sixteen colleges in the country had an enrollment greater than two hundred students in 1861 (2012), making Trinity College one of the largest institutions of higher education in the nation.

Trinity College received its status as a Methodist Episcopal Church affiliate in 1859, two years before the first shots were fired at Fort Sumter in the Charleston Harbor of South Carolina. Braxton Craven, a slaveholding Methodist preacher and Trinity College's first president, was troubled by the South's political difficulties and the dangers of a looming war. While teaching courses in ancient languages, ethics, law, logic, rhetoric, and philosophy, Craven found time to proclaim that the largely agricultural South had become economically subjugated by the industrial North but stated that secession was not a laudable idea. Rather, he favored a Union compromise intended to produce an economically independent South, an educated Southern workforce, and the perpetuation of cultural traditions in the Confederate states—namely, the institution of slavery (Craven April 6, 1860). During his tenure as president of Trinity College, the academy's faculty sought to engrain these ideas in all enrolled.

In 1860, the annual student residential fee at Trinity College was eighty dollars, with an additional seventy-five dollars for wood to burn in the winter, and a monthly charge of seventy-five cents for washing. To enhance affordability, students often paid via installments (Gannaway 1861). With the threat of war imminent, Craven noted that the number of applications were low for the upcoming 1861–1862 academic year. He surmised that Trinity College would have seen 250 students enrolled if the war had not drawn aspiring young men away from their studies (Craven 1861). This bleak observation would be the first of many in the coming years, as the end of the 1861 academic term saw the last prewar commencement of any considerable size. That year, eighteen young men received their degrees. Several Trinity College students were called to war immediately, and in his 1861 end of year report to the Board of Trustees, Craven noted that forty students left the academy to enlist. Despite these departures, no classes had been cancelled and day-to-day operations carried on as usual (Craven June 20, 1861). Subsequent graduating class sizes decreased over the coming years from twelve to nine and finally one. There were no graduates in 1865 (Board of Trustees Records 1863–1865). By the end of the war, thirteen Trinity College students had been killed in battle (Dowd 1939).

TRINITY COLLEGE'S WARTIME PURPOSE: THE TRINITY GUARD

Craven's diary, personal correspondence, and sermons reflected his early-Civil War fear that if the war moved into Confederate territory, Trinity College would play an integral, if not ill-fated, role. Most concerning to Craven was the fact that many college-age men were prime candidates for military enlistment—eighteen years of age or older (though many younger individuals managed to enlist or were involved in the war effort in some way) (Murphy 1990; Marten 2000). Compared to the Union army, the Confederate army had a much smaller pool of young men from which to draw. Whereas half of the eligible men in the North enlisted for the war effort, the South enlisted 80 percent of its white, adult male population—still, their number was insufficient to equal Northern numbers (a disparity approximated at two to one) (Cohen 2012; "Civil War Facts" 2020). Craven was well aware that a significant portion of the college's student body was eligible for conscription. He was also concerned that the campus might be commandeered by North Carolina military units and transformed into a military training base or prisoner of war camp. Craven believed that such disruptions would lead to the death of his Methodist Episcopal-affiliated institution (Craven Diaries 1845–1874). Ultimately, his fears came to pass.

Craven's speculations were based on similar events in South Carolina, Virginia, Mississippi, and Alabama. Operations at The Citadel military academy in Charleston, South Carolina, were hindered in April of 1861 as the governor regularly called on its cadets to serve the Confederate infantry (Baker 1989). Within the first month of the war, Thomas "Stonewall" Jackson led Virginia Military Institute cadets in a skirmish at Harper's Ferry (Thelin 2019). By the end of the year, every student at the University of Mississippi had left campus or joined the Confederate army. University of Alabama administrators converted the college's curricular structure to train student cadets to combat not only Union incursions but also any potential slave uprisings (Sellers 1953).

To secure Trinity College's endurance through the war, Craven proposed that the Board of Trustees allow him to organize an open-enrollment student military company. Cadet training, it was planned, would begin as early as the 1861 summer session (Board of Trustees Records 1861). The Trinity Guard, a student cadet company, consisted of current and former pupils as well as members of the faculty. In August of 1861, Confederate Capt. Henry Brevard Davidson called the Trinity Guard into service. Guard members were charged with quelling riots in the nearby city of Raleigh as well as communities in Montgomery County (Craven 1861). North Carolina governor Henry Todd Clark wrote to Craven in November of 1861. Clark offered Trinity Guard a second assignment at a large factory near Salisbury, North Carolina. The factory had been converted into a military prison, and the student cadets were needed to guard captive Southern defectors, Union prisoners of war, and oversee incoming inmate supplies from war prisons in Raleigh and Richmond, Virginia (Chaffin 1950). The governor assured Craven that the Trinity College cadets would be "precisely on the same footing as those in the service except they will be stationed entirely at Salisbury and not subject to be ordered away [to battle]" (Clark 1861). Craven responded to Clark and extoled that his students were eager to accept the new post. The college president volunteered to resign from the institution's administration in order to personally oversee the Salisbury military prison. Craven also requested that his student soldiers be granted proper uniforms. He did not, however, request munitions as the student cadets already possessed rifles, forty rounds of cartridges, lead, gunpowder, firing caps, twenty pistols, and swords (Craven November 9, 1861).

By December, members of the Trinity Guard were responsible for nearly three hundred war prisoners (Chaffin 1950). The student guardsmen were unusually kind to the inmates, letting them play baseball and, in Methodist Episcopal fashion, consciously developing a church-like fellowship among the imprisoned men. This goodwill was later repaid to Craven when Union

"Trinity Guard," c. 1861. University Archives Photograph Collection, Box 80. Duke University Archives, David M. Rubenstein Rare Book & Manuscript Library, Duke University, Durham, North Carolina.

troops occupied Raleigh, home to Craven's church on Edenton Street. One of the Northern soldiers stationed in Raleigh was a former Salisbury prisoner. He remembered the kindness shown by Craven's students-turned-soldiers and gifted the college president a horse, several small trinkets, and allowed him special accommodations under Union watch (Dowd 1939). Trinity Guardsmen's compassion to prisoners was, as has been mentioned, rather unusual given the harsh treatment of war prisoners at other Civil War sites. Indeed, inmates at Andersonville Prison near Andersonville, Georgia, were harshly treated, malnourished, and forced to reside in unsanitary conditions. Inmates were similarly treated at the prisoner-of-war camp established at the University of Missouri. In 1863, prisoners cut holes in the University of Missouri's main campus building while attempting to escape. Occupying troops also looted campus resources and bartered campus equipment for whiskey in local townships. The damage to the University of Missouri was estimated at $3,000 (Cohen 2012).

As the war raged, the question emerged as to whether the guardsmen were under the command of the state of North Carolina and Governor Clark, or the Confederate government and President Jefferson Davis. As a private, religiously affiliated institution, Trinity College was not beholden to state orders, but its students and faculty considered themselves men of honor and duty to the newly formed Confederate government. Craven wrote to Governor Clark in December of 1861 to determine Trinity Guard's governmental allegiance, his command of the Salisbury post, and to clarify a debate surrounding his military authority versus that of Adj. Gen. Martin. As Trinity Guardsmen were transferring into regular military units, confusion arose concerning whether Craven would remain in command of the cadets if Martin assumed control. Craven requested that the student cadets keep their status as college students first and military men second. Indeed, the student soldiers had not been paid for their military services. The college president ended his letter by requesting that he be named commander of the Salisbury prison to clear any confusion of who was in charge of both the Trinity Guardsmen as well as the military war prison (Craven 1861).

Soon thereafter, Craven appealed again and explained that Gen. Martin had ordered members of the Trinity Guard to leave the guardsmen and join the Confederate army. Craven was displeased with Martin and reminded the governor that the Trinity Guard accepted the Salisbury post on the terms that they were students, commissioned to serve at Salisbury alone, and that they could elect to return to campus after the post ended. Craven requested that the governor grant his students an honorable discharge (Craven 1862). In January of 1862, the Trinity Guardsmen were relieved of their duties. They returned to campus, and Capt. A. C. Godwin assumed Craven's role as overseer of the Salisbury prison (Dowd 1939).

In February, Craven wrote to Governor Clark to ask if there was any truth to local rumors that a draft was to be put into effect. Hoping the reports were false, Craven encouraged his students not to leave campus until they had received news from the governor (Craven 1862). Clark responded that regrettably, Trinity College students were subject to the Confederate draft. Further, students should expect to be drafted in their county of residence in the near future. Clark explained on February 25, 1862, "I regret the necessity for any draft, but the necessity of the Country now, can respect neither individuals or Institutions." In March of 1862, the governor of South Carolina, Francis Wilkinson Pickens, issued a draft order that conscripted men age eighteen to forty-five. Alarmed, Trinity College's faculty appealed to the North Carolina legislature. Chemistry professor I. L. Wright, on March

10, 1862, wrote to "His Excellency" Governor Clark asking if it might be wise keep some young men in their home counties "whose duty it shall be to preserve law & order within certain limits." Members of the Trinity Guard's first assignment, after all, was to quell insurrections in neighboring counties. Craven wrote again to Clark and informed the governor that, in Randolph County, there was a growing sense of Confederate disloyalty, that a "Deep, inveterate hate to this government abounds and the authorities of the County will never crush it." Though student members of the Trinity Guard were present to help quell possible insurrections, Craven requested that Clark send a permanent military company. Despite regional social tensions and attempts to exempt Trinity College students from conscription, the draft was enacted. Soon thereafter, several students and faculty were ordered to report for active duty. By April of 1862, Craven appealed to Governor Clark to form yet another volunteer military company. It was hoped that if Trinity College students joined this new company, they would be exempt from conscription (Craven 1862). There is no evidence, however, that Clark ever responded to Craven's letter, and the draft continued. While students left to fight in the war, financial hardships increased for the academy's faculty and administration.

WARTIME FINANCES AND CONCESSIONS

Before the war, Trinity College's faculty received $1,000 annually. In 1861, members of the faculty were given approximately one third of their salaries. As institutional finances decreased, salaries decreased, and for the duration of the war, instructors received whatever payments the college's administration could muster. As the academy's endowment dwindled, and Confederate currency proved remarkably unstable, funds were maintained, though at a diminished rate, primarily through tuition and boarding fees (Craven 1863). As student numbers decreased so too did tuition revenue. By the end of 1862, enrollment had decreased to 82, down drastically from 215 just prior to the start of war (Craven 1862). By the end of the 1863 spring term, only 40 students remained (Craven 1863). That spring, the cost for one month's board was increased to fifty dollars in order to increase revenue (Gannaway 1863). To complicate matters, the college had accepted war refugees in its boardinghouses who consumed the institution's provisions at an unsustainable rate (Craven 1863).

Despite the loss of financial and human resources, Craven navigated the wartime climate while justifying the continued operation of Trinity College. Under these circumstances, maintaining enrollment was essential. Prior to the war, students were expelled for various infractions such as imbibing alcohol. In the early war years, six students were caught drinking liquor. Instead of expulsion, Craven temporarily suspended the students. While the faculty and president relaxed rules in order to preserve student numbers, the college's Board of Trustees approved steep tuition and fee increases for the 1863–1864 academic year (Craven 1863). Due to Confederate monetary inflation, the spring semester's boarding cost was raised to $100. If students and their families could not pay the entire amount, the administration accepted donations of firewood in exchange for a $75 credit (Gannaway 1864). In an effort to recruit additional students, advertisements were printed in local Christian newsletters to convince readers that there was a social and moral imperative to educate their children (Chaffin 1950). Despite the fact that enrollment remained a problem, Craven continued to support the war effort. Trinity College's president coordinated the preparation of seventy-one quilts, eighty-nine pairs of socks, and thirteen pairs of pants to be sent to a Capt. Wilson (Craven March 20, 1863).

LOSS OF A LEADER

The 1863–1864 academic year marked a downturn for Trinity College. That year Craven abruptly resigned from his post as president. At the 1863 North Carolina Conference of the United Methodist Church, several charges were brought against Craven in his capacity as president. Craven was charged with neglecting the institution's financial state by incurring significant debts. Leading conference members argued that, due to these debts, the Methodist Episcopal Church did not outright own Trinity College. To conference members, the bank and other debtors were, in essence, the academy's owners. Craven was also accused of failing to acquire donations from regional Church members to pay off said debt. In short, members of the Methodist Episcopal Conference had lost faith in Craven and blamed him for the institution's fiscal condition (Chaffin 1950). Thereafter, the college's Board of Trustees ruled that the collection of funds to repay institutional debts was Craven's responsibility. Craven defended himself to the board. He provided evidence that the college's title of ownership was intact and that there was no threat that any debtor would lay claim to the physical property. He also argued that donations were practically impossible to acquire due to the ongoing war (Board of Trustees 1863). Nevertheless, several conference members aligned themselves against Craven and published a libelous article concerning the college president in Church newsletters. An ally of Craven penned a response in an attempt to correct the damage, but it was too late. Rumors circulated that the college might close due to said debts. In an attempt to silence rumors and preserve Trinity College's regional reputation, Craven resigned in November of 1863 (Chaffin 1950).

On February 3, 1864, the college's trustees determined that it would be imprudent to elect a new president given the institution's financial and wartime circumstances. Instead of electing a new president, the governing board deemed that a faculty member would serve as interim president (Gannaway 1864). On February 13, 1864, an announcement was printed in the *North Carolina Christian Advocate* that extoled the board's confidence that "the institution will be managed to the entire satisfaction of all who may give it their patronage" (quoted in Chaffin 1950, 240). The newly appointed interim president and classics professor, William Trigg Gannaway, knew otherwise. Gannaway lamented the scarcity of food and absence of dormitory furniture. The war, Gannaway explained, rendered it "next to impossible to procure, for the students, the necessary accommodations." The interim president pleaded with the Board of Trustees to help sustain the college "through its present crisis" (Gannaway 1864).

Trinity College's dire straits were standard for Southern institutions of higher education that had survived the war thus far. In 1864, the president of the University of North Carolina wrote to Confederate president Jefferson Davis requesting draft exemptions for his students, particularly those studying medicine. As the 1862 Confederate Conscription Act provided exemptions for teachers and druggists, the request was reasonable. Davis agreed to exempt junior and senior students only. However, the underclassmen were too indispensable in the war effort to exempt from military service, whatever their major might have been (Cohen 2012). It does not appear that Gannaway applied for draft exemptions, and it is uncertain that such a request would have been granted given Governor Clark's earlier interactions with President Craven.

STUDENT LIFE IN THE LATTER YEARS OF THE WAR

By the 1864 spring semester, only forty-six students were enrolled at Trinity College. Days before Gannaway addressed the Board of Trustees in June of 1864, a new draft order was announced, and twenty additional students were taken from the academy (Gannaway 1864). To replace these lost pupils, Gannaway veered from conventional Trinity College norms and admitted approximately twenty young women (Chaffin 1950). The admission of women to a men's institution was a rare occurrence in the nation, especially the American South, and was, given period social norms, generally considered an extremist practice (Thelin 2019). Before the Civil War there were approximately forty-five colleges for women nationwide, many of which were in Confederate states. Very few Southern colleges and universities allowed women to be educated alongside men. Southern states were more likely to host women's colleges that imparted the import of religion, Southern traditions, and homemaking rather than vocational studies or scientific investigation. Indeed, Southern women's colleges were created to perpetuate "microcosms of the antebellum world" (Cohen 2012, 20) and to keep women from enrolling in Northern institutions of higher education (Farnham 1994). While enrolled, Trinity College's men and women studied and worked alongside each other on minor campus restoration projects, making small repairs to the academic buildings and grounds. Gannaway later wrote concerning these female students: "Their presence was like an oasis in the Sahara of War, and their instruction was an antidote for the hardness, roughness, and inhumanity of the conflict" (quoted in Chaffin 1950, 241).

In the same report in which Gannaway complained of food and furniture scarcity, he noted that student spirits were generally light: "Indeed the whole term has been characterized by undisturbed quiet, pleasantness, and harmony" (Gannaway 1864). Minutes from the 1863–1864 assemblies of the Trinity College Hesperian and Columbian Clubs indicate that student literary societies continued to meet throughout the war. Members of the Hesperian Club inducted Confederate general Robert E. Lee as an honorary member in 1864. That same year, the college's only graduate was admitted to the Columbian Club (Chaffin 1950). Like literary societies at other Southern colleges and universities, the Hesperian and Columbian Clubs debated classical subjects and practiced their oratory and rhetoric skills. In addition to maintaining student morale and literary society meetings, courses were offered as usual, despite the marked reduction in enrollment (Gannaway 1864).

Despite low enrollment, campus social life continued. Glimpses of Civil War-era student life at Trinity College have been captured in letters and college records. A local resident, Mollie Alforce wrote to John Franklin Heitman, a Trinity College student called to serve in the Confederate army, about his classmates. In a letter dated April 28, 1864, Alforce assured Heitman that his friends were well and that she had visited with them often at church. Things were not going so well, however, for W. A. Wester, a Trinity College student who was suspended following the spring term of 1864. From April to June, Wester's disciplinary record reflected the following negative marks: absent from Latin hall, absent from prayers, absent from preaching, suspended in Algebra, publicly reprimanded in English literature, and demerits in composition. Despite low enrollment, Gannaway deemed that Wester should be expelled for his infractions (Gannaway "Deportment" 1864).

As the 1863–1864 academic year came to a close, the college's faculty planned a commencement for its sole graduate, E. H. Tapscott. Maintaining institutional tradition, several Randolph County residents traveled to the campus to celebrate the scholarly achievements and good character of Trinity College's newest alumnus. Former college president Braxton Craven was invited to deliver the commencement address to a war-weary crowd. A twenty-two piece military band led the audience in celebration activities until midnight (Chaffin 1950). This celebration would be one of the last Trinity College would host as the war raged, and the Confederacy began to crumble.

THE LAST YEAR

In June of 1864 the Trinity College Board of Trustees met and approved that faculty would continue to perform their academic activities despite decreased resources. Interim president Gannaway continued to teach history, philosophy, and classical languages in addition to maintaining administrative responsibilities. Members of the governing board appointed the college's math professor, Lemuel Johnson, as the campus's first librarian and treasurer. I. L. Wright was again recorded as professor of both chemistry and literature, while recent Trinity College graduate C. C. Lanier was hired to oversee the academy's preparatory department. The faculty were to be compensated via an equal division of the meager tuition surplus. Gannaway, cognizant of the conditions under which he assumed the role of interim president, evaded incurring new debts during his tenure. He wrote to the governing board that the institution's finances had not worsened since his appointment, but that he was disheartened that the faculty could not be compensated adequately for their continued efforts (Gannaway 1864). Professor Johnson, however, was compensated an additional 5 percent for the supplementary duties of college treasurer and librarian (Chaffin 1950). During this meeting, decisions were made to address the college's ongoing debt of $10,000—the subject of which was cause for Braxton Craven's resignation. A motion was passed that Craven, the college's prior financial agent, should assume full responsibility for the debt (Board of Trustees 1864). On July 30, 1864, Craven paid $10,986 to cover both the academy's debt as well as accrued interest from his personal funds (Dowd 1939).

Though free of debt, Trinity College still faced wartime economic hardships. By the start of the fall 1864 semester, tuition was increased from eight to ten dollars (based on academic class) and was owed in advance. Dormitories were available to students for one hundred dollars a month or eighty dollars in provisions. However, by the spring semester, boarding dues rose to two hundred dollars per month (Gannaway 1864). To offset the cost of tuition, the college's administration continued to barter for goods in lieu of printed money. Wounded Confederate veteran John B. gave the college 7 bushels of wheat and 250 pounds of salt to cover his own residency cost. Under these circumstances, Gannaway appealed to Confederate president Jefferson Davis for institutional tax exemption, but to no avail. In a September 21, 1864, bulletin in Raleigh, North Carolina's *Weekly Confederate,* students were asked to bring any textbook in their family's possession when they returned for the fall semester. This request was made because a Union blockade halted textbook shipments (Chaffin 1950).

A STUDENT-SOLDIER'S WARTIME EXPERIENCE

While Trinity College faced war-related issues, several of its students experienced the war firsthand. John Franklin Heitman, future president of Trinity

College, was a student at the institution when the war began. He joined the Confederate army during his freshman year as a sergeant in Company H of North Carolina's 48th Regiment (Munson 2019). He eventually earned the rank of captain. His letters from Mollie Alforce offer telling insights about war life, while Heitman's personal diaries reveal intimate details pertaining to this former college student-turned Confederate officer. Heitman was injured on December 13, 1863. He was hospitalized several times during the war for fever and diarrhea and was granted a thirty-day medical leave in August of 1864. While home, Heitman spent time with his mother, aunts, and church members, and attended a funeral with a eulogy delivered by Craven. Returning to the army, he wrote of time spent in the trenches, marching, guarding railroads, artillery shooting, drills, dress parades, and, at times, boredom. He was again hospitalized during November of 1864 and once again in January of 1865. While recovering from his wounds, he wrote that several other men had received similar injuries while engaged in battle. Heitman also noted that his hospital had few provisions in the way of clothing, food, and firewood (Heitman 1865).

On February 5, 1865, Heitman engaged with Union forces at the Battle of Hatcher's Run. After the skirmish, he recounted that fifty-two men from his unit had been killed, wounded, or were missing. Approximately one thousand Confederate soldiers were killed at this particular battle ("The Battle of Hatchers Run" 2020). Heitman survived without physical injury. His hat had been shot through, yet he was unscathed. In the days that followed, Heitman and his fellow troops trudged through hail, rain, sleet, and snow in defense of Confederate railroads. In February of that year, he was called to testify in the court martial of Capt. John R. Potts in Petersburg, Virginia. Even so, Heitman did not recount the reason for the court martial. Soon thereafter, he applied for another leave of absence, but to no avail. In March, Heitman's men began rationing hardtack, sugar, and coffee. The next month, on April 6, 1864, he and the rest of the 48th Regiment were captured at the Battle of Sayler's Creek near Farmville, Virginia, as a part of the Appomattox Campaign and were held with other Confederate prisoners at Johnson's Island, Ohio. Members of the 48th Regiment marched for several days while captured, passing through Washington, DC, on April 16, where Heitman observed the citywide mourning of president Abraham Lincoln. Heitman and his fellow captives arrived at the Johnson's Island prisoner of war camp on April 17, his twenty-fifth birthday. He recorded that he had nothing useful to celebrate and hoped that by his next birthday he would be employed in something "useful & wise & good." In May, rumors circulated of a Confederate hunt for deserters. At the prison camp, Southern officers spoke of swearing a Union loyalty oath to return home. Heitman took the oath in front of two witnesses on September 14, 1865 to "faithfully support, protect and defend" the US Constitution and the Union. They also swore to follow all laws created "during the existing rebellion with reference to the emancipation of slaves." Heitman arrived home on June 26, 1865 after having been away for eight months (Heitman 1865). In time, the Trinity College student would return to the academy to guide its curricular and economic progress.

TRINITY COLLEGE, CLOSED AND REOPENED

In the winter of 1864 and spring of 1865, Union troops under the command of Gen. William Tecumseh Sherman blazed through Georgia and South Carolina on a march to expedite the war's end. By April 3, 1865, Union general Ulysses S. Grant captured Richmond, Virginia. Confederate soldiers under the direction of Gen. William J. Hardee retreated to the campus of Trinity College. According to interim president Gannaway, Gen. Hardee pitched his personal tent within yards of the main college building's door. Twenty thousand weary Confederate troops accompanied by thousands of emaciated horses sought refuge on the campus. For approximately one month the college resources were shared with the "half-clad and half-fed" troops and steeds. Gannaway was forced to suspend college activities, writing that "the presence of the soldiers, the excitement of the students, the anxiety and consternation of the people, rendered further college exercises useless, if not impossible. It was determined to close till the storm should pass, peace be made, and civil order once more restored" (quoted in Chaffin 1950, 247–48). It was not unusual for troops to occupy college grounds during the war as institutional resources such as food, shelter, and occasionally medicine made colleges prime targets for for soldiers (Cohen 2012). In May, one month after the Confederate surrender at Appomattox Courthouse in Virginia, Gen. Hardee received word of the war's end and relieved his troops of their duties. Gannaway recorded that the soldiers left behind their arms, cannons, and war paraphernalia for the Union enemy to collect (Chaffin 1950).

On August 31, 1865, the college's Board of Trustees reconvened to discuss reopening Trinity College. They also received the resignation of Lemuel Johnson, math professor and acting college treasurer and librarian, and discussed Craven's debt payment. Members of the board ultimately decided that the college would reopen on January 11, 1866. In a unanimous vote, financier Craven was restored to his former presidency. The board, now indebted to Craven for paying the academy's debts, returned his administrative duties. Gannaway stepped down as interim president and was made acting chair of languages and history. Afterwards, a search was launched for a mathematics instructor to replace Professor Johnson. When Trinity College reopened, it did so with a total staff of three: Craven, Gannaway, and O. W. Carr (Board of Trustees Records 1865).

Craven was disappointed with the postwar physical state of the campus. Conditions following the month-long occupation of Confederate soldiers left the landscape resembling a battlefield. The theft of library books as well as dormitory and classroom furniture disheartened Craven so much so that he used his personal funds to refurnish the buildings (Craven June 13, 1866). That spring, fifty students enrolled. The boarding fee for four and a third months was set at sixty-three dollars, with a three-dollar charge for firewood (Gannaway 1866). Tuition revenue was used to finance faculty salaries. Craven was allotted three-sevenths of the accrued tuition while the other professors were granted two-sevenths. Gannaway's salary increased slowly from ten dollars in April 1866 to fifty dollars in January of 1867 (Gannaway 1866). In the spring of 1866, Trinity College's administration hosted the institution's first postbellum commencement ceremony. Three bachelor's degrees and eleven master's degrees, including one to war veteran J. R. Cole, were conferred (Board of Trustees Records 1866). Confederate Capt. John Franklin Heitman himself graduated two years later. The college's governing board hired additional faculty in the years following the war, and enrollment returned to its antebellum rate by the end of 1870. Likewise, the college's financial situation greatly improved. Assets were estimated at $12,000 in 1874 for land, $35,000 for the two brick buildings and library, and $3,000 in furniture. The chapel, Craven opined, remained one of the best in the nation and could accommodate two thousand patrons (Dowd 1939).

REEVALUATING THE DIRECTION OF TRINITY COLLEGE

During Southern Reconstruction, colleges and universities across the former Confederate South debated the addition of vocational curriculum to existing traditional liberal arts curricula (Thelin 2019). Before the Civil War, the University of Virginia was uniquely structured among its contemporaries, with eight colleges of science, law, medicine, and other practical areas of training. No other Southern institution followed such a decentralized model, including Trinity College (Bowman and Santos 2015). Incorporating new courses would bring administrative and structural concerns to the North Carolina campus. The faculty mused: should courses of a practical nature be interwoven with the existing liberal arts curriculum? Similarly, the faculty debated about crafting new degree programs to be housed in new academic units. In a meeting with members of the college's governing board on June 13, 1866, Craven proposed a few considerations for the institution's reopening that regarded "the future character of the Institution in its application to the education of the public" (Craven 1866).

As early as 1853, neighboring University of North Carolina had created a college of applied science. With the war over, Craven and his contemporaries surveyed the academic landscape and queried if Methodist Episcopal-affiliated Trinity College should adopt the public university land grant model and begin to offer agriculture studies, mechanical sciences, and other practical programs of a secular nature. Southern agrarians were skeptical that scientists and scholars were sages of farming, especially those who advocated for a Northern industrial approach to the planter tradition (Thelin 2019). Historically, Southern planters sent their sons to college as a social rite of passage. The traditional purpose of higher education in the American South had been to forge networks among elite peers and train in the social conservatism that perpetuated their status, not to create a business class of laborers. But now that the war was over, Southern colleges and universities needed to adapt to the changed social, political, and economic climate (Frost 2001).

At the dawn of Trinity College's 1866 reopening, there was an opportunity to restructure the academy's religious-infused vision to support the higher education of North Carolina's clerical and political leaders. Ultimately, Craven posited that Trinity College should become a full-fledged university, with modern curricula that met the postwar South's economic and vocational needs. Scholars of Civil War higher education have argued that the American Civil

War benefitted Southern institutions by decimating the traditional liberal arts system of instruction and facilitated the inculcation of the scientific university model (Frost 2001). Despite Craven's aspirations, Trinity College continue to struggle throughout the latter half of the nineteenth century. To enhance the academy, it was decided to relocate the college to Durham, North Carolina, in 1892. The physical relocation was made possible by funds provided by industrialists Julian S. Carr and Washington Duke. In 1896, 1899, and 1900, Duke made three $100,000 gifts to the relocated college with the stipulation that women would be continuously admitted. In 1924, Duke's son, James Buchanan Duke, established "The Duke Endowment" via a $20 million donation, which helped the academy to become a leading Southern research university. The next year, to honor Washington Duke, the institution's name was changed to Duke University (King 2002). Following its service to the failed Confederacy, Duke University continued its long tradition of educating only white, mostly male, students for the next century. It was not until 1961 that Duke University was racially integrated, making it one of the last major research universities in the American South to officially desegregate (Kean 2008).

Given the college's transformation from a predominantly religious liberal arts academy for white Confederate sons into an inclusive world-renowned research university, how, then, should wartime Trinity College be remembered? Like other Southern colleges and universities that persisted through the perilous Civil War years, Trinity College, its faculty, and administration struggled with severely low enrollment, military occupation, and shortages of supplies: all symptomatic of wartime higher education. Interim president Gannaway's attempts to belay the college's closure via female student enrollment, tuition increases, and the accommodation of Confederate soldiers mirrored actions taken by peer administrators at other Southern institutions of higher education. Even so, the Civil War administrations of both President Craven and interim president Gannaway went far to keep the college afloat. In addition to the college's persistent administration, faculty willingness to accept reduced salaries, and the accommodation of female students to increase enrollment, the surrounding community continued to provide students (though at a reduced number) throughout the war. Indeed, local residents supported the institution, kept abreast of the college's progress by means of church bulletins and newsletters, and attended commencement ceremonies. In the years of rampant Confederate financial inflation, families paid their tuition in kind, providing resources such as food and firewood that were crucial to sustaining the institution. Trinity College, despite its wartime hardships, grew in the latter half of the nineteenth century and progressed exponentially in the twentieth century. Today, Duke University remains a significant example of successful, private Southern higher education.

REFERENCES

Alforce, Mollie J. April 28, 1864. Letter to Capt. J. F. Heitman. John Franklin Heitman Papers. Correspondence, 1863–1865. Box 1, Folder 1. Duke University Archives. David M. Rubenstein Rare Book & Manuscript Library, Duke University.

Baker, Gary R. 1989. *Cadets in Gray*. Columbia, SC: Palmetto Book Works.

"The Battle of Hatcher's Run." 2020. American Battlefield Trust. Last modified October 27, 2020. https://www.battlefields.org/learn/articles/battle-hatchers-run.

Board of Trustees Records. 1861, June 19. "Board of Trustees Minutes, June 19, 1861." Board of Trustees Records, Volume 1, Duke University Archives. David M. Rubenstein Rare Book & Manuscript Library, Duke University.

Board of Trustees Records. 1863, June 17. "Board of Trustees Minutes, June 17, 1863."

Board of Trustees Records. 1864, June 9. "Board of Trustees Minutes, June 9, 1864."

Board of Trustees Records. 1865, October 26. "Board of Trustees Minutes, October 26, 1865."

Board of Trustees Records. 1866, June 13. "Board of Trustees Minutes, June 13, 1866."

Bowman, Rex and Carlos Santos. 2015. *Rot, Riot, and Rebellion: Mr. Jefferson's Struggle to Save the University That Changed America*. Charlottesville: University of Virginia Press.

Chaffin, Nora Campbell. 1950. *Trinity College, 1839–1892: The Beginnings of Duke University*. Durham, NC: Duke University Press.

"Civil War Facts." 2020. American Battlefield Trust. Last modified November 27, 2020. https://battlefields.org/learn/articles/civil-war-facts.

Clark, Henry T. November 5, 1861. Letter to Capt. Craven. Braxton Craven Papers, 1838–1882, Box 1. Braxton Craven Records and Papers, Duke University Archives, David M. Rubenstein Rare Book & Manuscript Library, Duke University.

Clark, Henry T. February 25, 1862. Letter to Capt. Craven.

Cohen, Michael David. 2012. *Reconstructing the Campus: Higher Education and the American Civil War*. Charlottesville: University of Virginia Press.

Craven, Braxton. Braxton Craven Diaries, 1845–1874. Braxton Craven Records and Papers, Box 2, Folders 30–34. Duke University Archives, David M. Rubenstein Rare Book & Manuscript Library, Duke University.

Craven, Braxton. April 6, 1860. "The Civilization of the Southern States." Braxton Craven Records and Papers, Box 1. Duke University Archives, David M. Rubenstein Rare Book & Manuscript Library, Duke University.

Craven, Braxton. June 20, 1861. Report of the President of the Faculty to the Board of Trustees. Braxton Craven Records and Papers, Duke University Archives, David M. Rubenstein Rare Book & Manuscript Library, Duke University.

Craven, Braxton. August 5, 1861. Letter to Governor Henry T. Clark, August 5, 1861. Braxton Craven Papers, 1838–1882, Box 1. Braxton Craven Records and Papers, Duke University Archives, David M. Rubenstein Rare Book & Manuscript Library, Duke University.

Craven, Braxton. November 9, 1861. Letter to Governor Henry T. Clark.
Craven, Braxton. December 30, 1861. Letter to Governor Henry T. Clark.
Craven, Braxton. January 22, 1862 Letter to Governor Henry T. Clark.
Craven, Braxton. February 24, 1862. Letter to Governor Henry T. Clark.
Craven, Braxton. March 12, 1862. Letter to Governor Henry T. Clark.
Craven, Braxton. April 17, 1862. Letter to Governor Henry T. Clark.
Craven, Braxton. March 20, 1863. Letter to Wilson.
Craven, Braxton. June 17, 1863. "Report of the President of Trinity College for the Collegiate." Braxton Craven Records and Papers, Duke University Archives, David M. Rubenstein Rare Book & Manuscript Library, Duke University.
Craven, Braxton. June 13, 1866 "Annual Report to the Board of Trustees of Trinity College." Board of Trustees book, No. 12, 1860–1879. Braxton Craven Records and Papers, Duke University Archives, David M. Rubenstein Rare Book & Manuscript Library, Duke University.
Dowd, Jerome. 1939. *The Life of Braxton Craven: A Biographical Approach to Social Science.* Durham: Duke University Press.
Durden, Robert E. 1993. *The Launching of Duke University, 1924–1949.* Durham, NC: Duke University Press.
Farnham, Christine Anne. *The Education of the Southern Belle: Higher Education and Student Socialization in the Antebellum South.* New York: New York University Press, 1994.
Frost, Dan. 2001. *Thinking Confederates: Academic and the Idea of Progress in the New South.* Knoxville: University of Tennessee Press.
Gannaway, William T. "Account Book, 1861–1865." William T. Gannaway Papers, Box 1. Duke University Archives, David M. Rubenstein Rare Book & Manuscript Library, Duke University.
Gannaway, William T. 1864. "Deportment of W. A. Wester." William T. Gannaway Papers, Box 2. Duke University Archives, David M. Rubenstein Rare Book & Manuscript Library, Duke University.
Gannaway, William T University Archives, David M. Rubenstein Rare Book & Manuscript Library, Duke University.
Harrison, Jennifer. 2000. "Nineteenth-century Virginia Female Institutes, 1850–1890: An Analysis of the Effect of Education on Social Life." Master's thesis. University of Richmond.
Heitman, John Franklin. August 12, 1864. "Transcript of Diary, 1864–1865." John Franklin Heitman Papers, Box 3, Folder 42. Duke University Archives. David M. Rubenstein Rare Book & Manuscript Library, Duke University.
Heitman, John Franklin. September 14, 1865. "Loyalty Oath." John Franklin Heitman Papers, Box 1, Folder 1. Duke University Archives. David M. Rubenstein Rare Book & Manuscript Library, Duke University.
Kean, Melissa. 2008. *Desegregating Private Higher Education in the South: Duke, Emory, Rice, Tulane, and Vanderbilt.* Baton Rouge: Louisiana State University Press.
King, William E. 2002. "Duke University: A Brief Narrative History." *Duke University Libraries.* Last modified November 21, 2020. https://library.duke.edu/rubenstein/uarchives/history/articles/narrative-history.
Marten, James. 2000. *The Children's War.* Charlottesville: University of North Carolina Press.
Munson, Barry. 2019. *North Carolina Civil War Obituaries, Regiments 47–70, Volume 2: A Collection of Tributes to the War Dead and Veterans.* Morrisville, NC: LuLu.com.
Murphy, Jim. 1990. *The Boys War: Confederate and Union Soldiers Talk about the Civil War.* New York: Clarion Books.

Sellers, James Benson. 1953. *History of the University of Alabama.* Tuscaloosa: University of Alabama Press.

Thelin, John R. 2019. *A History of American Higher Education.* 3rd ed. Baltimore: Johns Hopkins University Press.

Townsend, J. H. August 25, 1861. Letter to Cousin. Braxton Craven Papers, 1839–1882, Box 1. Braxton Craven Records and Papers, Duke University Archives, David M. Rubenstein Rare Book & Manuscript Library, Duke University.

Wright, I. L. March 10, 1862. Letter to Governor Clark. Braxton Craven Papers, 1839–1882, Box 1. Duke University Archives, David M. Rubenstein Rare Book & Manuscript Library, Duke University.

Contributors

Christian K. Anderson is associate professor of higher education at the University of South Carolina. He earned a PhD at Penn State in 2007. He served as associate editor of *Perspectives on the History of Higher Education* from 2007 to 2017. His research focuses on the history of faculty and student roles in university governance in the United States and Latin America. Anderson also researches higher education in popular culture.

Marcia Bennett is a museum professional at the Dahlonega Georgia Gold Museum. A graduate of the University of Nebraska-Omaha, she is pursuing an MA in history at the University of North Georgia. Her main area of research focuses on WWII and the American West, as well as the digital humanities and public history.

Lauren Yarnell Bradshaw is an associate professor at the University of North Georgia. She is a graduate of Georgia State University with a PhD in social studies teaching and learning. She has published on topics related to educational biography, the history of education in the American South, and social studies curriculum.

Holly A. Foster is an assistant professor of student affairs and higher education administration and coordinator for the higher education graduate programs at the University of Southern Mississippi. She holds a PhD in higher education administration from the University of Virginia and researches college student life, past and present.

Tiffany Greer serves as a preschool teacher for the developmentally delayed at South Jones Elementary School in Ellisville, Mississippi. She also works as an early intervention special instructor for the Mississippi Health Department. Tiffany is currently pursuing a PhD in higher education administration at the University of Southern Mississippi. She has researched the history of medical higher education in the American South and is currently studying college stereotypes in horror films.

Don Holmes is a lecturer of English at Carnegie Mellon University. He earned his PhD in English at the University of North Carolina at Chapel Hill. His research centers on the early formation and evolution of the Black rhetoric tradition and early American cultural and intellectual history.

Donavan L. Johnson serves as dean of students at Baton Rouge Community College in Louisiana. He earned an EdD in higher education administration from the University of Southern Mississippi. His research interests include higher education history, college student judicial affairs, and academic conduct/misconduct.

Lauren Lassabe is the coordinator of student accountability at the University of New Orleans. She earned her PhD in higher education administration from the University of Southern Mississippi. Her research interests include student activism, the politics of education, and the history of US higher education.

Sarah Mangrum serves as access services librarian and clinical associate professor with University Libraries at the University of Southern Mississippi, where she earned an EdD in higher education administration. Her research interests include the role of academic libraries in higher education, the theory of library as place, and academic library leadership.

R. Eric Platt is associate professor of higher and adult education and chair for the Department of Leadership at the University of Memphis. He holds a PhD in educational leadership and research/higher education administration from Louisiana State University. He specializes in the history of higher and religious education in the American South and is the author of *Sacrifice and Survival: Identity, Mission, and Jesuit Higher Education in the American*

South (2014) and *Educating the Sons of Sugar: Jefferson College and the Creole Planter Class of South Louisiana* (2017).

Courtney L. Robinson serves as an academic advisor in the College of Business and Economic Development at the University of Southern Mississippi. She earned an EdD in higher education administration from the University of Southern Mississippi. Her research focuses on the implementation of artificial intelligence to improve college enrollment and retention and the improvement of academic advising and communication outreach strategies.

David E. Taylor is an instructor at Northshore Technical Community College in Louisiana and teaches courses in human development, social psychology, and introductory psychology and sociology. He has taught at Mississippi Gulf Coast Community College, Gulf Coast Baptist Institute, the University of Southern Mississippi, and the Universiteti Aleksander Xhuvani in Albania. He earned a PhD in higher education administration from the University of Southern Mississippi and researches Civil War-era college instruction and Baptist-affiliated higher education.

Zachary A. Turner is originally from Alabama and graduated from Huntingdon College, located in Montgomery, Alabama. He has an MA in student affairs administration from the University of Southern Mississippi. Most recently, he served as assistant director in the Office of Leadership and Student Involvement at the University of Southern Mississippi, where he is currently pursuing his EdD in higher education administration.

Michael M. Wallace is a retired military intelligence officer. Currently, he is a professor of practice and director of the emergency and security program at Tulane University in New Orleans. A graduate of the Virginia Military Institute, he holds an MLA degree from Tulane University, an MA in Military History from the US Army Command and General Staff College and an EdD in higher education administration from the University of Alabama.

Rhonda Kemp Webb is a history teacher and the Social Studies Department chair at Lassiter High School in Marietta, Georgia. She earned a PhD in history education from Georgia State University, where she was also the university's grant coordinator for *Courting Liberty: Slavery and Equality Under the Constitution*—a National Endowment for the Humanities Summer Institute project. Webb also worked with the Georgia Department of Education to develop US history curricula and volunteers as a docent and researcher at Bulloch Hall, a site on the National Register of Historic Places located in Roswell, Georgia.

Index

References to figures appear in *italics*.

CPSIA information can be obtained
at www.ICGtesting.com
Printed in the USA
BVHW032311290821
615262BV00003B/10